A DANCE WITH FRED ASTAIRE

First Published in the United States of
America in 2017 by Anthology Editions, LLC

87 Guernsey Street
Brooklyn, NY 11222

anthologyeditions.com

Edited by Johan Kugelberg, Jonas Mekas,
and Sebastian Mekas

Editorial Assistant: Mark Iosifescu

Creative Director: Johan Kugelberg
Art Director: Bryan Cipolla
Design: Nicholas Law

First Edition
ARC 042
Printed in China.

ISBN: 978-1-944860-09-7
Library of Congress Control Number:
2017940293

# A DANCE WITH FRED ASTAIRE

## Jonas Mekas

Anthology Editions

New York

# TABLE OF CONTENTS

**an·ec·dote** \\'a-nik-ˌdōt\ *n, pl* **anecdotes**
*also* **an·ec·dota** \ˌa-nik-'dō- tə\ [F, fr. Gk
*anekdota* unpublished items, fr. neut. pl. of
*anekdotos* unpublished, fr. *a-* + *ekdidonai*
to publish, fr. *ex* out + *didonai* to give
— more at EX-, DATE] (ca. 1721) : a usu. short
narrative of an interesting, amusing, or
biographical incident

2

The author, in the Fred Astaire scene in *Imagine* (1972), a film by Yoko Ono.

# A DANCE WITH FRED ASTAIRE

"I need you in a scene for a film I am shooting. Come to the St. Regis Hotel."

So I come. Yoko Ono is shooting a scene for her new film, *Imagine*.

"You'll have to dance with Fred Astaire," said Yoko nonchalantly.

"OK" I said. I don't react too much to such surprises; I have been around Yoko and John long enough.

Fred Astaire comes.

Steve Gebhardt is ready with his camera.

We are supposed to dance across the room.

Fred Astaire says, "No, not yet. Let me do some rehearsing."

So he rehearses. He dances across the room three, four times, maybe five. He has to know exactly what he is doing. Then he turns to me, indicating that it's OK now for me to rehearse.

"No, thank you," I said. "I'll just do it."

The actor training of my young days informed me that a professional can learn from rehearsals, but an amateur only gets worse.

So there we go. Astaire dances across the empty room. I follow him. With no rehearsing.

Later Ken Jacobs, who saw it all on TV, said to me:

"You know, I think you did a better job than Fred Astaire."

I was very flattered by that, of course.

That was the highlight of my dance career. Beginning, end, and highlight at once. Brief but memorable...

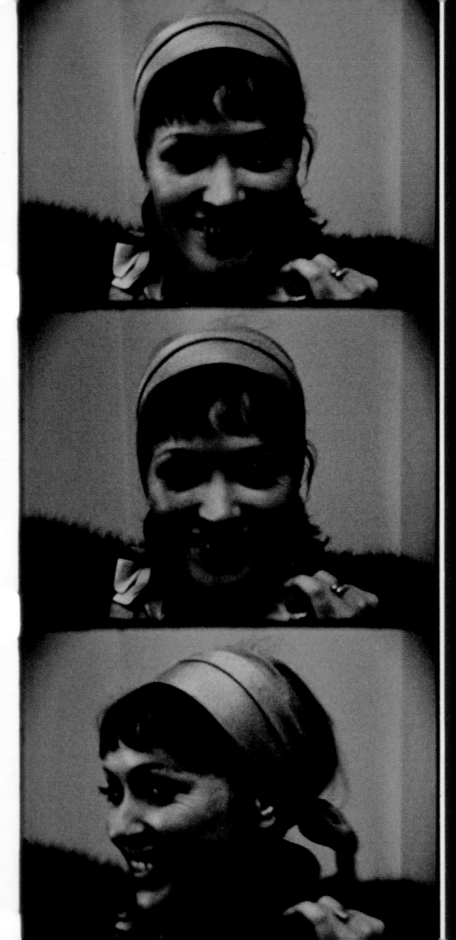

4

December 27, 1973

JONAS: Could you name, without thinking, from the top of your head, three colors?

KARINA: Blue. Red. White.

JONAS: Could you name three objects or anything that are blue?

KARINA: The sea. The sky. And... I don't know (*thinks for one minute*). I don't know. I don't know. Of course I can find something, but I don't know.

JONAS: Red?

KARINA: Red? Fire. Revolution. Anger. And optimistic. Blue makes me sad. Red makes me optimistic.

JONAS: White?

KARINA: It's a pure color. Purity. Sand. (*Pause*) I don't know... I feel well in white. It's like being pure; it's like life. It's like life because it's pure. And, snow.

JONAS: Say ten words. They could be nouns, verbs, anything.

KARINA: Love. Children. Mother. Father. Sister. Brother. Family. House. Nature. Brotherhood. And, No More War.

5

JONAS: Are you aware that besides being an actress, and now also a director, you are also considered by many, and, of course, by me as one of the most beautiful women whose face we've seen on the screen? Louise Brooks and you.

KARINA: I don't feel beautiful. I feel very different every day.

JONAS: I realize that today, with the women's liberation movement in full swing, any reference to the beauty of a woman can be taken as male chauvinism. But I know that we can speak about beauty of men and women, of certain men and certain women.

KARINA: Beauty is the way people are, the way they move, the way they do things. I always thought that Jean-Luc Godard was good-looking... But nobody else thought so. He is very good-looking. If you really look at his face, he's got a perfect face. Usually you can't see his face because he's wearing black glasses.

JONAS: I always was of the opinion that intelligence is beauty. And Jean-Luc is very intelligent.

KARINA: He has a very perfect face. And the eyes, the expression of the eyes, too. And I always thought so, even when I didn't know him. He's got one of the greatest faces.

OPPOSITE: Anna Karina in New York, December 27, 1973.

6

Watercolor of the Anthology Film Archives lobby at 425 Lafayette Street, by Jerome Hill.

# JOSEPH CORNELL'S INVISIBLE STRINGS

Joseph Cornell was known for his secluded life. It was very seldom that he made appearances outside of his 37-08 Utopia Parkway home in Flushing, Queens.

But he came to the opening of Anthology Film Archives on November 30, 1970.

Most of the evening he remained sitting on the steps, just in front of the Invisible Cinema space designed by Peter Kubelka. Not many people knew who he was.

Parker Tyler, who had known him for many years, came and sat next to him. They conversed for a while. I was standing a few steps further down and I didn't hear the conversation that was taking place between Parker and Cornell, but suddenly it seemed that there was a little argument ensuing. As it happened, P. Adams Sitney was sitting on the other side of Cornell, and now I'll relate to you what P. Adams Sitney observed.

At some point in their conversation, Cornell turned to Parker and, in his slow Cornell voice, said:

"Parker, you know, maybe you could give me back that box I gave you, you remember..."

There was a slow surprise shock emerging on Parker's face. Parker is also slow, like Cornell, but with a kind of intellectual slowness.

"Yes, Joseph..." he said in a surprise voice which was both real and theatrical. "But, Joseph, I thought you gave it to me as a present, for good..."

A Cornellian silence followed. Then, Cornell, without looking at Parker, said:

"But, Parker, you didn't see the invisible strings attached to it."

Cornell, this I found out later, didn't particularly appreciate what Parker had written in some art magazine about one of his favorite Hollywood stars.

From *Un Chant d'amour* (1950), a film by Jean Genet.

## A NOTE ON GENET'S FILM
## *UN CHANT D'AMOUR* AND HAROLD PINTER

The year was 1964, early January. Barbara Rubin and I had created a scandal at the Knokke-le-Zoute Experimental Film Festival when they forbade us from showing Jack Smith's film *Flaming Creatures*, so we proceeded to Paris. There, we spent some time with Roman Polanski as our driver. He had a car—a tiny car, but a car. Eventually he gave up when Barbara decided to go swimming in the Seine. We could not persuade her not to do that. So we left her by the Seine and went to La Coupole.

It was during that trip that I revisited Nico Papatakis. I had met him some years earlier, during the re-shooting of Cassavetes' film *Shadows*. In 1950 Nico helped Jean Genet to make his only film, *Un Chant d'Amour*. It was a legendary film, which few people had seen even in Paris. The censors did not allow it to be shown in the theaters. So I asked Nico if I could take a print of it to New York. Nico wondered why I wanted to take that kind of risk, but I was very determined about it. So now we were at Café de Flore and in my huge raincoat pockets I had the film. To make the transportation safer, we divided the print into several rolls.

Since the travelers from Paris to New York usually were checked very thoroughly, I decided to go first to London for a day and arrive in New York from London instead. You have to know that Paris in 1964 was considered by the customs people a smut city. On my previous return from Paris to New York, they confiscated two Olympia Press books I was carrying in my bag. London travelers were not being checked so carefully at the customs. That was the advice given to me by Brion Gysin, in whose home I was staying in Paris. So that's what I did.

On the plane from London to New York, I got into a conversation with my seat neighbor. My neighbor happened to be Harold Pinter on his way to New York for the opening of one of his early plays. As we were talking, we discovered we knew some of the same people, including Nico. So I told him what I had in my pockets. We discussed the best strategy to deal with the customs guys. The plan we devised was that he'd go first. He had more stuff. I usually travel very light. I was to follow after him.

9

And that's what we did. He got his huge suitcase down from the running belt and we moved towards the customs guy of Pinter's choice. I followed him almost like a servant. The customs man surveyed us and asked Pinter to open his suit-case, which Pinter did. The customs man peeked in and his face went strange: There was nothing in the suitcase but some thirty copies of Pinter's play.

"What are these?" asked the customs guy.

"It's my play that is opening on Broadway next week," said Pinter calmly.

You had to see the face of the customs guy! He lit up, his eyes lit up, he went all gaga. Here is a real Broadway playwright, a celebrity, a suitcase full of plays! All excited, he motioned to a couple of other customs guys:

"Come, take a look: This guy has a play on Broadway. No joke."

They all surrounded the suitcase, staring at it in an awe that I cannot describe to you. And since they seemed to ignore me completely, and I had no suitcase, I just walked through. Then I turned around and waved to Pinter. I could see from his face that he enjoyed the way the affair went.

I proceeded towards the exit with the print of *Un Chant d'Amour* in my rain-coat pockets.

# MIKE WALLACE JACK SMITH SHOW

I have no record of the exact date—I was so busy during the mid-sixties that it wouldn't have been possible for me to keep any records of my activities—but it had to be around late 1964. In March 1964, I was arrested for screening Jack Smith's film *Flaming Creatures* and, a couple of weeks later, for screening Jean Genet's *Un Chant d'Amour*. Now, these arrests, that came on the tail of the Lenny Bruce arrest, had produced so much press and pro and con that the story had reached the TV guys. And, of course, there was none more important in 1964 than Mike Wallace.

One day as I was doing my work at the Film-Makers' Cooperative, I receive a call from Wallace's office. They want me and Jack Smith to be on their program to tell all about *Flaming Creatures* and everything. "OK," I said. "It sounds interesting. I'll talk to Jack."

I reported this to Jack. He, of course, being a born phlegmatic, thinks slowly, talks slowly, but eventually he came to the same conclusion: *It's interesting. Let's see what happens.*

So it's all arranged. We come to the TV station, everybody's ready. We take our seats—it was supposed to be a live show—and we go.

First it's me. Mike wants to know what this thing called underground film is all about. So I tell him, I sum it up, it takes like one minute. Then Mike turns to Jack and asks one simple and short question about his film *Flaming Creatures*.

I would give a thousand bucks now if I could remember that question word for word. It may be in Wallace's archives, but the question contained a reference to *Flaming Creatures* as an obscene film offending public morals.

At that point Jack stood up from his chair and shouted out a tirade at Mike to the effect that he was an absolute mongoloid moron. Jack spewed it out in a torrent of Smithsonian venom at poor Mike, who watched us in disbelief. Then Jack turned around and walked out of the studio. I had no choice but to do the same. I have no idea if all of this exists somewhere on tape.

12

Mike Wallace (*center*) at Anthology Film Archives' celebration of the films of the brothers Lumière, May 1990.
Photo: Ron Galella.

13

Jack Smith, 1962. Photo: The author.

That was our Mike Wallace show.

Thirty years later.

Anthology Film Archives hosted one of its notorious fundraising events. I say notorious because they never brought in any monies. But we always had a good time and some great people came to give us a good time. On this occasion it was a very special event organized by Jane Safer, our managing director at that time. Mr. Pépin cooked Lyon specialties for a hundred people in honor of Auguste and Louis Lumière, with Louis Malle very graciously introducing the event and making comments on the Lumière movies.

14          The evening went great.

As I was walking around the room with a glass of wine, thanking the guests, I came to a table rich in celebrities and who is sitting there with a glass of wine in the company of Cronkite, Bob Towbin and Kurt Vonnegut? Yes, it's none other than Mike Wallace himself. I had not met him since the Jack Smith event. So I come to him and say:

"You may not remember it, but we have met once…"

Mike practically jumped up and practically shouted: "Remember? How could I ever forget it! You were the only ones who ever walked out of my show! How could I forget it!"

OPPOSITE: Jacques Pépin, Anthology Film Archives, May 1990.

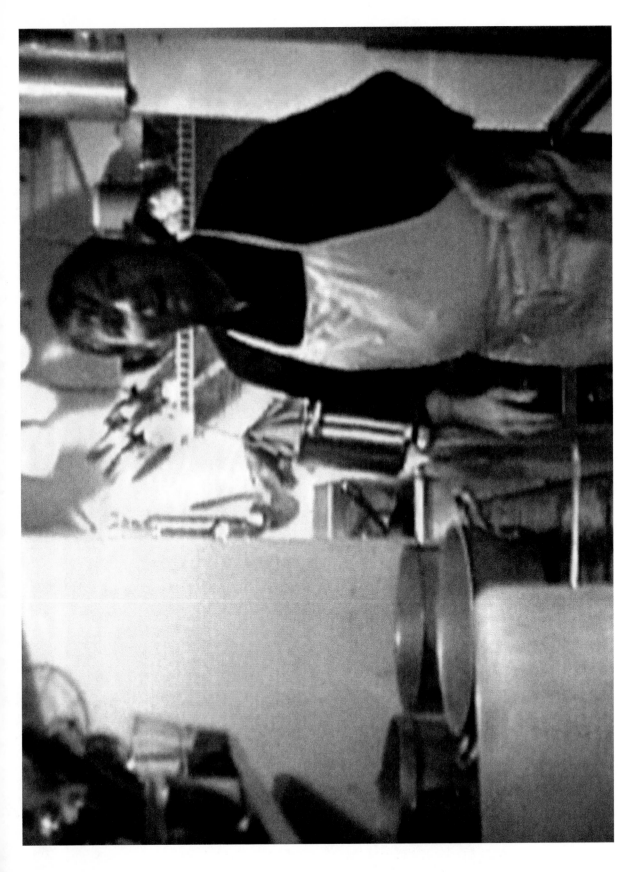

15

16

# HOW GREGORY CORSO SAVED MY LIFE

From 1967 to 1974, the Chelsea Hotel room 725 was my home. Harry Smith lived just around the corner, same floor. Behind a thin wall separating us, next door, there was Janis Joplin practicing her amazing voice, but I could hear all the other sounds too, her bed being next to my bed... And there was Patti Smith, and higher up there was Shirley Clarke and the guy with the python snake which knew how to escape and cause some panic occasionally. And there was Gregory Corso and strange happenings in Harry's room with smoke and burning mattresses... But Gregory Corso was also instrumental, indirectly, in what I consider saving my life.

This is how it happened.

It was a late, late night at the Chelsea Hotel. I had worked hard that day. Now I was tired and wasted. I needed some change of pace.

It was already after midnight but I had to do something. I had to go out and shake myself up. I had read my Francis Bacon.

I decided to go to Times Square and see what's happening there. I needed some night action.

So I put on my coat, I got my hat. It was a cool late fall night.

I opened the door, I was about to close it, when I heard a strange, strong thump. I looked back and I was surprised to see a book, amazingly fallen out from a tightly stacked shelf of books. One managed to slip out and fall on the floor.

I closed the door and went to the shelf. I was perplexed and amazed: How could a book jump out from such a tightly, nicely packed shelf? Yet there it was—the book was on the floor.

I picked up the book. It was Gregory Corso's *Happy Death*.

I held it in my hands and I read the title again.

Then I took off my coat, I took off my hat, and I said to myself, no, I am not going out tonight to Times Square or anywhere else. Some angels must be warning me. I ain't going out tonight.

Even today I believe that Gregory's book must have saved me from some disaster that night.

I told Gregory this story, a week or so before he died. He nodded weakly, and said he was pleased that he had saved my life... He was beautiful, Gregory, a beautiful poet, smith of words.

OPPOSITE: Gregory Corso, 1975.

The author exiting the Chelsea Hotel, 1967. Photo: Gideon Bachmann.

HOTEL CHELSEA

WEST TWENTY THIRD STREET
AT SEVENTH AVENUE
NEW YORK, N. Y. 10011

"A LANDMARK OF N.Y.C."

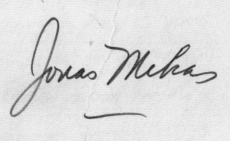

725

HOTEL
CHELSEA
23RD ST. AT 7TH AVE.
NEW YORK
N. Y. 10011

Keychain from the author's room at the Chelsea Hotel, where he lived from 1967 to 1974.

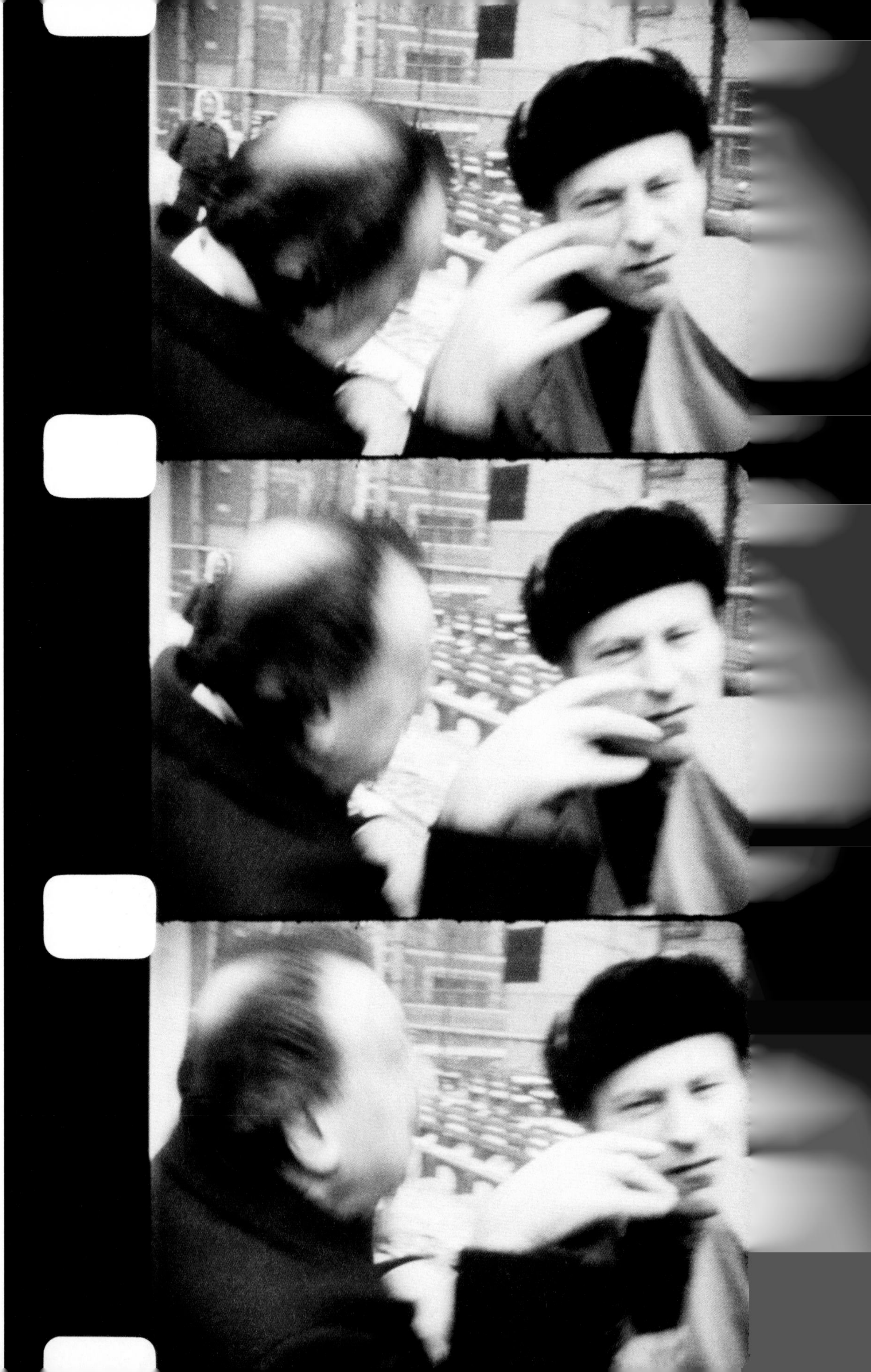

## SALVADOR DALÍ, PETER BEARD,
## MARIA MONTEZ AND JACK SMITH

It was in 1961 that I had moved into the third floor loft of 414 Park Avenue South. It was just across from the Belmore Cafeteria, a cab drivers' night stop. Belmore was also the downtown bohemians' late-hours hangout, after all the downtown places, including Cedar Bar, went dark. Belmore was open twenty-four hours and the food was cheap. I could see it all through my window. But nobody bothered me, there in my loft, which was also the editorial office of *Film Culture* magazine.

But in early 1962, Film-Makers' Cooperative was created and my loft became also the office of the Cooperative. Which also meant that it became a nightly hangout of the New York film undergrounders. But not only the film-makers: painters, musicians, poets, and film-makers, they were all intermingled in the sixties. Every night there were meetings, arguments, exchanges of works. I managed to retain a back corner for myself. The rest of my place became public property.

That's where I met Andy Warhol for the first time. And you could see on any regular evening Allen Ginsberg, Jack Smith, Bob Kaufman, Robert Frank, Angus MacLise and, of course, Barbara Rubin, who was my helper and keeper of the house at that time.

So it was there that one of such evenings, *clank clank* with his cane came Salvador Dalí with his escort, Miss France, Dufresne, a.k.a. Ultra Violet. He wanted to know what was happening in the New York art underworld. He was talking in four languages at the same time and we had a good time.

I had met Dalí only once before. It was in 1956. For the *Film Culture* magazine benefit premiere of Hans Richter's film *8x8*, he had written a little funny incomprehensible text. We read it at the screening of the film at the Museum of Modern Art. George Fenin, one of my editors, took the letter with him after the screening. I do not know what happened to it.

A couple of weeks after Dalí's visit to my 414 Park Avenue South place, Peter Beard calls me. Dalí had decided to do a series of happenings and he wants me to participate in them and film them.

I filmed several of Dalí's events. He was always fun to be with. Always an actor, a performer. An actor not in the Actors Studio style, but maybe more from the school of circus clowns... He always knew he was acting, acting to entertain.

OPPOSITE: Salvador Dalí and the author during the 1963 filming of Dalí's performance piece.

But even when he was clowning, you never knew what was really going on in his head. Occasionally, he didn't act, he sat there very alert and very much in himself, observing, very serious and very vigilant. But you couldn't read him.

The events that he did were dominated during that period by shaving cream, loads and loads of it. On cars, furniture and on beautiful women of which, thanks to Peter Beard, who was acting as his production manager of sorts, there was an inexhaustible supply at *Vogue* magazine. But there was also Taylor Mead, and myself, and Peter himself—we were all part of Dalí's cast.

I should tell you how I met Peter.

It was in 1962. My brother Adolfas was searching for a lead for his film *Hallelujah the Hills*. He needed someone physically flexible, someone with a good sense of humor, and an even greater sense of adventure. I mentioned this to my good friend, film-maker Jerome Hill, while visiting his studio. So he picks up an issue of *Life* magazine from the table, opens it, and there is Peter Beard, full-page, *Life* magazine's Young American Man of the Year. "That's my nephew Peter Beard, I think he is the man Adolfas is looking for."

That's how Peter Beard became the star of *Hallelujah the Hills*. Peter is still one of my best friends and whenever we meet, we have fun. He is great, Peter.

But let me return to Salvador Dalí for one more moment, because my story is not yet finished.

I had several occasions to spend some time in the company of Dalí and his wife, Gala, at his place at the St. Regis Hotel. Dalí was usually more subdued in a home situation. Despite all his clownings I had a feeling that basically he was very shy. Stan Brakhage also spoke to me on several occasions about his own shyness and how difficult it was for him to deal with it without resorting to clowning when in public.

One day when I arrived at Dalí's place there was a young woman there.

"Meet Tina, the daughter of Maria Montez," said Gala.

Daughter of Maria Montez! I could hardly believe it. I had to tell this to Jack Smith. Maria Montez was Jack's life obsession. He had dedicated his life and his art to her.

I told all this to the young woman. She became very curious about Jack. She asked if she could meet him.

**HALLELUJAH THE HILLS** Written and Directed by Adolfas Mekas

**With PETER H. BEARD SHEILA FINN MARTY GREENBAUM PEGGY STEFFANS**

Produced by DAVID C. STONE

Peter Beard in *Hallelujah the Hills* (1963), a film by Adolfas Mekas.

24

When I told this to Jack he got very, very excited. He even cooked some soup for me, which I ate despite a couple of roaches that were looking hungrily at me and my soup from not too far a distance.

Anyway, I arranged a meeting between the two. And I know they met. I wanted to join them but had to be in Paris and when I returned I was immediately drowning in an ocean of problems and tasks—my normal life in those days— and I forgot to ask how it went. It will always remain a secret, what happened when Jack met the daughter of his Muse.

June 12, 2011

As I was waiting in the ticket line at JFK, the man next on line introduced himself to me. Ivan Galietti, a photographer. We have met before, he said, at Salvador Dalí's place. He was there when I introduced Jack Smith to Tina Montez or, as he knew her, Tina Aumont. "Do you know what were the results of that meeting?" I asked him. "They struck quite a good friendship," he said. Later, in Rome, where they supposedly met again, Jack tried to persuade her to be part of a Tango piece he was planning to do, but she refused.

Helen Adam. Photo: LaVerne H. Clark.

## MEETING ROBERT DUNCAN

Helen Adam was one of the great Scottish poets of the New York sixties. She lived with her sister in a small Upper East Side apartment. I don't know how but we had become very good friends and whenever she had something special going on in her house she used to call me. By the way, she was also known for the hypnotic, remarkable singsong reading of her poetry.

Anyway, this was one of those evenings. I had to come, she said. Robert Duncan, the poet, was visiting and she wanted him to meet some of her friends.

Duncan was sitting on the edge of Helen's large bed that took up half of the room, leaving little place for chairs—her place was that small. He was sitting there and looking straight in front of him. We were introduced by Helen; I had never met him before. Duncan looked at me, but he was not really looking at me. His eyes were totally blank. I suddenly realized he was blind. I wondered why nobody had told me that. The evening went, we talked, and, of course, I paid attention to his blindness and acted accordingly. I don't think he left the bedside spot he was sitting on all evening. I found him like that and I left him like that.

Next day I called Helen. "Helen, you never told me Duncan was blind," I said.

"What?" exclaimed Helen. "Didn't you know he is cross-eyed? He isn't blind, no. He's only cross-eyed. When one is cross-eyed one's eyes are never focused on you."

That is how my first meeting with Robert Duncan went.

223 E 82nd St.
N.Y.C.
Oct 14th

Dear Jonas,

I can't tell you how much my sister & I enjoyed your lovely & mysterious letter from Spain. Pat is as enchanted with it as I am.

If, by any chance, you happen to be free on Thursday evening, the 19th, we are having a small party. (It has to be small in our tiny apartment) for the poet Robert Duncan, who is in town for one night. Do come if you can, any time after 9 o'clock. We are just off 3rd avenue, & on the second floor.

Best wishes always,

Helen

P.S. I am sorry to let you know so late but Duncan only phoned me yesterday.

223 E.82nd St.
Oct.11th

Dear Jonas,

It was such a pleasure to meet you again at Barbara & Howard's.

I enclose your Tarot reading & hope it will come true. It is one of the best anyone I know has had for a long time.

I was fascinated by your wonderful story of St.Teresa and the mysterious roses. It is wonderful to feel the goodwill of a great being from the supernatural world.

Very best good wishes always

Helen

P.S. Your most beautiful & haunting M.S.S. has just come. I was enthralled by it. The strange ritual of the long walk in the footsteps of the Saint, & the little dog licking the dust of your boots , & the bells echoing through the empty city early in the morning!

It is like an eerie & magic poem.

I do indeed hope you will truly make a film about St.Teresa. Only you could do it as beautiful as it should be done.

About the dragon dream. The oldest dragon of all is the Worm Curoborus who bites his own tail, & is one of the mighty symbols of Eternity. My own favorite dragon is "Smaug" in Tolkien's The Hobit! an adorably awful creature.

Thank you again for your lovely @ inspiring story.

Helen

Jonas

Tarot reading, Oct. 1967

1. First card. THE SIGNIFICATOR. The basis of things in both the Astral world and on the Earth.

THE LOVERS. The greatest love card in the pack. Love, beauty, trials overcome.

2. The card that covers. This means the atmosphere in which all the other currents work.

THE STAR , another great major card. The angel is pouring forth the waters of

life & blessing inspiration, & attainment.

3. The card that crosses. The opposing forces, but this card is also wonderful. THE WORLD.

THE WORLD. Fame, travel, success, happinness, great good fortune.

4. The best that can be expected in the circumstances, ACE OF SWORDS (reversed). A card of great force used ruthlessly. You are capable of taking of the Kingdom of Heaven by storm with your own strength, or of snatching the crown of triumph by sheer will power. But because this card is reversed the sword could be two edged & you yourself could be hurt by using it.

5. The base of things in the past. THE EMPEROR again a major card, meaning you have an Emperor's strength, & royal power.

6. The more immediate past. VII SWORD. Blindfolded among swords. Difficulties & not knowing just what way to turn. But not defeated, still on your feet.

7. The influence which is coming into play in the near fuure.

VI CUPS. New & happy relationship. Cups filled with stars & talents. The only problem, which to choose.

8. Yourself as the Tarot says you are now. V CUPS (reversed) a card of hesitation, having drunk of many cups & exausted them, you are not yet turning round to taste two more.

9. Environment. THE HIGH PRIESTESS. The great Queen of the world of mysteries. She could indead be Saint Theresa, as you sggested. Anyway she is watching over you.

10. Hopes & Fears. VII wands. Struggle, but with blessening wands, which means the struggles are somehow good.

11. The culmination of the reading . VI wands (reversed). Riding in triumph & covered with laurel. But because it is reversed this triumph, though sure, will be long in coming.

Alltogether a splendid reading, all sort of powerful beings of love & magic raining blessings on you.

Helen Adam

A letter from Helen Adam.

30

Christiane Rochefort, Cannes, 1963. From the author's unedited film footage.

# MY NIGHT IN JAIL AND LENNY BRUCE

I remember very well my father's advice when I was still a child: Whatever you do, see that you never end up in jail.

I remembered my father's words in March 1964 when I was sitting in my tiny prison cell in the Tombs. That's the name for the New York City prison. I ended up there because of the screening of Jean Genet's film *Un Chant d'Amour*. I did not have any regrets; I believed I did my citizen's duty. But I knew I would have had a great difficulty explaining it to my father.

Anyway, here I was in jail.

I had already been arrested two weeks earlier, for screening another film, Jack Smith's *Flaming Creatures*. Those were bad times. Same time as I was going through my censorship trials, Lenny Bruce was going through his. I survived mine. He was crushed.

Anyway, that evening, before screening Genet's film, knowing that I'd be arrested again, I had prepared myself by stuffing into my raincoat pocket half of a chicken. Jail food, you know, is horrible.

To make the story short, I was arrested, and I was now sitting in this cold, miserable cell. Suddenly I remembered the chicken. So I pulled it out of my pocket and began unwrapping it. And suddenly a virtual miracle happened. The stale, boring prison air was pervaded by the chicken aroma! To call it a smell would not be telling the truth. Yes, it was an aroma!

I was about to get my teeth into this piece of aroma when I perceived a noise by the iron bars separating my cell from the neighboring cell. This black guy, obviously awakened by the miraculous aroma, was looking through the bars at me. He was looking at me but he was really looking at my chicken.

So I broke the chicken in half and I squeezed one half through the bars, to the guy. He was elated.

"This is great chicken, man, this is great chicken," he kept saying.

So that was it. We ate our chicken and we slept. The next day I was bailed out.

Months passed. Maybe a year.

I was walking down Broadway, downtown.

Suddenly I heard a voice—a guy was running after me, all excited:

"Hey, man, do you remember me?"

"No," I said. I was trying to remember.

"I am the guy you gave half of your chicken to, in the Tombs, remember?"

Yes, now I remembered!

We had to go into the next whiskey bar and have a drink. Which we did.

I mentioned Lenny Bruce.

I had seen him perform only once and I didn't even know he was Lenny Bruce.

During the summer of 1962, one day I happened to be in Greenwich Village, and it was hot and I was thirsty so I walked into a small club or bar of sorts, for a drink. As I was drinking my beer I began to focus on this guy at the end of the place telling jokes. I moved closer. This guy was really outrageously funny. Not in the way that one usually tells jokes. He was just talking, in a very personal sort of way. I can still remember his voice, even now.

So I had my drink and I continued my walk.

It was later, when I saw the pictures in the papers, after his arrest, that I recognized the guy I saw that day in the club.

Sometime during the last days of Bruce's trial, Barbara Rubin, who was sort of helping me in those days with various tasks and who considered Lenny Bruce one of her heroes, went with her friend Rosebud to see him in court. They managed to get close enough to him to hand him a picture for an autograph. But neither they nor Bruce had anything to write with. So Barbara gave him her lipstick. Bruce smudged his name across the picture with it and then, in what looks like a violent outburst, stuck the lipstick though the picture, through his own face, obliterating his mouth. As if to say: *They are shutting me up!* And it's amazing to see this picture today. It's a picture that embodies the same violation as was performed by the justice system on him. I think he really meant it that way. It was his statement on the justice system of New York City that day.

The last time I saw Barbara, just before she left for France in 1972 (or was it in 1973?) she gave me that picture, together with her film *Christmas on Earth*. I still have it.

43 rue Piat Paris 20.

PARIS LE 16 AVRIL 1964

Monsieur le Rédacteur en Chef

La nouvelle est parvenue ici que le jeune réalisateur Jonas MEKAS est l'objet d'un procès pour avoir présenté une oeuvre de Jean Genêt, et nous en sommes attristés.

Les oeuvres des poètes appartiennent à l'esthétique et non à la morale; les faire connaître est toujours un bien, et un acte honorable. Jean Genêt est un grand poète, dont l'oeuvre théatrale est représentée à Broadway depuis des années.

Nous devons remercier Jonas MEKAS d'aider à la connaissance de Jean Genêt. Nous pensons que l'on ne peut dans aucun pays, sans encourir le blâme de l'Histoire, emprisonner un homme pour activité poétique, et nous souhaitons tres vivement que Jonas MEKAS ne soit pas condamné en Amérique de ce fait.

Simone de BEAUVOIR, Jean-Paul SARTRE,
Christiane ROCHEFORT

Cette lettre a été adressée au N.Y Times.

1. C. Rochefort

34

Photo of Lenny Bruce autographed with lipstick to Barbara Rubin.

OPPOSITE: Barbara Rubin in *Walden*, a film by the author.

# OFFICE MEMORANDUM

UNDERGROUND CINEMA                    (from Memo of August 1, 1963)

Jonas Mekas, who writes a disputatious Film Journal for the

Village Voice, said not long ago (May 2): "Perhaps you have noticed

that most of the time, lately, I have been writing about movies which

you can't see anywhere. I think it is a very bad state of affairs when

the best of contemporary cinema cannot be seen at all." Mekas went on

to say: "The movies I have in mind are Ron Rice's The Queen of Sheba

Meets the Atom Man; Jack Smith's The Flaming Creatures; Ken Jacobs'

Little Stabs at Happiness; Bob Fleishner's Blonde Cobra - four works

that make up the real revolution in cinema today. These movies are

illuminating and opening up sensibilities and experiences never before

recorded in the American arts, a content which Baudelaire, the Marquis

de Sade, and Rimbaud gave to world literature a century ago and which

Burroughs (Naked Lunch) gave to American Literature three years ago.

It is a world of flowers of evil, of illuminations of torn and tor-

tured flesh; a poetry which is at once beautiful and terrible, good

and evil, delicate and dirty. A thing that may scare an average

viewer is that this cinema is treading on the very edge of perversity."

These four films were made by members of the New American Cinema

Group, founded by Mekas in 1962. Their films are distributed (if

that is the right word for "movies you can't see anywhere") by the

## TIME
INCORPORATED

36

schedules: of trials:

Flaming Creatures    : May 18th June 2nd
Genet         ————  May 12th  June 2nd

Jacobs-Perlman  June 8th
Naomi.  June 2nd
Genet  June 15
FC.        "  10

Aug 11 13 F.C.
19. June- Genêt

Lve Marcuson 30th
July 30th- Jacobs
Aug 11th- JONAS
Aug 18th - JOEL

STATE OF NEW YORK
EDUCATION DEPARTMENT
DIVISION OF MOTION PICTURES
STATE BUILDING, 80 CENTRE ST.
NEW YORK 13, N. Y.

TM 3442
Serial No.
(16MM)

# ORIGINAL LICENSE

FILM-MAKERS' COOPERATIVE ................................................is hereby granted a license,

pursuant to the provisions of article 3 of the State Education Law and the Rules of the Board of

Regents adopted thereunder, for the exhibition of one print of a motion picture entitled

A MOVIE BY BRUCE CONNER    (MUSIC & SOUND EFFECTS)

made and produced by.....BRUCE CONNER.........................................................and

consisting of........414.........feet of film, for and in consideration of the required license fee duly

paid in the amount of $.3.50.................... .

The Division reserves the right to revoke this license.

STATE EDUCATION DEPARTMENT
DIVISION OF MOTION PICTURES

DEC 22 1964
Date of issue

*Director*

It is necessary to preserve this certificate.

Form 2.  Mp72-S62-9000  (2A4-37)

38

---

STATE OF NEW YORK
EDUCATION DEPARTMENT
DIVISION OF MOTION PICTURES
STATE BUILDING, 80 CENTRE ST.
NEW YORK 13, N. Y.

TM 3443
Serial No.
(16mm-gauge)

# ORIGINAL LICENSE

FILM-MAKERS' COOPERATIVE ................................................is hereby granted a license,

pursuant to the provisions of article 3 of the State Education Law and the Rules of the Board of

Regents adopted thereunder, for the exhibition of one print of a motion picture entitled

HENRY GELDZAHLER    (SILENT)

made and produced by.....ANDY WARHOL.........................................................and

consisting of.....1,186.........feet of film, for and in consideration of the required license fee duly

paid in the amount of $.7.00.................... .

The Division reserves the right to revoke this license.

STATE EDUCATION DEPARTMENT
DIVISION OF MOTION PICTURES

DEC 22 1964
Date of issue

*Director*

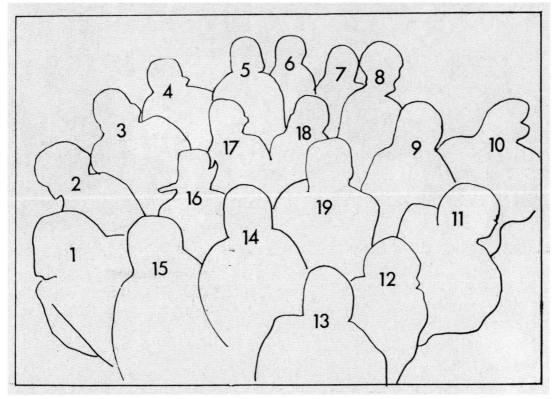

*Popular Photography*, April 1968: 1. Peter Max; 2. Anthony Johnopoulos; 3. Richard Leacock; 4. Ken Jacobs; 5. Robert Downey;
6. Andy Warhol; 7. Nico; 8. Paul Morrissey; 9, 18, 19: USCO, anonymous; 10. Cyril Griffin; 11. Jacques Katzmacher; 12. Paul Kim;
13. Jonas Mekas; 14. Stan Vanderbeek; 15. Don Snyder; 16. Barbara Rubin; 17. Jerry Brandt.

40

New American Cinema Group meeting, October 1960. FROM LEFT TO RIGHT: Seymour Val,
Ed Bland, Adolfas Mekas (*in back*), Lionel Rogosin, Alfred Leslie, unidentified, Shirley Clarke (*back to us*),
Gregory Markopoulos, Sheldon Rochlin (*in back*), unidentified.

**LOVE & KISSES TO CENSORS FILM SOCIETY**
(Division of the New American Cinema Group)

1963 MEMBERSHIP CARD NO. 1547

**SHOWINGS**
Every Monday Evening at
**THE GRAMERCY ARTS THEATRE**
127 East 27th Street, New York City

Jonas—

two plainclothes detectives visited
the Factory a few days ago ;
tried to get into the film. The film
I've left with you is most of
which ~~is~~ might be called pornography

or such. I've contacted the
Castelli Gallery re future
legal assistance. Andy
(says Gerard) is supposed to
return ca. May 21.

Billy

J Solanas
110 Greenwich [...] N.Y.
NYC 10071

New York
N.Y.
PM
15 APR
1969

U.S. POSTAGE
6¢

to Jonas Mekas
222 W 23
NYC 10011

42

## VALERIE SOLANAS AND ME

I had met Valerie Solanas, the author of *S.C.U.M. Manifesto*, a good number of times during my Chelsea Hotel period. We had drinks and conversations at the Chelsea's El Quijote bar. She was not crazy. I would describe her as a fanatic Dostoyevskian feminist. When I look back at my life, I have always attracted to myself unbalanced, extreme people.

Anyway, I think she considered me her friend. So when, after the shooting of Andy Warhol (June 3, 1968), she ended up in women's prison, which at that time was still on the Sixth Avenue and Eighth Street corner, she decided that I should be her confidant via whom she could communicate with the world. She sent me a number of letters which I was supposed to pass to the press, specifically to *The Village Voice*, where I was a columnist at the time. I passed the letters to the publisher but he didn't think they should be published. Now, reviewing her letters from the prison, I noticed that they were quite threatening. Actually, three years after her release from prison (for "reckless assault with intent to harm"), she was rearrested for threatening letters and calls to various people, including Warhol.

Solanas died in San Francisco from emphysema (April 26, 1988). Here is one of Valerie Solanas' letters to me:

TO ALL *VV* EDITORS & WRITERS

Dear sniveling cowards, liars, & libelers:

I was just informed that someone from the *VV* called Lorraine Miller, the lawyer the court appointed me to be my advisor (even though I didn't want an advisor, &, by the way, she's my advisor only; I'm representing myself) & asked her for a statement about me.

I DON'T want an article written about me, but I realize that, being I'm poverty-stricken & in jail, my desires count for nothing & that you'll go ahead & write an article anyway, &, further refuse, as you & the staffs of all other papers have always refused, to extend to me the simplest courtesy, which is also the most basic & minimal journalistic obligation to both the one written about & the readers, of contacting me, to verify the "facts" you print about me, even though my whereabouts since I shot Auntie Wahov have been both known & nearby.

Few journalists on this paper or any other would ever dare print anything about me other than the enormous, lavish lies (& the "facts" Howard Smith related in his last two SCENES articles about me are among the most enormous & lavish I've seen) your masters (Wahov & the vilest & toadiest of all toads, the GREAT TOAD, Maurice Girodias) pay you to print. If you did, Big Daddies Wahov & Toad would take you off their payrolls & withdraw their promises to publish your shit books.

I say few, rather than no, journalists because there are some (for example, Letitia Kent, who wrote the article about Wahov shortly after he got out of the hospital) whose mindlessness, who willingness to believe whatever anyone—Wahov. Whose very essence is a lie or his trained dog, the Great Vacuum, Viva, who salivates whenever Wahov rings the bell, or any other nonentity, who spoke to me once briefly &, therefore, "knows" me—tells them, makes it unnecessary to bribe them.

If you're the rational people you think you are, you'd realize that one's potential power is directly proportional to the number of bribes & lies it takes to try to squelch it, &, having realized that, you'd realize that a little groveling in my direction might be expedient, to phrase it delicately. Like all cringing cowards who kick those who are down & slobber & fawn over & hop to do the bidding of the wealthy & influential those same editors and journalists who are now disseminating the lies & aggrandizing at my expense the egos of their masters will someday, when scum secures power, lap away at my ass whenever I lift my finger.

4-12-69

Dear Jonas,

The enclosed letter is to all New
editors & writers. I'm sending it to you,
because if I sent it to the W office,
it might get intercepted by
you-know-who.

You're to show this letter to all
the editors & writers. If you don't, I'll
find out. The Great Toad isn't the
only one with a private central intelligence agency. And this
letter had better not find it's way
into the Toad's hands. If it does,
I'll not only find out, but I'll hold
you responsible.

I already know & have known for
quite some time of your dealings
with the toad regarding me.

Valerie Solanas.
VALERIE SOLANAS
Women's House of Detention
10 Greenwich Ave.
NYC 10011

Drop me a note as soon as you get
this.

# SCUM MANIFESTO

Presentation of the rationale and program of action of SCUM (Society
for Cutting Up Men), which will eliminate through sabotage all
aspects of society not relevant to women (everything), bring about
a complete female take-over, eliminate the male sex and begin to
create a swinging, groovy, out-of-sight female world.


by

VALERIE SOLANAS

You're probably snickering to your low-grade, spineless selves, secure in the knowledge that Toad & Wahov have me so sewed up by the shit contract I signed that I could never be other than either nothing or their total slave, but your smugness rests on your ignorance of my PH technique that I hit on in the course of developing my scum therapy, based on & derived from scum principles. My PH technique enables <u>any</u> male of <u>any</u> age to get a hard on any <u>time</u> he wants & sustain it as long as he wants. The personality changes brought about by achieving PH vastly increase his sexual feeling. I intend to give the Toad intensive scum therapy & teach him the PH technique, which will effect great changes in his personality, which will, in turn, render him manageable & easy to deal with, & I will as a result, get my works back.

Would you like to do something highly innovative? Have a journalistic first? Next time you print your string of filthy lies or mindless prattle about me—spell my name right.

Valerie Solanas
VALERIE SOLANAS
Women's House of Detention
NYC   4-5-69

<u>Definite</u> <u>proof</u> <u>of</u> <u>the</u> <u>gross</u> <u>inferiority</u> <u>of</u> <u>all</u> <u>of</u> <u>you</u> <u>to</u> <u>myself</u>: You wouldn't have the balls to engage me in debate—a freewheeling ad lib session with <u>no</u> moderator—on <u>live</u> t.v. with me. You would only dare attack me if I'm locked up (&, further, you feel confident that I'll be locked up for quite some time), &, therefore, unable to counterattack.

48

## TINY TIM AND MY BRIEF CAREER AS MUSIC AGENT

If you were at the Living Theatre, or some other similar downtown New York venue, in the early sixties, and if by an unfortunate chance the lights happened to go out, and the audience was beginning to get nervous, there would suddenly come up, from somewhere in the first row, the gentle sound of ukulele and an equally gentle falsetto voice of Tiny Tim. Tiny Tim was a familiar fixture at many downtown New York events of the early sixties. He was always there with his big paper bag in which he carried his ukulele, and nobody knew what else, always ready for the occasion.

I do not remember exactly how we met, but we became good friends. He came to many of the shows I was running. For the premiere of Gregory Markopoulos' film *Twice a Man*, Barbara Rubin, who was my helper at the Film-Makers' Cooperative at that time, got him to carry a large banner advertising the film at the yearly Polish parade, with Tiny Tim at one end of the banner and Cynthia McAdams, a budding photographer, at the other end. Barbara and Cynthia had struck a very unique friendship with Tiny Tim. He was mad about them, and they were mad about his music and his unique, childlike personality. He was their doll—he permitted them to give him baths, they washed him, they groomed him, and he enjoyed it all, and he played his ukulele for them in the bathtub, and he laughed and he giggled for them nonstop.

Since I thought he was an amazing singer, I decided that the whole world should hear him: I decided to become Tiny Tim's music agent. He liked the idea. Barbara found an empty loft, we got Ken Jacobs to bring his tape recorder, and in one nonstop, three-hour session, we recorded his entire repertoire of songs, fifty-five in all. He never stopped, he just went from one song right into the next, with no pauses in between.

It was an amazing session.

OPPOSITE: Tiny Tim, 1964.

So there I was, a budding music agent, with two hours of the most beautiful ukulele music and equally most beautiful Tiny Tim voice, ready to bring him to the wide world. To help me to do that, I got help from Marvin Karpatkin, a lawyer friend who had handled some music people before and knew something about the field. For a year or so we tried to sell Tiny Tim to music companies. We worked hard at it. But the answer we got was always, "No, no, who wants to listen to a guy playing ukulele, and with that weird falsetto!" After a year or so we decided to drop the idea, we were going nowhere with it. And that was the end of my career as a music agent.

Four or five years later, Tiny Tim was "discovered" and signed up by a big music company. Signed up and destroyed. The music business people didn't see the beauty of the pure Tiny Tim: They made him sing with an orchestra... He was still good, even commercially presented. They could not destroy him completely; he still shined through. He even seemed enjoying doing it. But the innocence and purity was gone, the beauty of pure ukulele was gone, the Tiny Tim of our downtown memories, the Tiny Tim that I knew, was gone.

But he still exists in the tapes that we with Barbara recorded that evening, and the first lines of all fifty-five songs are written in Barbara's hand on the reel-to-reel boxes, beginning with "I don't care if the sun don't shine," and ending with "Dina, is there anyone–fina."

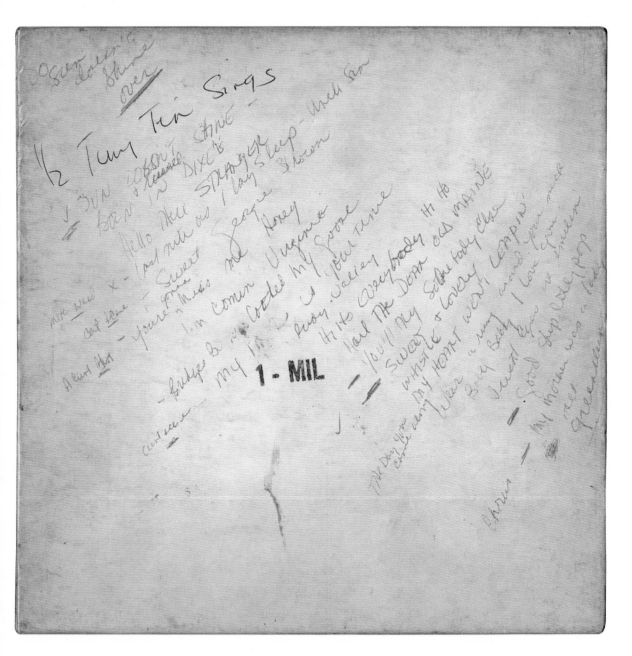

½ Tiny Tim Sings

1 - MIL

51

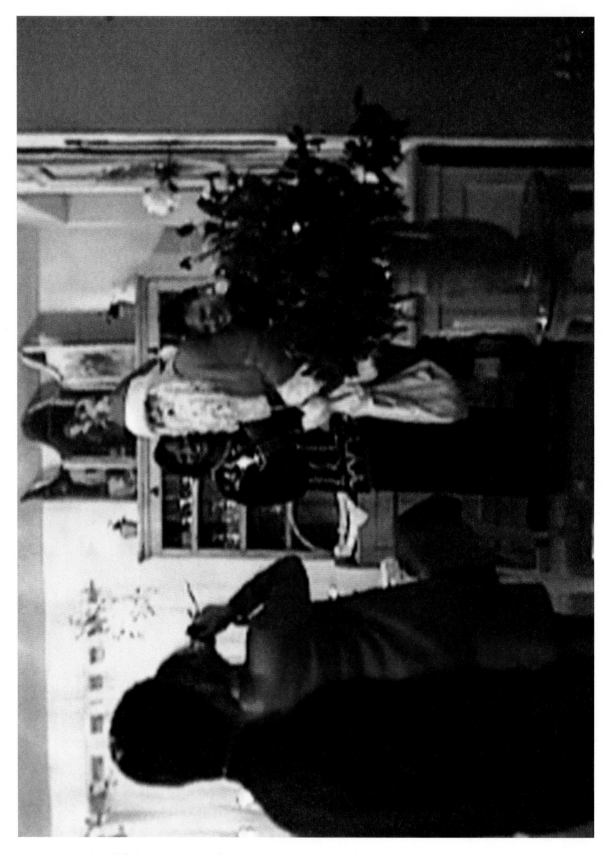

Arnold Schwarzenegger as Santa Claus, Los Angeles, 1998. From the author's video archives.

# MEETING ARNOLD SCHWARZENEGGER

It was just before Christmas. The year was 1994. I was in Los Angeles, visiting my friend Hiro Yamagata.

I was still deep in my sleep when I was woken up by a powerful thundering noise of motorcycles. Later I asked Hiro about it. "Ah," he said, "every Sunday morning we go riding into the desert with Arnold. Arnold Schwarzenegger. For fun."

"Do you want to go to a children's Christmas party? It's at my friend's home," he said later that day. Having nothing else to do, I said, "Yes. That would be great."

The evening proceeds, children are having a great time—Hollywood children, but children are always children.

It was a real children's Christmas party including, of course, the Santa. And what would be a children's Christmas party without a Santa! But there he comes, jolly, laughing *ho ho ho*, and the children like him very much because he is so funny.

A woman next to me whispers in my ear, "Do you know who he is?" "No," I say, "I don't. Who is he?" "It's Arnold," whispers the woman.

Yes, I looked at the Santa closer now. Yes, it was Arnold, there was no mistake. And he was having a great time!

Then he put the bag of gifts on his big shoulders and he walked out to treat other children with gifts and joy. He was beautiful, Arnold.

I have to tell you another anecdote involving Hiro Yamagata.

The first time I met Hiro he told me that one of the people he would really like to meet was Allen Ginsberg. Could I introduce him to Allen? That is the easiest thing to do, I said, I will take you to Allen right now. Allen had called me earlier that day, asking me to come to the New York University gallery where he was hanging his photo show.

So we go, and sure, Allen is there. So I introduce Hiro to Allen and I leave because I have many other things to do.

Next day Allen calls me. "Who is this?" he says. "He just bought my entire show!"

And that was the truth; that was Hiro's way of doing things. Hiro liked Allen and he liked his photographs. And he knew Allen was broke. Later Hiro arranged a show of Allen's photographs at the Venice Biennale. He also paid Allen's cancer bills, as he later did for Gregory Corso. Allen wrote a beautiful piece about Hiro's show *Earthly Paradise* in the show's catalogue.

54

Hiro Yamagata with the author, 1998.

OPPOSITE: Allen Ginsberg and Peter Orlovsky, Central Park, c. 1980.

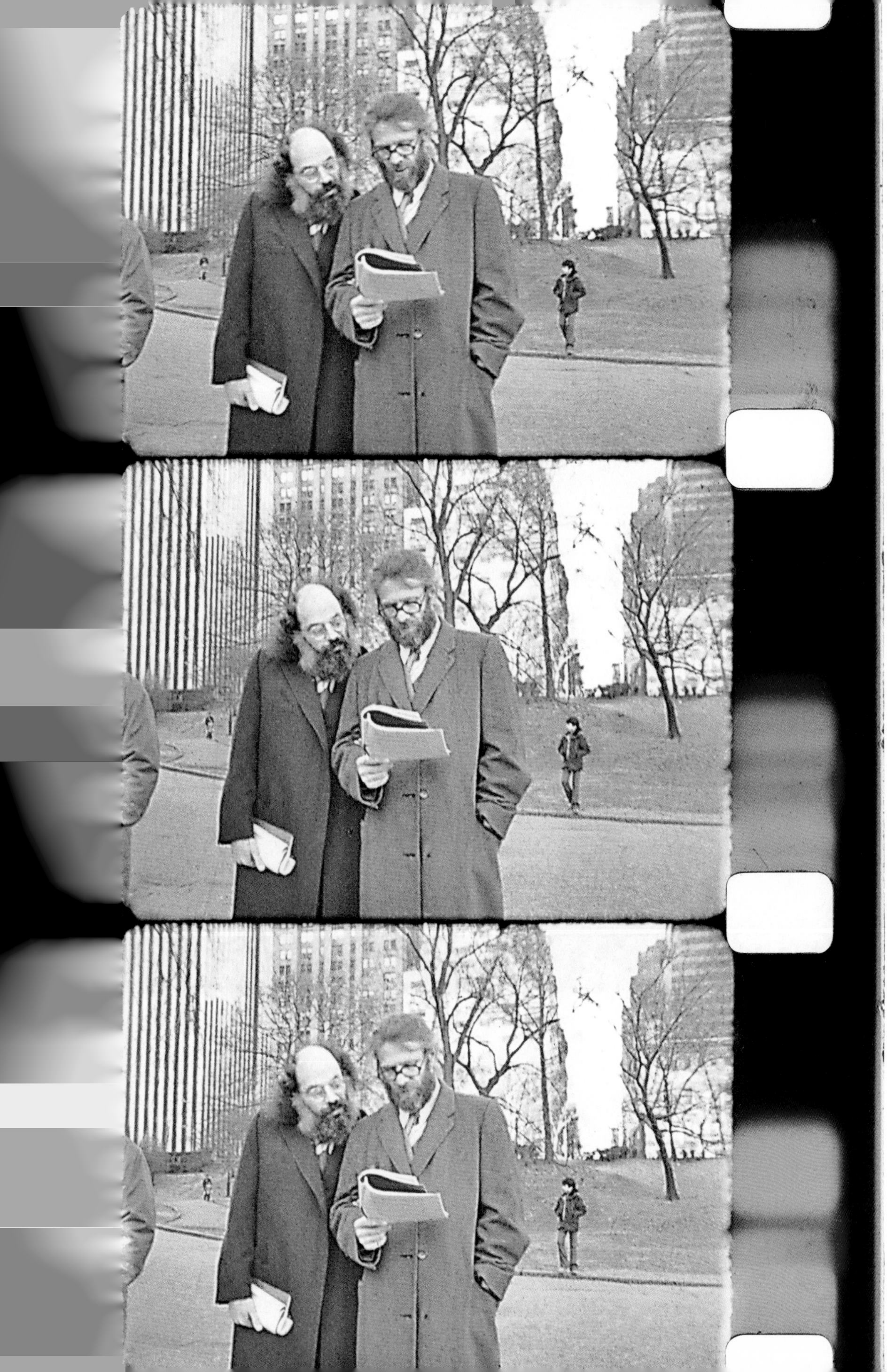

The author with Andy Warhol at the Factory. Photo: Stephen Shore.

## ANDY'S MIAMI AFFAIR

So this woman calls Anthology Film Archives and she says, "I want to talk to Jonas, I have something very important to tell Jonas, could I get his telephone number?" So they say, "No no no, Jonas will call you."

So I call her. The message said it was very important. I am very curious. Who knows, maybe it's really important. She sounds, from her voice like she could be seventy or seventy-five, and she speaks very, very slowly. So I say to myself, it's OK, I have to give time to it. I resigned to it.

So she says, "When I was seventeen I was studying art and I ended up some-how in Miami Beach. I was in Miami, I was swimming, and there I met a young man who said he lives in a wooden cottage there on the beach and his name he said was Andy Warhola. And I was seventeen and he was some three years older than me. So he invited me to his place, and I visited him several times, he made some drawings of me, very detailed, very detailed, and I made some drawings of him, and there were always some young men around him, and one day when we were alone he says to me, 'I have to tell you, I don't want to be a homosexual, could we...' and he made some passes at me. But you know, I was seventeen, and I was very shy, I was very shy, I was seventeen. I did not know what to do, he said, 'I do not want to be a homosexual.' I saw him a couple more times. But you know, I am Jewish. Are you Jewish?" "No," I said, "I am Lithuanian." She continued, "I am Jewish and I have this guilt thing, you know? For many years I have been carrying this guilt that if I would have made love to him, the whole history of art would have changed." "Probably, yes," I said. "Probably, yes..." "I have told this story to many," she continued, "to many who have written books about Andy, and they all said 'No no no, he has never been in Miami, you are inventing this story.' But you know, I am not inventing it, it's true." "I know," I said. "I believe you."

We talked for a while longer, then we hung up. I believed her—her voice told me she was true.

58

## A DAY IN MY LIFE AS A DOG

I don't really know how it happened, but one day in 1967, I decided to try a dog's life. I mean, to live like a dog among dogs.

I was helped in this idea by the fact that I was staying at the house of Minnie Cushing—actually it was an old mansion, in Massachusetts, and there were many dogs in it, big and small, old and young, and they seemed to be all of a family, a family of dogs.

It was not really my idea. It was an idea of Peter Beard's, who often gets such crazy ideas. But I liked it.

So I spent most of my day on all fours. That is, running around with other dogs on all fours. It was a grueling task, but I was in perfect physical shape so I had no problem with that. More of a problem was the fact that the dogs were usually running faster than I could—that is, on all fours. And what's worse, they were not in favor of sitting still for too long: They preferred just running around all the time, the whole bunch of them. I had no choice but to stay in the game with them, including chasing after cars, which drove me really nuts. The other problem was drinking water out of the bowl. I just couldn't squeeze myself between their snouts, my head always got in the way. But I was not bad in the bone-catching games, which surprised Minnie. Things like that.

I have to tell you that in spite of the grueling day, I ended up feeling great. I thought that a dog's life, after all, was not that bad; actually, it was great compared to the lives of the humans around me. I'll never say again, "Oh, this is a dog's life."

59

PAGES 58, 60–61: The author as a dog, with Minnie Cushing, Newport 1967. Filmed by Peter Beard.

60

61

# WEEGEE'S AND MACIUNAS' ASHES
## AND GINSBERG'S BEARD

October 6, 2004

A headline in *The New York Sun* says:

VERONICA LAKE'S ASHES LOCATED...
IN UPSTATE ANTIQUE SHOP.

This reminded me of an anecdote that I cannot restrain myself from telling you.

I think it was 1974. It was a beautiful summer day. Hollis, my wife, and myself thought it was a perfect day for a picnic in Central Park. So I packed my picnic basket. I was in my Italian period, so it consisted of pepperoni, Italian cheeses, Dapolito's bread, and a bottle of Chianti (it's very good on a hot summer day).

After a couple of hours in the park, we decided to pay a surprise visit to our friend Cornell Capa, at ICP (The International Center of Photography), just across the street from the park.

Cornell enjoyed the surprise. Especially when we laid out on his office table our picnic supplies.

We had a great time.

I don't remember how the talk turned to Weegee. During the mid-sixties, when I ran Film-Makers' Cinematheque on 41st Street, we became good friends with Weegee and his funny wife. They came very often to see films and hang around.

"You must have some of his work at ICP," I said.

Capa laughed:

"His work? Not only do I have his photographs, I have his ashes. Look."

And he opened his desk drawer. It was a huge, old-fashioned office desk with huge drawers. It was full of routine office drawer junk—pencils, rubber bands, pencil sharpeners, old batteries, etc.

"Look, here are Weegee's ashes." And he pointed to a little urn. "I didn't know where to put it, so I stuck it in the drawer..."

OPPOSITE: Cornell Capa at his office at the International Center of Photography, 1974.

He closed the drawer and we continued our picnic.

You may not find this story funny but that afternoon we all thought that it was very funny.

Now, after telling you this anecdote about Weegee's ashes, I must tell you another story. I must.

It's about the ashes of George Maciunas.

In 1997, the young people of Vilnius were celebrating Fluxus and its creator George Maciunas. Tomas Venclova, a poet who was teaching at Yale University's Slavic department, was about to visit Vilnius around that time. He decided to bring a present to the Vilnius Fluxus enthusiasts. He decided to bring George himself back to Lithuania by way of his ashes.

64

But he faced a problem: The ashes of George Maciunas, according to his wishes, were cast into the Atlantic Ocean in Greenwich, Connecticut. Venclova turned to Yale's scientists and posed a question: Suppose I fill up this little flask with the water from the Long Island Sound bay. What is the probability that some of George's ashes would appear in this flask? Professor Chikanyan of Yale's physics department came to the conclusion that yes, some atoms of George definitely had to be in that flask. As a matter of fact, millions of them.

So Venclova took the flask to Vilnius and, in a special celebration, it was emptied into the Vilnelė River that runs through Vilnius, symbolic of George Maciunas' return to Lithuania, his native country.

P.S. December 29, 2009

The other day, as I was sorting out some old papers, my eye stopped on a clipping, a photograph I had cut out from the May 15, 1983 issue of *Vienybė*, a Lithuanian weekly paper that used to come out in Brooklyn, now defunct. The caption to the picture which I am reproducing here read:

Weegee at a 1957 screening (a benefit for *Film Culture* magazine) of Hans Richter's film *8x8*. Photo: Elliott Landy.

66

Friends of George Maciunas, after casting his ashes into the Atlantic Ocean.
Reproduction of a photo from *Vienybė*, May 15, 1983.

67

The ceremony of emptying the flask of George Maciunas' ashes
into the Vilnelė River, Vilnius, Lithuania. Photo: Romas Lileikis.

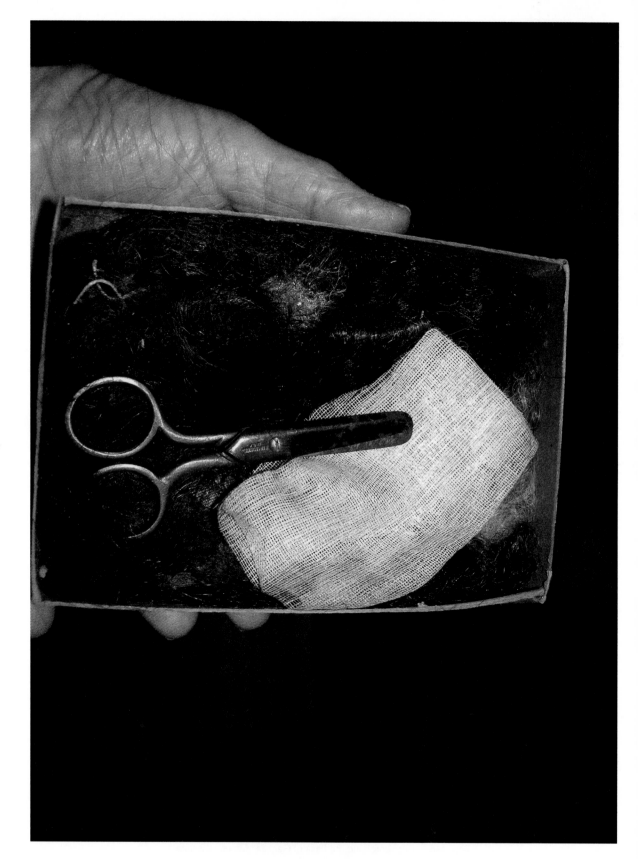

The beard of Allen Ginsberg.

"It's five years since the death of George Maciunas, the initiator of the Fluxus movement. His last wish was that his ashes be cast into the Atlantic Ocean. This photograph was taken near the Greenwich, Connecticut lighthouse. In the picture from left to right: Barbara Moore; a writer from *Artforum* magazine; composer Yoshi Wada who during the casting of the ashes into the ocean performed a moving, sad piece; the artist Ay-O; Nijole Salcius; and Nijole Maciunas-Valaitis, George's sister."

OK, this will be the last footnote on this subject. Not exactly the same, but similar.

In 1963 Barbara Rubin persuaded Allen Ginsberg to shave off his beard. She did it herself at the Film-Makers' Cooperative when it was still at 414 Park Avenue South. She put the beard in a little box and placed it on the shelf next to the film cans. As years went by everybody forgot about it. But the other day, as I was sorting out my books and stuff, I came upon a little box. I opened it: It was Allen Ginsberg's beard... I closed the box and put it back next to his books.

70

# NAM JUNE PAIK'S POLITICAL PERFORMANCES

January 5, 2005

We did many things together with Nam June Paik over the years. There is nobody greater than Nam June Paik...

But I am most fond of our political Fluxus performances. After all, we both were, and probably still are, exiles.

One thing that we used to do is to remind audiences of human rights as defined in the United Nations Charter. One of the last such performances we did was at the University of Cincinnati in March of 1968. We went onstage and I read the United Nations Charter in Lithuanian, while at the same time Nam June read it in Korean. I say read, but what we actually did was struggle through it, trying to translate it from English into Lithuanian and Korean. And I have to tell you that it's hard to imagine a harder task. Reason for that being that the language of the United Nations Charter is incredibly bureaucratic and convoluted.

So there we were, Nam June Paik and myself, onstage, struggling with the text. And, of course, we did a horrible job of translation. But, of course, nobody knew it—the audience spoke neither Lithuanian nor Korean. But we didn't care about that. We had to make our political statement and we did it in a Fluxus sort of way.

I have to tell you about another political performance of Nam June Paik's. I wasn't part of this one. It took place in Washington, D.C. When I tell people about this performance not everybody believes me. And it was only in a paragraph in the *New York Post* that it was reported. No one else, as far as I know, dared to report on it. Unfortunately, I have misplaced the *Post* clipping [included].

In 1998, the president of South Korea was visiting President Clinton at the White House. I do not have the exact date with me as I am writing this down, but anyone interested in it can find it easily. Anyway, the president of South Korea was meeting President Clinton. For that occasion a dozen prominent Koreans living and working in the United States were invited to the White House. And, of course, none is more prominent than Nam June Paik.

OPPOSITE: Nam June Paik, Soho, c. 1976.

As some of you may know, in 1996 Nam June Paik had a stroke, as a result of which he was restricted to a wheelchair. So here he was, at the White House, in a wheelchair. President Clinton approached each of the Korean guests and greeted them. Noticing that Nam June Paik was in a wheelchair, he indicated that he should remain seated. But Nam June Paik insisted that it was only proper for him that he gets up to receive the president's greetings. And so he did. And as he did stand up, his pants fell down. His pants fell down! In front of all the dignitaries and all the TV cameras. An immediate brief explanation of the happening came from I am not sure whom, Paik himself or the person in charge of the wheelchair, the explanation being that Paik had lost so much weight because of the stroke that most of his clothes had become too large for him...

Now you have to remember that this event happened during the Lewinsky affair period...

I asked Nam June Paik, some years later, if it was really an accident or a planned event. He laughed but did not offer an explanation. But I am absolutely sure that it was all very carefully planned, all of it. It's 100 percent Paik. Outrageous and totally innocent at the same time. But right to the point.

P.S.

On May 26 of this year (2006), the Guggenheim Museum held a memorial evening in honor of Nam June Paik. There were several speakers telling a lot about Nam June Paik's eventful life. On that occasion, I decided to tell to the friends of Paik, crowded in the Guggenheim Museum's spaces—the balconies were opened to the attendees of the memorial—yes, I decided to tell them about Paik's White House event. The story was well received, as it should have been. I added that the story may be completely invented, even if it seemed to be in a perfect Paik/Fluxus style.

But the audience was in for a surprise. Ken Paik Hakuta, Nam June Paik's nephew, came to the mike and admitted, "Yes, it was me who pulled up Nam June's trousers. It all happened as you told. President Clinton's face did not betray any reaction one way or the other during the incident, but I saw Hillary's face and she looked mad as hell."

72

Hermann Nitsch, Nam June Paik and the author, Anthology Film Archives, 1994. Photo: Arunas Kulikauskas.

DEAR SHIGEKO & NAM JUNE PAIK:

Just to tell you that you are the Best
Be it the East or be it the West.
Forgive me that I so seldom talk to you
but I think of you often, dear Friends, I do.
My life keeps me busy more than I can take
even this hot August when I sweat and bake
and drink water and Pelegrino and beer
and nothing helps. But we are still here,
while so many good friends are gone away
in time and space -- but we are still here, we still play
our Fluxus games. Aren't we lucky, my friends!
Ah, we never know, where it begins or where it ends,
so I said to myself, drinking my glass of wine,
I should write to you this note, and wish you a very very
summer, wherever you'll be -- both of you --        /fine
because both of you have given me so much, it's true,
it's very true -- good memories of the good past
time we spent together -- yes, good memories will last
long long after everything else will fade away
in time and space -- yeas, yes, what else can I say
but one thing: as the time goes, and the game ends
there is nothing more important than good, old
friends!

August 1, 2002

# Page Six ®

### By RICHARD JOHNSON
with Jeane MacIntosh

## Dropped trou

IT'S one thing to forget to zip up your fly. What happened to **Nam June Paik** is on a whole other level. The avant-garde video artist, now a bit frail at 65, had his pants fall down — all the way down to his ankles — as he shook hands with **President Clinton** at the state dinner for Korean leader **Kim Dae Jung** Tuesday night. Paik, who had evidently lost some weight since he last wore his tuxedo, was in a wheelchair being escorted by his nephew **Ken Hakuta**. But Paik stood up to shake Clinton's hand in the receiving line. That's when his beltless, and suspender-less, pants headed south, revealing to one and all that he wasn't wearing any underwear. Clinton handled the episode with aplomb, basically pretending nothing out of the ordinary was going on as Hakuta pulled up his uncle's trou. Lots of still and video cameras recorded the scene, making it a tough decision for editors whether to use the images.

75

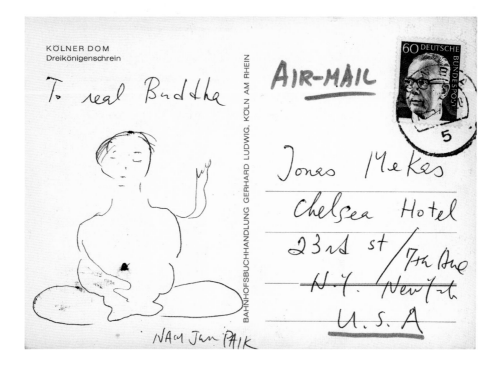

KÖLNER DOM
Dreikönigenschrein

To real Buddha

NAM June PAIK

AIR-MAIL

Jonas Mekas
Chelsea Hotel
23rd st / 7th Ave
N.Y. New York
U.S.A

# A VISIT TO HELEN LEVITT

February 13, 2002

Visited Helen Levitt. I asked her to help Anthology to match Robert Frank's endowment grant by donating some photographs. Robert had just given us a grant from a humble foundation he had established in memory of his daughter, Andrea.

Helen called me yesterday. "Of course I'll give you some photographs," she said. So this morning I went to her East 12th Street place, where she has been living for the last several decades. The door was open; a brown cat met me at the door.

She hasn't changed since I saw her last, some fifteen years ago. Looks very happy, very much in herself, and hasn't lost her sense of humor.

I asked if I could take some video shots of her room and herself. She firmly refused. She said, for her new book, *Crosstown*, they wanted to interview her, but she refused. Helen is a person who sees everything while herself remaining totally invisible.

When I had Helen at my ICP series, in the seventies, she said she had a camera with a lens on the side of the camera, not in front, so people won't suspect she is photographing them.

Anyway, we had a nice meeting. Later I went to the Strand bookshop to see her friend Devereau. Helen said, "See my friend Devereau. He'll give you my new book."

"Did she ever show you her footage for a never-completed film on Central Park?"

"No," I said, "I didn't know she did filming in Central Park."

"It has some images that are as strong as some of the images in her book," said Devereau.

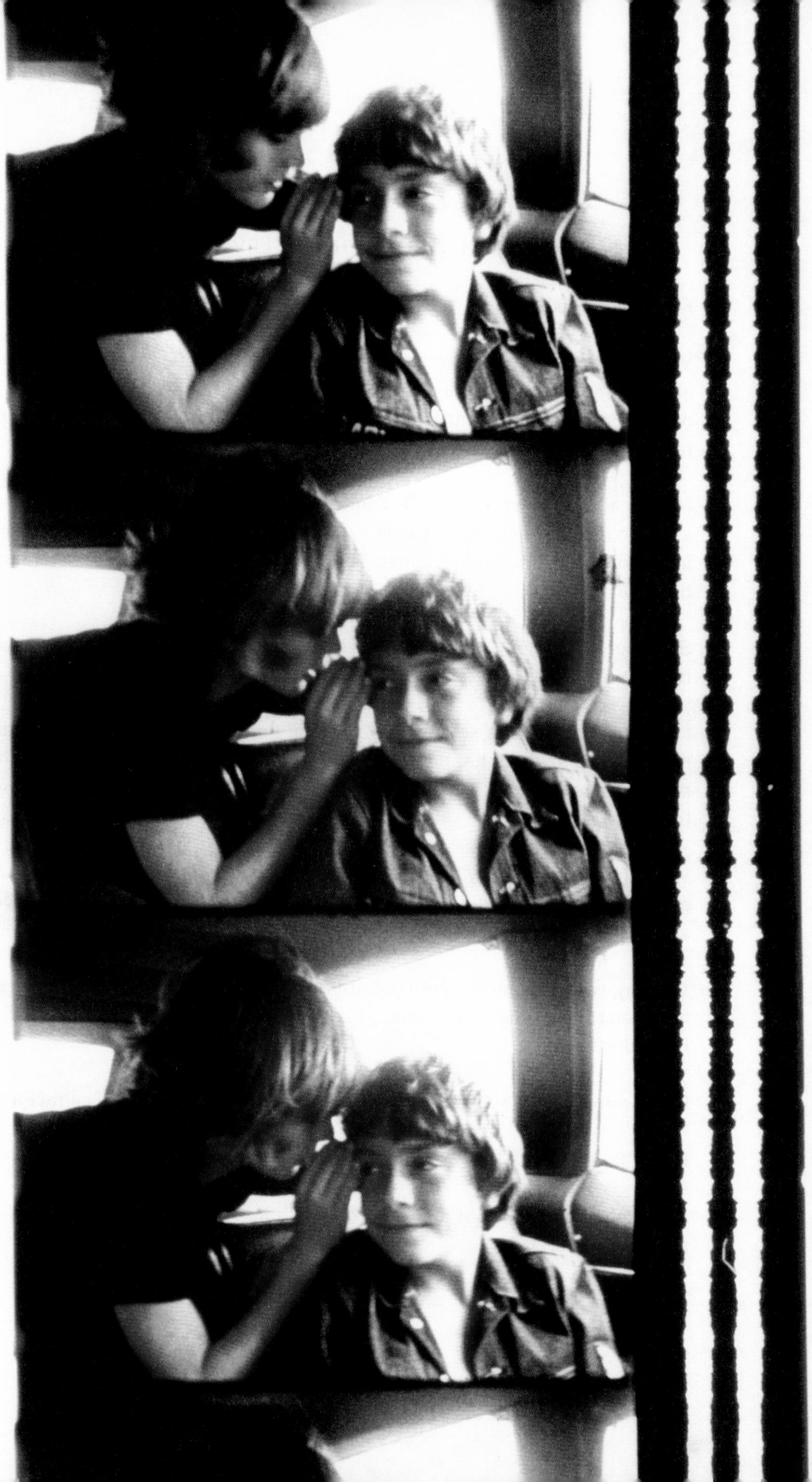

# A CLOSE CALL:
## PETER BEARD AND THE KENNEDY CHILDREN

The summer of 1972 was a very happy time in Montauk for Caroline and John Kennedy Jr., and Tina and Anthony Radziwill. Lee Radziwill had rented one of Andy Warhol's houses on the shore of Montauk's Atlantic coast—a large, beautiful seashore house where Lee stayed and where now the Kennedy and Radziwill kids spent much of their summer. Andy stayed there too during much of the summer, in one of the houses. And so did Peter Beard. Peter, besides being a tutor of the kids, was also a sort of bodyguard. I had a similar function sometimes during the summer. There were also occasional other visitors, especially during weekends.

That summer—I am not sure about the exact date—it was only a weekend or two after Peter's return from Kenya. What I want to tell you happened one weekend during that summer. Lee had some business to attend to in New York and she had to leave earlier that Sunday. Peter was entrusted to drive me and the children back to New York in his car.

Somehow it was still bright, an early evening, as we were reaching a midway point of our journey, when by chance I lifted my eyes from the book I was reading and I couldn't believe what I was seeing: Peter was driving on the wrong side of the road! Momentarily he had slipped back into Africa! I saw that Peter was totally oblivious to that fact and also, at the same time, I saw a car coming full speed our way. It all took place in a split second. "PETER, WATCH!" I shouted.

Of course, Peter being Peter, his reaction was as speedy as it had to be—that is, light speed. He turned to the right in just enough time to avoid a head-on crash.

We continued as if nothing had happened. Only later, at home, and during the coming weeks, actually years, that moment kept coming back to me. I've never asked Peter how he remembers it. Knowing his adventurous style of life, he probably took it as a very routine event. To Peter it was only one of hundreds of such split-second escapes.

I never mentioned this event to Jackie or Lee, not wanting to upset them.

OPPOSITE: Anthony Radziwill and John Kennedy Jr., 1971.

80

# FILMING POETS AND JEROME HILL'S CAMERA

The year was 1959. The Living Theatre had just moved to their corner of Sixth Avenue and 14th Street location. A poetry evening was taking place. The Living Theatre was very open to manifestations of whatever was new and exciting in the other arts. In 1954, the very first screening of Stan Brakhage's films, a landmark in the history of American avant-garde film, took place at the Living Theatre's Broadway and 100th Street corner place.

So now, in its new home, downtown, a very special poetry reading was taking place. Allen Ginsberg, Frank O'Hara, LeRoi Jones (Amiri Baraka), Ray Bremser. I had to record it with my camera. I had to!

Only a few days earlier Jerome Hill had lent me a small US Signal Corps 35mm Eyemo camera—you know, the one if you'd drop it from a plane it would certainly survive. They were that solidly made.

So the reading begins, and I push the button and the camera rolls. But I had never used this camera before and I didn't know how loud these cameras were, the sound that they made! And I was, of course, sitting in the first row in order to catch it all. Suddenly everybody turned toward me, including Allen, who was reading. For a moment I was determined not to be distracted from my documentary mission. I kept my finger on the button. But some twenty seconds later I had to admit to myself that I was making a real nuisance of myself. I had to quit. I did some more filming that evening, but I did it during the intermission, backstage.

Many years later Allen saw the footage I took of the reading. "Why didn't you take more of it? This is very important stuff," he said. "How could I? You yourself were panicking about the sound the camera was making." "You should have continued anyway," said Allen insistently. Allen always had this documentarist's streak in him. When in 1987 I got my first video camera, he saw it on my table and asked me to show him how to use it. Once I showed him how, he began videotaping my loft, in one long twenty-minute nonstop take, recording everything in it.

81

OPPOSITE: LeRoi Jones (Amiri Baraka) and Frank O'Hara.
Poetry reading at the Living Theatre, November 2, 1959.

"This is very important for the history, it must be videotaped, everything in this room," he said. He got so excited about it that he asked where he could get a video camera for himself. So during the next days I managed to get one for him from Sony, for free. "Just in time," he said. "Tomorrow I am leaving for Israel. I'll record my trip."

I saw Allen again a month or two later. "How was the Israel trip? Did you get a lot of footage?"

"The camera was stolen from me the first day I landed in Israel," said Allen.

I want to return to Jerome Hill, who lent me the Eyemo camera.

He was a great guy, Jerome. He loved Greece. He spent a lot of time in Greece when he was younger and had some relatives there too who spent summers there. He took a lot of photographs there, which he published in a book called *Trip to Greece* (1936).

Then came the war. He was drafted into the Signal Corps and eventually ended up with a division that was destined to invade Greece.

So the army guys call Jerome and his buddies to prepare them for the landing. The lieutenant in charge has it all planned out. He has a big table covered with pictures of the coastline on which they are contemplating to land. These pictures were to help familiarize them with the coastline. So the lieutenant comes to Jerome and asks if he understood the instructions. At which point Jerome says to the lieutenant: "That house there, that is Tante Olga's house. That one is the fisherman's who is a very good cook. Ah, yes, but that house there is no longer there—I helped Tante to tear it down. They planned to build another one, but never did..."

All the pictures were from his Greece book!

Frank O'Hara reading, 1959. IN THE BACKGROUND, FROM LEFT: Ray Bremser, LeRoi Jones
(Amiri Baraka), Allen Ginsberg. Photo: Reproduction from *ARTS* magazine (April 1974).

84

# TO KEN JACOBS ABOUT OUR BLEEDING NOSES

Evening—as usual—of April 10. Now: Morning of the 11th, the year: 2001

Dear Ken:

My nose is bleeding. So I thought I will write you this little letter. Because you are my nose-bleeding friend. I remember you told me that. I even filmed you showing your bleeding nose in Binghamton.

Anyway, as far as I can remember, age seven, age ten, age twelve, fifteen—my nose was always bleeding, once a month or so. I used to sit on a stone, in the fields, watching the cows, shepherd that I was, and the nose used to start bleeding. It was always so upsetting and mysterious because there was so much blood and I used to run home to my mother who did everything to stop the blood running, with cold water, pails and pails of bloody water. I still see those pails. Or lying on my back. Or stuffing the nose with cotton or some other stuff. But then it ran into my mouth. Ah, the smell of blood, I can still taste it in my mouth.

Anyway, it happened again and again.

All the blood I've left in the fields of my childhood, and in all the travels over Europe, war time—not blood of war, but blood from my own nose, how pathetic...

Then it stopped. Maybe for three decades.

But now for the last few months, my nose decided to get back at her bloody works, and today, I was walking down Mulberry Street, and it started again. I tried to keep my head sort of up—people looked at me, they thought I was weird—but it kept running. I had a napkin in my pocket, now it was all bloody, and the people looked at me—who knows, this may be contagious, AIDS or something—but then it stopped. By the time I arrived at Anthology it was sort of OK...

Later I asked Hollis, "Do you know why my nose is bleeding?" She thought, all her teachings tell her, that there must be something in my nose that demands more blood, or too much blood, run into it. But when I was a child I don't remember anything being wrong with my nose except that bloody bleeding.

So I thought I'll write you this note, brother in bloody nose, brother of bleeding nose. Do you have any theories or explanations for why your nose used to bleed? Is it still bleeding, sometimes? Things like that. We just have too much blood, somehow. Why? Why? Why? Why aren't we like other normal human beings? It would be so nice...

Jonas

OPPOSITE: Ken Jacobs, Vienna, 1971.

85

Ricky Leacock during the filming of Shirley Clarke's film *Skyscraper*, 1957. Photo: Anthology Film Archives.

# ON RICKY LEACOCK

May 5, 1971

Had a few Bloody Marys with Ricky.

"My only worry is that I never made a really personal film," said Ricky. "All my films were made for money. I made them because they paid to make them."

"What about *Toby*?"

"Yes, but they told me to make it, so I made it."

He said his biggest problem was the subject matter. He'd like to make a film now, but please give him a subject. "I don't know what to make it about," he said.

Sheldon Renan joined in: "I'll ask you a really personal question: How come you say you never made a film you really liked?"

"Because of all that equipment. Always so clumsy," said Ricky.

A pause.

"I, myself, I think I am an anthropologist," I said.

"I am also an anthropologist," said Ricky. "Only people who have a real insight, knowledge of something that is not like anybody else's, should make films."

He said the only people he really knows is the Middle America, Nixon people. He can make true and good films about those people because he really knows them. The film that he liked making most was *Happy Mother's Day*, he said. "It was fun."

We drank our Bloody Marys and rambled. We spent the earlier part of the evening talking on Channel 13 TV. We came to the Chelsea Hotel very depressed. It seemed to us so senseless to sit there in a TV studio and talk the way we talked and say nothing. Ricky said the best people for TV purposes would be people without legs. They wouldn't move, and the camera would be able to show them always in their entirety: top half, so to speak. They could even push themselves around on rollers. Anyway, we wanted to get drunk after the show, and Ricky was depressed about $12,000 worth of equipment stolen from his film class at MIT.

December 8, 1994

Who is Ricky Leacock? Which one is the real Ricky Leacock? The teacher? The cameraman? Film-maker? Video-maker? Documentary film-maker? Cinema verité film-maker? Home moviemaker? One who is very, very serious or one who likes to make a total fool out of himself? Top professional or top amateur? 35mm? 16mm? Super-8? Video-8? One who films nature? Prisons? Presidents? Musicians? Operas, farmers, babies, friends eating eggs? Home movies, TV? A great Portuguese cook, the most generous host, lover of beautiful women? Ah, there are so many Rickys, and they are all great.

An unforgettable image from *Primary*: Jackie Kennedy passes by mischievously throwing a smile—or was it a kiss?—at the cameraman who is there and from whom nobody wants to hide anything because he is so nice, such a nice person, and so unimposing. The most subtle moments of life that would break to pieces in front of any other camera offer themselves alive and joyfully to Ricky. Because he passes no judgment. He is the camera eye. Wherever he is, he becomes part of it and nobody minds him. And that is very, very difficult to achieve: to film it and still keep it alive! But Ricky does it. I lift my hat to you, Ricky!

Ricky Leacock, April 14, 2003:

"I saw *Turksib* when I was ten, I was ten, and I said, I could make a film like that too. That was the first film that made me want to make a film. So when I was twelve or thirteen I made the banana film."

OPPOSITE, FROM LEFT: Donn Alan Pennebaker, Victoria Leacock, Ricky Leacock, Rebekah Maysles, Albert Maysles. Photo: Robert Haller.

89

# John and Yoko Film Festival

# ELGIN THEATRE

## EIGHTH AVENUE AND 19TH STREET

## FRIDAY, DEC. 18—program no. 1

## SATURDAY, DEC. 19—program no. 2

## SUNDAY, DEC. 20—program no. 3

### All Programs 8:30 PM

*For the Benefit of the
Film-Makers Cinematheque

all seats

**$2**

---

## HARBURG ROAMS WORLD OF LYRICS

### Composer Initiates Series Spotlighting Songwriters

**By JOHN S. WILSON**

A series of monthly programs designed to put the spotlight on the forgotten man of songwriting, the lyricist, was inaugurated Sunday night at the 92d Street Young Men's-Young Women's Hebrew Association, with Yip Harburg onstage.

Mr. Harburg is known formally as E. Y. Harburg but there was nothing formal about his presentation as he rummaged through his four decades of lyric writing, reflected about his craft ("To be a lyricist, you've got to be a euphoric masochist") and burst into illustrative song in an earnest, somewhat quavering, but very expressive voice.

He began at the beginning with his Depression hit, "Brother, Can You Spare a Dime," which J. J. Shubert wanted to cut from the revue "Americana" because, he complained, "It's too sorbid." And he reminisced about and sang songs from his notable scores for "The Wizard of Oz" and "Finian's Rainbow."

He rekindled fading memories of other shows—"Jamaica," "Flahooley" and the charming lyric he wrote to Offenbach's "Barcarole" for "The Happiest Girl in the World."

## Mayor Calls 6-Month For Knapp Commis

**By DAVID BURNHAM**

Mayor Lindsay said yesterday that a six-month extension in the life of the commission investigating allegations of corruption in the New York Police Department was "vital to the public interest."

Mr. Lindsay made the statement in a letter to Thomas J. Cuite, the City Council majority leader, in which he urged the Council to extend the commission's subpoena power from Dec. 31, 1970, to June 30, 1971.

Such an extension by the City Council is required if the commission is to use a $215,037 grant offered by the Law Enforcement Assistance Administration, a branch of the Justice Department.

Though eventual passage of the legislation sought by Mayor Lindsay is expected, two Councilmen have introduced bills that would in effect kill the commission by denying it the right to subpoena witnesses.

The chairman of the commission, Whitman Knapp, a Wall Street lawyer, said in a letter forwarded to the Council by Mayor Lindsay that the investigation so far "has focused on gambling operations, the sale of narcotics, organized crime, vice and other criminal activities as well as business operations allegedly making illegal payments in order to conduct their business free of police harassment."

"Mr. Knapp's letter," Mr. Lindsay said, "details the cur-

Though
nevolent
fighting
in testin
Council a
actions
last May
became i
troversy
weeks ag
of an aff
sion pror
men in th
upper Ea
walk the

The a
commissi
moves b
the subpo
there we
numbers
systemat
policeme
reason
vising
taking
covering

Obvic
spread
affidavi
full pa
assertin
investig
fective,

"No
relati
poenas
investi
made
except
has be
by v
subp

M
be

## YOKO ONO: *FLY* AND *LEGS*

In December 1970, Ben Berenholtz, who was running the Elgin Theater (now home of Feld Ballet), called me to say that he had some empty days to fill. Would I like to organize some screenings?

With not a second of thought, I said yes, of course, I will do it.

I called Yoko Ono. "I would like to show some of your films. Which ones would you like me to show?"

Yoko being Yoko, with not a second of thought, says, "No, I don't want you to show my old movies: I will make some new movies for you." "But we have only one week," I said. "That's a long time," says Yoko. "I will have two new movies for you!"

Yoko and her cameraman Steve Gebhardt went immediately to work. And that's how two new films by Yoko Ono, *Fly* and *Legs*, came into existence.

Jack Smith also produced a new film, *No President*, for the occasion. He was still editing reel two in the projection booth while reel one was being projected.

A few days later I had the following conversation with John and Yoko:

JONAS: The importance of your legs film will increase with time. There will be meanings and values imposed upon it, art or no art. It will be a valuable and curious document of legs of artists and intellectuals—they were not exactly from the street—New York anno 1979.

YOKO: It has to be intelligent legs, I thought. First of all, I asked them to collect intelligent legs. And now, when people come and see the legs, they suddenly see that they are just ordinary legs.

JONAS: But they don't care about their legs, they don't take good care of their legs.

YOKO: They don't.

JOHN: It was very interesting. A lot of people, they were saying, "Oh, can't I leave my underpants on?" A sign of individuality. Or some wanted to leave their boots on. A lot of people think that with clothes on, the clothes become their individuality, they really suspect that they would all look alike without it. It's strange.

YOKO: And the thing is that it's just very nice to film legs. One person said: "I wonder if Nixon has very ugly, violent legs." But there is no such thing as ugly legs. Even Nixon, if you see his legs, they would look the same. And I just wanted to show that all of us are all right. We are all very peaceful. Even the meanest person, when he's asleep, he'll look beautiful, like a baby, or naïve. Because our body is very naïve, you know. And when I saw the film, I thought, very, very sad, very sad, because of the deformity, you know.

JONAS: It is a very sad film.

YOKO: The deformity. And everybody's so insecure. They don't want to look that ugly, and everybody's out there. And it's sad. Because in this world they are desperately trying to hide that ugliness and they are trying to look beautiful.

JOHN: They struggle to be beautiful.

YOKO: And it's not their fault that their legs are ugly, that they are ugly. People have to suffer for being ugly. Even if it's not their fault. They feel ashamed. And it was a very sad film. People showing their ugly bodies. But also, at the same time, when it was under that light, I thought they were all beautiful.

JONAS: When I was watching them, during the filming, when I saw them in their totality, with their faces and all, and in that context, they looked all right. But when only the legs are framed in front of you, right there on that screen, they become more exposed to scrutiny.

YOKO: There was one producer who has millions and millions, and he came and he showed his legs—he was too shy to... but he showed his legs, and I saw that with all his money he couldn't change his legs, and also his legs showed that he was too fat and was getting into old age. And he couldn't do anything about it, with his money and power. So, actually, everybody is like, very vulnerable. Like, we showed our bottoms, too, they didn't look anything special.

JONAS: They were... you noticed, you got a big applause... (*Laughs*)

YOKO: But also, there was a big silence, when we were on...

JOHN: All day, there were a lot of jokes, and talking about us being in the film. But then we went on, and there was this silence, very, very silent... *Hmm, what kind of legs do they have... Maybe they'll look like insect legs or something...*

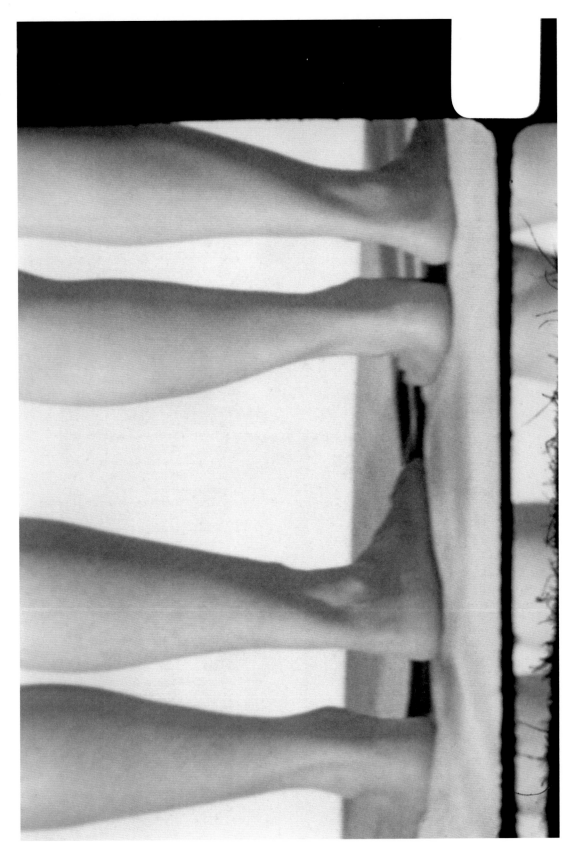

93

Guess which legs belong to John and which to Yoko...

94

1. Harvey Kramer
2. Ann Nagy
3. Shelly Petnov
4. Kathy Cox
5. Jonathan Cott
6. Dan Richter
7. Donna Gray
8. Jim Moore ✓
9. Lorraine Knox
10. Michael Cuscuna
11. Taylor Mead ✓
12. Lindsay Marasotta
13. Jim Moran ✓
14. Peter Delacort
15. Susan Pinsker
17. Noel Behn
18. Bruce Litmin
19. Michael Turner
20. Larry Rivers ✓
21. Brendan Atkinson
22. Tom Lightburn
23. Garth Summerville
24. Kristin Steen ✓
25. Beth (c/o Norm Seaman)
26. Lisa Negrin
27. Gay Seaman
28. Evelyn Seaman (c/o Norm Seaman)
29. Vali ✓
30. Jim Rich
32. Norvel
33. Michael Ridley
34. Richard Ryan
35. Dean Buck yes
36. Sam Jones
37. Yvonne Ruskin ✓
38. Ira Cohen ✓
39. Andy Smith
40. Patti-Lee Chenis ✓
41. Piero Heliczer ✓
42. Peter Hansen
43. D.A. Pennybaker
44. Cynthia Pennybaker
45. Pete Bennett
46. Jeff Hewitt
47. Utah Phillips
48. Mike Kramer
49. Harriett Black
50. Beryl Stone
51. Randy Brown
52. Bici Hendricks ✓
53. Geoff Hendricks
54. Danny Cohn
55. John Storyk., 1700 Broadway, New York. N.Y. 1001

56. Ralph Shultz
57. Tomi Riley
58. Suzannah Sedgewick
59. Al Steckler
60. Renie Bergen
61. Lillian Ocasio
62. Ellen McDonald
63. Basil Cox
64. Asha Coorlawala
65. Jann Wenner
66. Derek Carter IV
67. Donora Johnson
68. Denise Johnson
69. Richard Jones
70. Diane Newman
71. Alan Newman
72. Malcolm Bailey
73. Dave Kroll
74. Ken Reiderman
75. David Bergen
76. Dick Bellamy
77. Joe LaGuidice
78. Walter Kellery
79. Anna Pomaska
80. Secondhand Rose
81. Joe Butler
82. Letty Eisenhauer
83. Sandy Noyes
84. David Kurzman
85. Rhett Brown
86. Bob Brown
87. Velvert Turner
88. Gustav Sjoberg
89. Andrea Zlatkin
90. Howard Zlatkin
91. Ronnie Rosenblatt
92. Peter McGullam
93. Ziska
94. Loren Standlee
95. Austin Chinn
96. Jack Smith
97. David Poisal
98. Don Plumleigh
99. John Miele
100. Henry Geldzahler
101. Gordon Minard
102. Susan Buck
103. Jerry Cole
104. Jane Rose
105. David Simon
106. Jillian Hewitt
107. Michael Findlay
108. George Catha
109. Peter Ferrara Broadway, New Y
110. Michael Page

List of Yoko Ono and John Lennon's New York friends whose legs were featured in their film *Legs*, December 1970.

YOKO: We have very modest-looking bodies, you know... And despite all that, we love each other's bodies. So I felt very sad at the same time. I know that every one of those legs is something very, very special, to that person who loves. I mean, John's body is very, very special for me, I love him very much. And to me, it's a very special body. Of course, it doesn't have a silver lining, or something...

JOHN: I think it's a rather special body...

YOKO: Yes, it is very special. So, people are very fat beings. But they create poetry about each other's legs, you know.

I think of *Legs* film also as an event. It has a lot of elements of an event, in a sense that everybody came there and became a star and they were all happy that they were stars, they were all happy on that stage. Another thing is, one of the critics called me up. Well, she went to see the legs film but didn't stay until the end, it's a film mainly for the people who are in it, you know... so they still have that kind of concept.

JONAS: Like with *Apotheosis*. The camera went into the cloud, they couldn't see anything for a minute or two, so they immediately started shouting.

JOHN: The screen was white. But it was moving all the time. It was real clouds.

JONAS: Though one couldn't see them on the Elgin screen. For two or three minutes or so. So the audience went into attack.

| | |
|---|---|
| 111. Livy Merchant | 167. Jerry Parker |
| 112. Patrick Firpo | 168. Fumio Yoshimura |
| 113. Susanna De Maria | 169. Robert Mollot |
| 114. Leslie Talbot | 170. Jan Van Raay |
| 115. Fred Raskind | 171. Poppy Johnson |
| 116. Michael Gassman | 172. Silviana |
| 117. Judy Kramer | 173. Laurie Deutsch |
| 118. Pat Farrell | 174. Nancy Salzman |
| 119. Mary Pat Haberle | 175. Bruce Gedman |
| 120. Paul Krassner | 176. Evelyn Oliver |
| 121. Gerald Weiner | 177. Jim Buckley |
| 122. Mary Jane Hayes | 178. Fonje de Vre |
| 123. Joe Dragon | 179. Beverly Tangen |
| 124. Elena Hernandez | 180. Stewart Krane |
| 125. Mark Sloane | 181. William Brownrigg |
| 126. Fred Billingsley | 182. Linda Patton |
| 127. Jann Hodenfield | 183. Charles Bergengren |
| 128. Michael Thomas | 184. Ron Rosenbaum |
| 129. Deborah Gwyneth | 185. Countess Svietlana vonStritez |
| 130. Lillian Roxon | 186. David Lee Bergen |
| 131. KAREN/BACK//K/  George Back | 187. Eileen Smith |
| 132. Karen Back | 188. Kevin McCarthy |
| 133. Mark Rutzky | 189. Roy Robinson |
| 134. Don Schaffer | 190. Jan von der Marck |
| 135. Kathy Streem | 191. George Segal |
| 136. Lee Jaffee | 192. Peter Max |
| 137. Carol Friedlander | 193. William Holderith |
| 138. Willoughby Sharp | 194. Peter Beard |
| 139. Tom Lea | 195. Jeff Rose |
| 140. Liza Bear | 196. Tim Lippman |
| 141. Robert Polidori | 197. Diane Ostendorff |
| 142. Donny Burks | 198. Valery Herouvis |
| 143. Andy Harlow | 199. Arthur Tarres |
| 144. Pamela Francis | 200. Sylvain Mizorahi |
| 145. Steven Drangel | 201. Bill Murcia |
| 146. Barbara Clark | 202. Jeffry Lewis-Green |
| 147. Peter Yokum | 203. Al Goldstein |
| 148. Andy Siehel | 204. Mallory Geitheim |
| 149. Mark Monstermaker | Bob Linderman |
| 150. Jonas Mekas | 206. Pete Gaylor |
| 151. Richard Robinson | 207. Debby Ross |
| 152. Lisa Robinson | 208. Robert Acciani |
| 153. Julia Leonard | 209. Michael Acciani |
| 154. Susan McLaughlin | 210. Richard Dostal |
| 155. James Pietsch | 211. Shirley Clark |
| 156. Dave Walley | 212. Temple Boon |
| 157. Jon Hendricks | 213. Stanley Amos |
| 158. Elliot Ingber | 214. Gary Williams |
| 159. Dick Beahrs | 215. Bob Fall |
| 160. Carl Mirasola | 216. Bill Collins |
| 161. Harvey Stromberg | 217. Daphne Erwin |
| 162. Linda Jackson | 218. Patrick Hulsey |
| 163. Glenn Doddo | 219. Berta Orsita |
| 164. Eugene Seaman | 220. Jim Everett |
| 165. Glenn Johnson | 221. Bruce Bettinger |
| 166. Des Eisenstein | |

96

222. David Robinowitz
223. Emil Schau
224. Jerry Marcel
225. Mark Cerge
226. Peter Moore
227. Hala Pietkiewicz
228. Victor Herbert
230. Wm. Rockmacher
229. Jerry Ordover
231. Julie Hymen
232. Sue Shenn
233. Ralph Severini
234. Nancy O'Connor
235. John Lobsitz
236. Ann Silverstein
237. Grace Charleton
238. Shirley Basler
239. Virginia Lust
240. Susan Anderson
241. Jud Yalkut & Jeni Engel
242. Allen Kline
243. Howard Smith
244. Patti Oldenburg
245. Bunny Dexter
246. C.H. Ford
247. Paul Mozian
248. Al Aronowitz
249. Larissa Jarzombek
250. Bob Rosen
251. Jan Spiegelman
252. Bob Adleman
253. Walter Gutman
254. Cyrinda Hatzikian
255. Pedro Meroney
256. Dave Stein
257. Gabriel Stenziano
258. Joe Shepherd
259. Marc Stanton
260. Steven Hirsch
261. Chas. Rose
262. Katherine Dunfee
263. Christopher Makos
264. Kevin Donnelly
265. Gregory Shepard
266. Rick Salmon
267. Jack Hopkins
268. Emily Shin
269. John Cain
270. Paul Shepherd
271. Jerry Singley
272. Diane Meltzer
273. Louis Newman
274. Isabel Questell
275. Les Waldbauer
276. Steve Black

277. Ron Anderson
278. Dolly Latzonic
279. John Amon
280. Bob Hankins
281. Seth Feigenbaum
282. Maureen Simone
283. Lennie Gruen
284. Richard Rheem
285. Jan Teitelbaum
286. Joel Homer
287. Diane Friedman
288. Jon Gaynin
289. Gail Gaynin
290. Roy Manvell
291. Leonard Wienstien
292. Dusty Moss
293. Francesca Moss
294. Allen Taylor
295. Michael Chender
296. John Buscemi
297. Sid Bernstein
298. Joel Weinstein
301. Shelly Landers
299. Tony Biel
300. Diana Biel
302. Phylis Banek
303. Tamil Tormos
304. Isabel Figuredo
305. Rudi Echeverri
306. Jeff Dubron
307. Rachel Dubron
308. Milton Schneider
309. Peter Morris
310. David Smith
311. Barb Sellwin
312. Pat Depew
313. The Orr.
314. Bob Fries
315. Joshua Deutsch
316. Chris Fries
317. Marilyn Landers
318. Annie Leibovitz
319. Barbara Neidleman
320. Biguel Wiea
321. David Johansen
322. Diane Podlewski
323. Merlo
324. Trisha Podlewski
325. Phyllis Vampolsky
326. Bert Shavitz
327. Bill Sontag
328. John Southard
329. Janet Rodolico
330. Steve Gebhardt

97

YOKO: Somebody who saw it said, "Why was it completely white?" He felt like he was suffocating. Provocation. And then, when it came out into the blue sky, out of the cloud, he just felt like, *aah*, the suffocation is over.

JONAS: Somebody sitting next to me turned to me and said something nasty about the film. So I said, "Don't you like a nice white screen?" And he said, "Oh, but cinema is mo-ve-ment, the cinema is *mo-ve-ment*!" So I had to step aside, he was hopeless. Today, I just came from Jack Smith's show, and he had announced that he'll show *No President*. He had shown that film before, on a number of occasions, and he always changes it, makes changes. It's never the same. So, now, everybody, two hundred or so people, are sitting there, and Jack comes, and he's very late, and he's in the projection booth, still making splices, and finally the film comes on, but those two hundred, everybody wants to see it exactly the way they saw it the last time, you know! But Jack had not only reedited it; he continued working on it even while it was being projected. He covered the image here and there, and fooled with the music—he continued editing the film right there on the projector, and the film we had all seen before now became slightly something else, like I never saw that film before. So somebody stood up, angrily, and started shouting: "It was great before, when I saw it. What is he doing, why is he destroying it?" "Sir," I shouted at him, "is it every day you get a great artist like Jack Smith to come here and edit, make a film right for you, right here, aren't you lucky?" And the man kept squeaking: "I have seen this film, it was great, and what is he doing now?" They are so used to... They always want to see the same and the same. Even if they see it only once, they are so easily... We talk about Pavlov's dogs. But this is worse! No dog will ever ask for the same after only one impulse. But these people refuse to see, they remain blind to whatever is happening right there before their eyes. Smith or no Smith. And Jack was working there, upstairs, in the projection booth, going through his trances, just to make it greater for them, and it was very great to see it.

99

# NOVA

### WOMAN IS THE NIGGER OF THE WORLD

SHE: "WOMAN IS THE NIGGER OF THE WORLD..."
MARCH 1969 THREE SHILLINGS AND SIXPENCE

### JOHN LENNON/PLASTIC ONO BAND

with
Elephant's
Memory
and
Invisible
Strings

Apple

1848

100

August 19, 1962

Dear Jonas,

Are you on vacation? Why don't I hear
from you any more? Please, do say something!
Just let me know that you're not mad at me,
or you are mad at me from some specific reason
or non-specific reason, etc.

We are now planning a symposium of Japanese
avan-guard film-makers on the condition of the
Japanese film-makers. We will tape the whole
thing and send you the translation so that you
may probably be able to put it on some American
film magazine as "Symposium of Japanese Film-
makers". I do not know just how you feel about
it. I do know that Japanese film makers are
eager to have this symposium since they want to
reach the American film-makers and others who
are interested in knowing the conditions of film-
makers in Japan. . . . .

How about the short shorts that we were going to get?
Are you objecting to the way it would be sent? Please
let me know as soon as possible since the Art Festival

is not too far ahead.

I'm coming to the end of my wits about staying in
Japan. This is horrible. New York is my only town.
But just today, I bought a beautiful plant spending
all my money. The plant looks so nice in my apartment
which is gradually becoming "my room". It is so simple
to get use to a room. That is how people wander and
that is how they settle down, I guess. It is rather
sad.

Kiss the pavements of New York for me.

As ever,

yoko

102

Pola Chapelle. Photo: Adolfas Mekas.

## ANAÏS NIN COOKIES

It was 1960. Ian Hugo had just completed his film on Venice. Anaïs Nin, his wife, was the star of the film. Few people knew about Ian Hugo, but Anaïs' reputation had already reached New York. None of her voluminous *Diaries* had yet been published; that was to come later.

Anaïs had invited a dozen people that had orbited around the avant-garde arts to her house, 3 Washington Square, for a special preview of the film.

That was a very hungry period of mine and my brother Adolfas' lives. We had no jobs, no money, and no food. As the film was being screened and everybody was involved in it, it took no time for me and Adolfas to notice that, in the back of the room, there was, prepared for the guests, a little delicate table with plates of cookies. We had not eaten anything that day. Three or four minutes before the end of the film we snuck to the table and began gobbling up the cookies.

Now what I'll tell you next comes from Pola Chapelle, presently Adolfas' wife, who happened to be at the screening. Anaïs wrote an endorsing blurb for the cover of her first song album. Pola was there but neither Adolfas nor myself knew her at that time—we met Pola some years later. So this is her report on the event:

The film ended. Anaïs invited the guests to have some wine and cookies. Pola looked towards the cookie table and saw these two shabby guys finishing gobbling up the cookies. There were practically no cookies left... Pola saw us finishing the cookies and sneaking away. She was amazed how fast those cookies were gone... Yes, some were still left, symbolically sort of...

She told us that story years later. She was wondering who those guys were. And I have always felt sort of guilty about Anaïs' cookies.

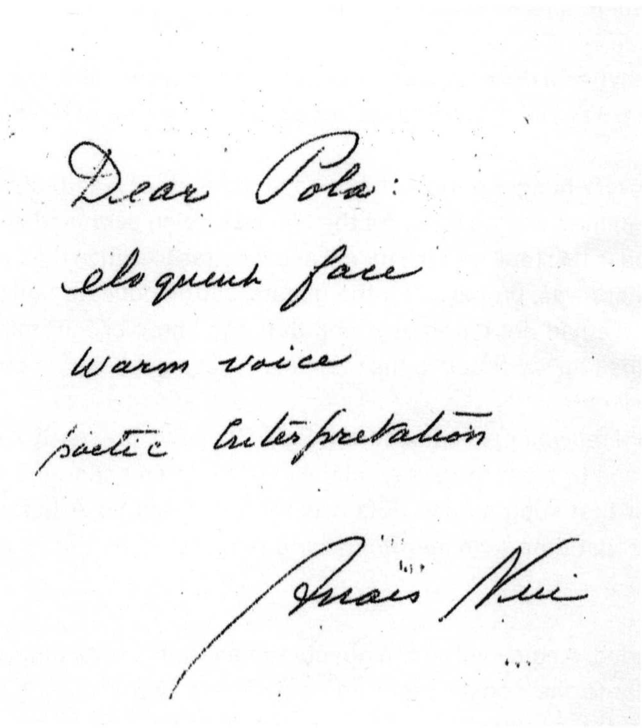

104

Dear Pola:
eloquent face
warm voice
poetic interpretation

Anaïs Nin

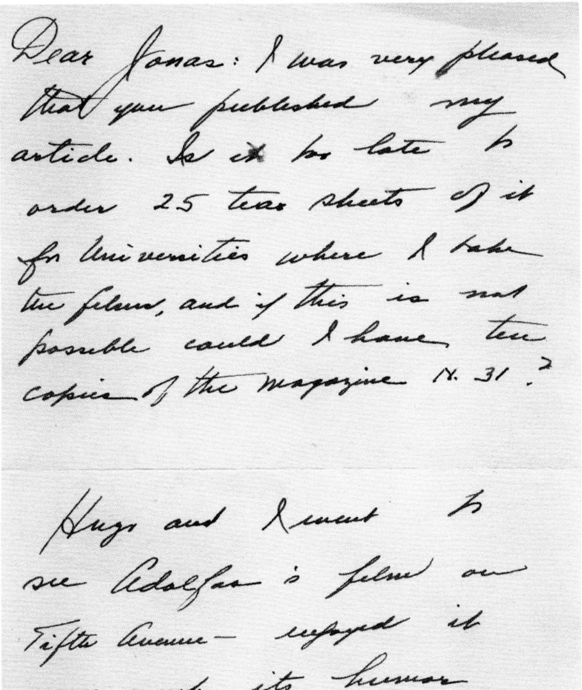

Dear Jonas: I was very pleased that you published my article. Is it too late to order 25 tear sheets of it for Universities where I take the films, and if this is not possible could I have ten copies of the magazine N. 31?

Hugs and I went to see Adolfas's films on Fifth Avenue — enjoyed it very much, its humor and freedom and fantasy. The score was excellent, really, and both sharp contrasts between wit and

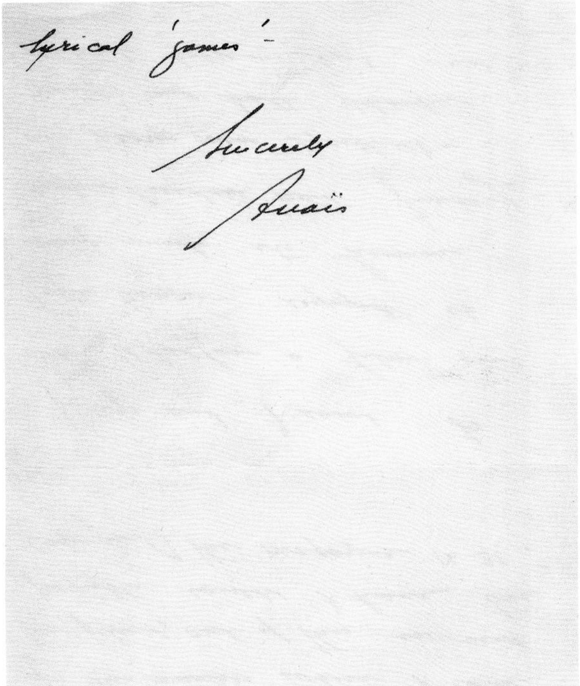

lyrical 'games'.

Sincerely

Anaïs

105

## ANDY WARHOL PRINT

In 1982, I needed money to renovate the Second Street Courthouse building, which I had purchased for Anthology Film Archives from the city. I decided to produce an art portfolio. Marian Goodman pointed to a pile of portfolios in the corner of her office and told me: "You see those portfolios? Some of the best artists are in them. I produced them to help Shapiro's Chair at Columbia University. Nobody buys them. Don't do it."

I went ahead and did it. I asked Andy to be in it. He said, "Why don't you choose an image from the *Chelsea Girls* and I'll make a print for you from the image?" So I did. I chose a few frames, Hollis Melton made slides and test prints, and I showed them to Andy. We decided on one with Eric Emerson, and I took it to Porter-Wiener Studios, Andy's silkscreen printer, to make some tests. Some six or seven different variations were made. I took them to Andy.

When I arrived at the Factory, corner of Union Square North and Broadway, second floor, there were some three or four "international" art dealers there. So I said, "Andy, can you interrupt the sales business and choose the print you like from these tests?" Andy looked at me with his famous Zen stare and motioned at the art businessmen: "Let them make the choice: They know it better." And he walked away.

OPPOSITE: Frames from *Chelsea Girls*, for a silkscreen print Andy Warhol produced in 1981 to benefit Anthology Film Archives.

So I laid out the prints on the table and invited the nicely dressed gentle-men—most of them were from Europe—to help me to make the right decision. I wish I had a video camera with me. I really wish. Because the men got really involved in the challenge of decision-making. They became vicious art critics. They attacked colors of Andy's recent prints; they thought they were too TVish and gaudy.

After some ten minutes or so, they all gravitated towards a pale red/pink as the preferred dominant color. They thought this was different from what Andy was doing. I thanked them for the choice and took it to Andy, who was munching on a sandwich in the back room. He looked at it for a second or two and said, "That's great. Print it that way."

That was it. By the way, I sold all the portfolios, all seventy-five of them, despite Marian's warning.

At the Factory, Union Square, Broadway and 17th Street.

Allen Ginsberg during the wake, April 6, 1997, in his old apartment at 405 East 12th Street.

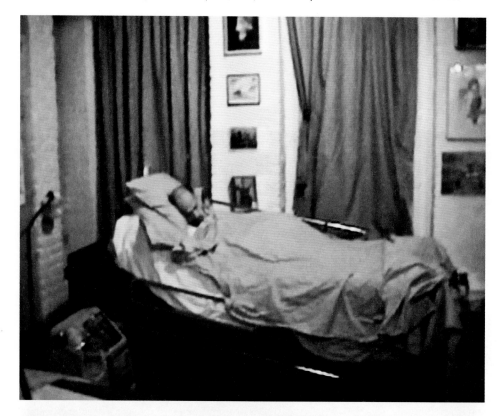

Peter Orlovsky, April 6, 1997.

## NOTES FOR ALLEN

April 2, 1997, 10 p.m.

Allen [Ginsberg] just called. His voice was very, very weak... He said doctors told him he had only about three months to live. Liver cancer, and other horrible things. But he was in a good mood. He said he had accepted death, and is not worried or panicking, it's all very normal. I asked him if he had enough care, if he needed anything. He said no, he has a nurse, and even a very special hospital bed that is very easy to control... no, he needs nothing. He said he's writing a lot of poetry, for a book which could be entitled *Poems from the Bed Thinking About Death*. I may be misquoting. Said, "Come and visit me." I felt he had some special need for me to visit him. I promised to visit him mid–next week. His new apartment is all cluttered, he said, but very comfortable, a lot of paper stuff. Bob Dylan called, and Hiro called and cried. We talked for some twenty minutes, and it wasn't a sad conversation, I just couldn't feel sad hearing his voice so relaxed. Actually, we both laughed a lot, talking about it, about him knowing that he has only three months to live, and all that unfinished business—which we both agreed was total nonsense anyway—as we go from here to there. We laughed; he only chuckled, with his familiar classic Allen chuckle. Anyway, it was not a sad conversation at all. I'd rather sum it up as a happy conversation, strange as it may sound to some. But that's Allen's special gift, I guess.

111

April 5, noon

Bill Morgan called. Said, "Sit down." I said, "Just say it." "Allen died last night, 2:40 a.m. Funeral service Monday 9 a.m. to 1 p.m., Shambala Center, 118 West 22nd Street. Wednesday he came back from the hospital. Was in good working spirit. Worked all day. Thursday he fell sick again. Friday night had a stroke, went into coma. Never woke up. Fell asleep..."

April 5, Saturday, 5 p.m.

Sent Message to Paris, Tokyo.

Hiro called. Said, "Come to Allen's place."

There were some ten of Allen's friends when I came, and four or five Tibetan monks sitting around a low tea table, chanting.

Allen's body was in his bed, where he died, by the north wall of the room, by the window draped blue. A light wind now was moving the drapes, gently—his head west, head turned sideways, sort of towards us, but not exactly. He was somewhere else. Rosebud was there, and she turned on some lights for a minute because the part of the room, a long room, where Allen was lying was in semi-darkness. She did that so I could film Allen. He was sleeping, and deep in thought, I thought. With a touch of romantic sadness in his face. But relaxed. Reminded me of Raphaelites. I don't know why.

ALLEN
GINSBERG
appears with his father
in behalf of McGovern.
Thursday, October 12
8:00 p.m. Loeb, student center
Eisner & Lubin
566 LaGuardia Pl.
sponsered by
Students for McGovern

Allen Ginsberg with his father, Louis Ginsberg, at a poetry reading at the New School, c. 1973.

114

The author, Allen Ginsberg and Richard Round, at the New York Film Festival. Photo: Elliott Landy.

The monks chanted all evening. Occasionally they held little conferences among themselves, trying, I guess, to determine if Allen's spirit had really left the body—because nobody should touch his body until the spirit leaves it. But since the results were negative, the monks kept chanting and ringing bells and burning stuff, etc., as we all sat around the room, silent, or talking quietly—Rosebud, Rani, Hiro, Patti, Anne (Waldman), Peter (Orlovsky), and a few others. Allen did not want, nor did the monks, to have any strangers or press or TV around; they wanted Allen's spirit to leave the body in quiet peace, with only close friends around. Peter, who said he himself was only sixty-eight, was deeply broken by it all. But he was happy at the same time. He was bent down in body but totally upright in spirit, I thought. He seemed to be completely somewhere else, only half-aware of what was really happening. He was in some kind of blissful dream.

It was about quarter to twelve when the monks decided that Allen's spirit had really left the body and it was OK to remove it from the premises. Funeral home people came, all neatly dressed, and in a very matter-of-fact way, very professionally and respectfully, wrapped up Allen's body in the funeral shroud, placed it on the stretcher, and wheeled it out. It was about five or ten after midnight.

I walked into the street. I caught a glimpse of the black limo, on my video, with Allen's body in it. Then I saw Peter, so sweet, so sweet, with his hands put together for prayer. Then the limo began moving away and Peter waved, bye-bye, in the sweetest possible way, I have never seen anything so sweet—bye-bye, Allen—and the limo disappeared among the street lights, and Peter went to the 405 East 13th Street door and began searching for a key in his pocket, and this action, somehow, searching for a key in his pocket, after all what had happened, this seemed to me suddenly so incongruous, so out of place and, at the same time, so totally returning back to reality.

I turned my video camera towards First Avenue. It was full of lights, taxis, and the Lower East Side life. I walked towards it, my camera still running.

**Dear agnes:**

The young people were young, their
happinness was totally and openly happy
and their beauty was beautiful &
exhilaratingly innocent and contageous as only
innocence can be.

I looked, I listened, I saw & it was
so freeing and so totally somewhere else
and so far from what's on TV and
newspapers,
the world of the mature & the grown-ups...


and as I contemplated it all like this
pushing casually through the crowd
I saw you, agnès -- unmistakingly you --
who else could be so relaxed, so totally,
and so totally there -- so totally yourself
so totally in it all at the same
time -- an image  of transparency and relaxation
and happinness -- Ah, you manage to become
so totally part of no matter what it is,
completely and totally with what is now, this
moment, embracing it, moving with it with
no effort, lightly and amazingly,
lightly and amazingly --

like I've seen same in some old Chinese
drawings, same radianc e and lightness
& happinness, the poetry of life in the faces,
postures & lines of poets and drunks and geishas
and haiku geniuses who all had transcended
-- like you -- the pain and absurdity of
Real Life --

I thought so as I was walking home through
a mild drizzle along the
late January Broome street -- thinking --
and happy.

Now I am typing this, and I have a glass of
Cahors, still full -- Arab drums on radio &
a Persian flute --

---

"it has a magic in it," says the musician and
then he plays -- and then he plays --
And it's all very amazing, dear agnes,
it's all very amazing, everything,
I mean, everything --

Feb.7.2003

The author with Agnès B. in Paris, 1997. Photo: Peter Sempel.

118

# FIVE ANECDOTES FROM
# THE LIFE OF GEORGE MACIUNAS

## 1

We were chiseling the walls of the AG Gallery space, on Madison Avenue; George didn't like plaster. He wanted the bricks exposed. So we had to chisel all that stuff off. It was hard work, it took us days and days. And all that dust! And it was a hot summer, too. Almus, George, myself, we worked and we cursed. The year was 1961.

A Lithuanian journalist assigned to the United Nations calls me, he wants to connect with Lithuanian immigrants doing cultural work. So I say come to AG Gallery, we'll talk.

I tell this to George and he gets very excited: "Good," he says. "We need him."

So the guy comes, obviously a dutiful Soviet apparatchik, and George immediately hands him a chisel and puts him to work. No culture talk, no nothing. For days he worked, poor guy, dusty, sweating.

A week or two later I receive a call from the CIA. They want to know all about this guy. "What kind of relationship do you have with the Soviet Mission?" they ask. "He is working for us," I say. "He is scrubbing our walls, he's working for us." "Do you pay him?" they asked. "No, no. Just the opposite: He treats us with vodka," I say.

George practically split his sides laughing when I told him about the call.

The local Lithuanian community got wind of the case and they immediately began spreading rumors that AG Gallery was a Soviet art front in New York.

## 2

A show was announced at AG Gallery and the press was invited to preview the exhibition. I can't remember who the artist was, but the artist backed out two or three days before the opening.

I walk in, and I see the entire floor covered with blank canvases. "Help me," says George, "help me to spray water on the canvases, I have to have them all ready by tomorrow."

OPPOSITE: George Maciunas, c. 1965.

So we sprayed them with water, all twenty or so canvases, and George went around, with color tubes, red and black and blue mostly, and dripped paint on them, and the paint spread on the wet canvases and made designs on its own. In fifteen minutes or so he had "painted" some twenty canvases. By the way, George was colorblind.

In the morning they were all dry and ready. We hung them and we stood there, waiting for the press.

No press came. But the show was on. Yes, I think Lil Picard came; she wrote for German papers on art in America.

3

George always had Big Money schemes. In 1960, he decided that one could become a millionaire by importing very special canned European foods. So he sent hundreds of form letters to European special food exporters and producers, offering to be their agent/salesman; and, "Please, send me some samples of your special canned foods."

And samples he got! Hundreds of canned food samples began arriving at his home.

I was living at that time with my brother Adolfas, on 515 East 13th Street. And we were poor and very, very hungry. So George says, "You need food? I'll get you food! I have these hundreds of cans of food, very, very special, and I am sick of it. You want it?"

"Yes, yes," we said, "We want it!"

So he brings and dumps in our place maybe a thousand cans of the most expensive, very, very special pâtés, nightingale tongues, all very, very special stuff. So we ate and ate, and we fed all the hungry Lower East Side poets for a year or two, and everybody was amazed when we used to pull out those French delicacies, which you could get only at the Waldorf Astoria.

I don't have to tell you that George couldn't sell any of it. He ate it all himself, with our help.

OPPOSITE: George Maciunas, Yoko Ono, and John Lennon
on a Hudson River Fluxus cruise, July 7, 1971.

In 1974, we had to build a projection room for Anthology Film Archives at 80 Wooster Street. The room had to rest on the slender cast-iron columns. In order to do this, holes had to be drilled through the columns. We all stood there, looking at the thin delicate columns, on which the entire building was resting, as George, with a powerful drill in his hands, approached them.

"Go out, all of you!" he shouted. "I don't know how these columns will behave. They may just crack and the whole building may collapse on my head. Go out!"

I knew there was nothing in the whole world that could persuade George not to do it. He had to do it, live or die. So we all walked out and stood across the street, staring at the building, while George proceeded with drilling.

The building held. The columns held. Everybody survived.

Only later, years later, after George died, as I was going through some of the stuff I had saved from the basement of 80 Wooster Street, after George moved out, I discovered a tiny flask, half-filled with black dust. It carried a label, in George's own careful handwriting: "Dust from the cast-iron column." Not only did he drill the hole in the column: With the danger of imminent death hovering over his head, he didn't forget to collect all the little particles, produced by his drill, in a little flask, as a Fluxus piece.

One thing George really hated was waste.

## 5

One night I was sleeping in the basement of 80 Wooster Street. I think it was late fall of 1967. George came in and said, "Come, help. I got these trees here, we have to plant them."

"What, at this hour of the night?" I hate to get up at night. But I did, and yes, he had these shabby trees lying on the sidewalk.

"I stole them from the parking lot on West Broadway," he told me proudly, laughing. "They were tearing up the whole place, with bulldozers, and I asked them to give me a couple of trees, and they said no! So I waited until the night, and I took them, you see? We have to plant them now while it's dark. It's against the law to plant trees in Soho."

123

The author and his brother Adolfas, sketched by George Maciunas, 1953.

The house where George Maciunas spent his childhood, Kalautuva (near Kaunas), Lithuania, July 11, 1993. Photo: Penkauskas.

George Maciunas' portrait of the author, AG Gallery, 1961.

OPPOSITE: To prevent policemen from using their shoulders to break his door, George Maciunas covered it with sharp printer's paper cutting blades. His room was in the Film-Makers' Cinematheque basement, 80 Wooster Street.

George's door
80 Wooster
May 11,1975

125

The staff of Anthology Film Archives in front of 80 Wooster Street, 1980. Photo: Amy Greenfield.

80 Wooster Street tree, April 2013. Photo: Sebastian Mekas.

J DUPUY
537 BROADWAY
NEW YORK NY 10012

western union Mailgram

UNITED STATES POSTAL SERVICE
U.S.MAIL

1-034827E133002 05/13/78 ICS IPMMTZZ CSP NYAA
2 2129252285 MGM TDMT NEW YORK NY 05-13 0135P EST

ANTHOLOGY FILM ARCHIVE ATTN FLUXUS HENDRIKS
80 WOOSTER ST
NEW YORK NY 10013

THIS IS A CONFIRMATION COPY OF A PREVIOUSLY PHONE-DELIVERED TELEGRAM

GOD IS AN INFANT DEVIL IS AN INFANT EAT BABY FOOD FROM
GEORGE MACIUNAS

13:36 EST

MGMCOMP MGM



5241 (R1/78)

TO REPLY BY MAILGRAM, SEE REVERSE SIDE FOR WESTERN UNION'S TOLL - FREE PHONE NUMBERS

The next day, or a day later, some city officials showed up. "No trees are permitted here," they told me. "You'll have to get rid of them."

I go down to the basement, to George. He was making his Fluxus boxes or something, and he says, "Tell them if they don't like our trees they can pull them out." So I pick up my Bolex camera and go back to the city officials. "No, George is not going to do it. He says you have to do it. And he wants me to take some pictures of it."

The city people looked at me, then at each other, turned around, and we never saw them again.

But the trees grew and prospered. Big, beautiful trees they are now, happy trees, the only trees on Wooster Street.

In April 2013, the City of New York decided that the two trees planted by George Maciunas in front of 80 Wooster Street belong to the City, and since their opinion was that they constituted a danger to the building and the people, they should be cut down. Decided, done. As Roslyn Bernstein, author of *Illegal Living: 80 Wooster Street and the Evolution of SoHo*, wrote:

"New York City Department of Parks sent six men and three trucks with two chain saws to cut down George Maciunas's trees. The noise was deafening as one of the men, in a cherry picker, wielded his saw while [the] other below was piling the falling limbs."

OPPOSITE: A telegram from George Maciunas delivered four days after his death to his friends gathered for his memorial at 80 Wooster Street, the first Soho cooperative building he created and in the basement of which he lived.

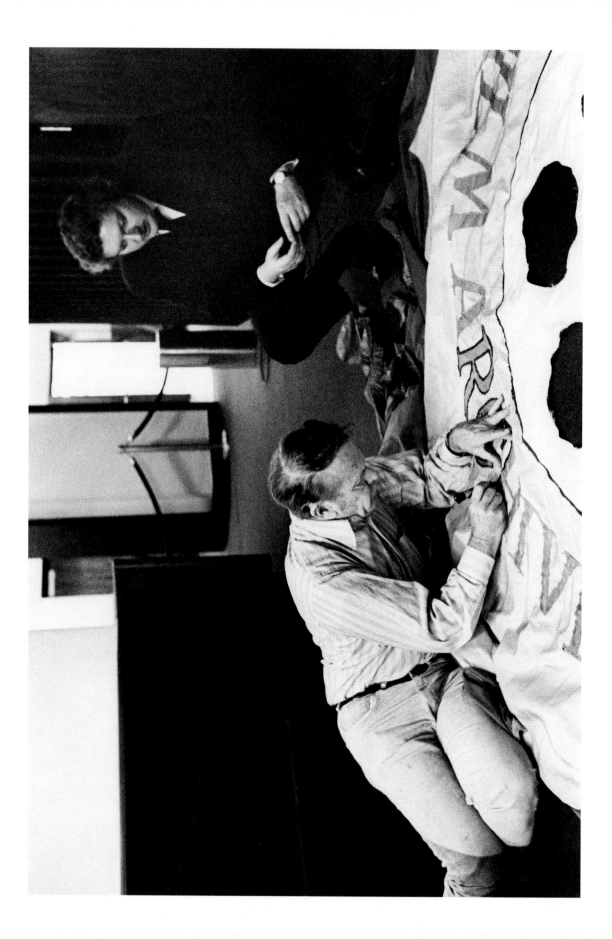

# A FEW NOTES ON JEROME HILL

It's so far away and so very close. Almost fifty years ago. That's when I met Jerome for the first time. I wanted him to do an article for *Film Culture* on the making of the Schweitzer film for which he had received an Academy Award.

I made the telephone call. He invited me to visit him at his Broadway and 61st Street office.

His office was a combination of a library, editing room, and a Japanese-style tearoom. The tea table, situated in a nice corner space with flowers all around it and a window view, was the most important part of the "office." That's where all "business" took place, as we sipped our teas. In all my fifteen years of doing "business" with Jerome, everything with him had to be light, unbusinesslike, a tea-table situation. There was a touch of Japan in Jerome. I don't know whether he had ever been to Japan, but in his early youth he had published a book of haikus. I still have a copy of the book, printed on Japanese paper.

The lightness: a little bit of Zen; a certain sweet carelessness and humor with which he did everything is what I remember now so well; the little funny routines he had set for himself and his coworkers in Cassis, New York, and Big Sur were light and full of humor. It was in his office library (I was in charge of his "office" for one summer) that I read my first Suzuki and Watts texts (Jerome was a friend of both) and the Bollingen Series books (Jerome helped to publish them).

Anyway, we met and I asked him to do an article on his Schweitzer film, which he did. But he also wanted to know more about *Film Culture* magazine. I told him that we were having big problems with paying printer's bills—actually, the printer was suing us. The Franciscan Brothers, the monks in Brooklyn whose printing shop we were using, were suing us for not paying our bills, so Adolfas, my brother, had to go to court, which was—you won't believe where—it was the Second Street and Second Avenue corner Courthouse building, Anthology's present home!

OPPOSITE: Jerome Hill and Peter Kubelka designing a banner for Anthology Film Archives, 1970.

Anyway, I told Jerome all about our problems. And I have to admit to you, when I was talking to him I had no idea who he was. I only knew that he was the film-maker who made the Schweitzer film. I knew nothing about his family fortunes inherited from the building of the transcontinental railroad system, bridging the east and west coasts of the United States. So I was very free and uninhibited in my description of our financial situation. When I finished my description, he asked how much *Film Culture* owes to the printer, and I told him, at which point he turned to his secretary and asked her to write a check for that amount. What was amazing was that he did it so casually, without making it look like anything special. It was simple and light and easy, and I accepted it as something very natural, no big fuss.

That's how our relationship began. I was very poor in those days, living on coffee and doughnuts. When Jerome found that out, he arranged for me to eat at his favorite restaurant, a free table, whenever I needed. Sometimes he joined me. We talked a lot about what was happening in New York's independent cinema scene. He wanted to know everything. His interest soon led him to wanting to meet some of the film-makers, so I introduced him to Peter Kubelka, Stan Brakhage, P. Adams Sitney. One day he asked me whether there was a way he could help some needy avant-garde film-makers financially. I proposed to create an Independent Film-Maker's Grant. This grant, that existed for some seven years (1960–1967), worked like this: I made up a list of twelve needy avant-garde film-makers. Each would receive forty dollars a month for a year. Each year I'd check the list and take off some and add some new names. Today you may laugh about the forty dollars. But in the early sixties it paid for a month's rent. Peter Kubelka even today talks with excitement about the days when he would receive the forty dollars.

Through all the early years of *Film Culture*, whenever I could not pay the printer's bill, Jerome picked it up. When the Film-Makers' Cooperative was created, it was Jerome who gave me money to pay the salaries of the Co-op workers during the first five years. When *Cahiers du Cinema* was about to sink (circa 1970), it was Jerome who saved it by inaugurating an English edition (edited by Andrew Sarris). (This fact is not known even in Paris...)

132

Jerome Hill, c. 1950.

The banner for the first international exposition of the New American Cinema, Spoleto, 1961, designed by Jerome Hill.

**FESTIVAL OF TWO WORLDS**
**FESTIVAL DEI DUE MONDI**

**A New Film Exposition**
**presented by David C. Stone**

**Rassegna di film**
**presentata da David C. Stone**

CINEMA-TEATRO SPERIMENTALE — SPOLETO

*PROGRAM*

JUNE 16 & JULY 3
Jerome Hill's *The Sand Castle*
John Korty's *The Language of Faces*

JUNE 17 & JULY 4
Jonas Mekas' *Guns of the Trees*
Dan Drasin's *Sunday*

JUNE 18 & JULY 5
Graeme Ferguson's *Downfall*
Richard Preston's *Nightscapes, The Maze, The Candidates*
*& Conversations in Limbo*

JUNE 19 & JULY 6
Robert Frank's *The Sin of Jesus*
Robert Frank & Alfred Leslie's *Pull My Daisy*
Edward O. Bland's *The Cry of Jazz*

JUNE 20 & JULY 7
Curtis Harrington's *Night Tide*
Ralph Hirshorn's *The End of Summer*

JUNE 21 & JULY 8 (matinee)
Ron Rice's *The Flower Thief*
Jerome Liebling and Allen Downs' *Pow Wow*
James Broughton's *The Pleasure Garden*

JUNE 22 & JULY 9
Peter Kass' *Time of the Heathen*
Hilary Harris' *Polaris Action Pilot & Highway*

JUNE 23 & JULY 10 (matinee)
Stan Brakhage's *Anticipation of the Night, Daybreak & Whiteye*
Robert Breer's *Recreation, Man and his Dog Out for Air, Jamestown, Cats,*
*Inner and Outer Space, Blazes, Homage to New York*

JUNE 24 & JULY 11
Allen Baron's *Blast of Silence*
Joseph Marzano's *When They Sleep, From Inner Space & Changeover*

JUNE 25 & JULY 12 (matinee)
Gregory J. Markopoulos' *Serenity*
Stan VanDerBeek's *What Who How, Ala Mode, Mankinda, Science Friction*

JUNE 26 & JULY 13
Erich Kollmar's *Changing Tides*
Madeline Anderson's *Integration Report 1*

JUNE 27 & JULY 14
Lionel Rogosin's *On the Bowery & Come Back Africa*

JUNE 28 & JULY 15
Sidney Meyers' *The Quiet One*
Michael and Philip Burton's *Journey Alone*
Helen Levitt, Janice Loeb & James Agee's *In the Street*

JUNE 29 & JULY 16
Morris Engel's *Weddings and Babies*
Warren Brown's *A Light for John*

JUNE 30 & JULY 10 (evening)
Ben Maddow, Sidney Meyers & Joseph Strick's *The Savage Eye*
Richard Leacock, Donn Alan Pennebaker & Albert Maysles' *Primary*

JULY 1 & JULY 12 (evening)
Bert Stern's *Jazz on a Summer's Day*
Stuart Hanish, Barbara Squire & Russ MacGregor's
*Have I Told You Lately That I Love You*

JULY 2 & JULY 8 (evening)
John Cassavetes' *Shadows*
Michael Blackwood's *Broadway Express*

**Daily at 5:30 & Midnight**
**Tutti i giorni alle 17:30 & 24:00**

PANETTO & PETRELLI-SPOLETO

Then, in 1967, came the idea for Anthology Film Archives. Jerome's buddy from his army days, Joe Martinson, the chairman of the Public Theater at that time, was renovating the building at 425 Lafayette Street to create a showcase for Joe Papp's Shakespeare theater productions. Martinson asked Jerome whether he would consider doing something for cinema in that building. So Jerome calls me, very excited, and we go to Ballato's Restaurant on Houston (that's where we met most of the time during those years) and we talked, and the more we talked the more excited we became about the idea of creating something very special for cinema, something like an Academy of Cinema. An idea that became the Essential Cinema Repertory collection.

The rest of this is history. The result of this lunch was the creation of Anthology Film Archives. Jerome put at my disposal his personal Avon Foundation to create a film projection space designed by Peter Kubelka that became known as the Invisible Cinema; he sponsored the creation and acquisition of all the film prints of the Essential Cinema Repertory collection; he sponsored the creation of a reference library (P. Adams Sitney combed the old bookshops of Europe for rare editions of early books on cinema). Until his premature death in 1972, Anthology was Jerome's love and dream. And it was a vision that was just too good to last. Our vision, my vision, Sitney's vision, Kubelka's vision, and Jerome's vision. This dream, the vision was cut short by Jerome's cancer. The creation of Anthology Film Archives and the Essential Cinema Repertory collection will remain in the history of cinema one of the most unique and heroic aesthetic undertakings. It was a misfortune of Olympian proportions when, immediately after Jerome's death, the Avon Foundation (ironically, renamed the Jerome Foundation) decided to phase out all support to Anthology Film Archives, betraying Jerome's vision and his heart's wishes.

Jerome's lunch meals in Cassis at Les Roches Blanches and in New York at Ballato's were times of meeting friends, telling jokes and relaxing. I can still hear the happy, open laughs of Jerome and P. Adams Sitney, himself an inspired joke-teller. We were never in a hurry; Jerome was a master in creating a relaxing atmosphere. On his way to Les Roches Blanches, he took his time to explore his garden for special herbs to sprinkle on our lunch dishes.

Jerome had an amazing knowledge of art and design history. In Torino, I remember, we would walk through art museums and he could tell paintings' ages within a ten-year span just from the designs of the clothes and shoes in the paintings.

Jerome Hill (*back right*) visiting Peter Kubelka (*front left*), Vienna, 1970. Also in the picture is
Peter Konlechner (*front right*) and P. Adams Sitney with his wife, Julie (*in back, left*).

ABOVE LEFT: Jerome Hill with Albert Schweitzer, during the 1956 filming of Jerome Hill's *Albert Schweitzer*.

ABOVE RIGHT: The author, as painted by Jerome Hill in Cassis, 1966.

Talking about Torino, it reminds me of Jerome's other contributions to the American independent avant-garde cinema: the traveling expositions. In 1961 Jerome asked me to curate the first major North American Cinema Exposition at the Spoleto Festival in Italy—a festival of arts run by Menotti and sponsored by Jerome. An exposition of some twenty-five film programs took place, introducing for the first time to the European audiences the New American Cinema.

In 1967, Jerome paid for another major traveling exposition of the American avant-garde film. P. Adams Sitney and I put together some twenty-five programs of films, which I took to Torino, then to Rome, and then P. Adams Sitney took it all over Europe, in some countries jointly with Barbara Rubin. For the Torino and Rome shows, Jerome made personal calls and contacts to assure that shows took place in visible, good places.

I could go on and on. I know I am missing mentioning many other contributions that Jerome has made to the American avant-garde independent cinema (such as many personal grants to individual film-makers). And I am writing here only about cinema. Others can tell what Jerome has done for music and the preservation of old manuscripts in monasteries, etc., etc., where his contribution is major and lasting.

One last story. In Cassis, Jerome was befriended by a family that had a little daughter. The family was a poor family. One day at Jerome's office, I found a fat bundle of letters, hundreds of them, written by a young girl's hand, and some, later, by a teenage girl's hand. I asked Jerome about them and he said he could not resist helping this family. He paid for the education of the girl, for all her schools. These letters were all the thank-you letters from the girl, telling all about her life in school and at home. Later, in Cassis, in 1966, I met her. She was already a beautiful young woman.

I have to end this story with another story. As I was preparing this little piece on Jerome and thinking about Jerome and how he relates to my life, I was called to the phone. It was her: Jerome's girl, now a woman, and a woman in her sixties, living in Provence, happily married, who suddenly (we haven't spoken in forty years) had decided to give me a call. It was as if Jerome himself were on the phone.

*Department of Cultural Affairs*
*City of New York*

*830 Fifth Avenue*
*New York, New York 10021*
*212 360 8125*

To Whom It May Concern:

(name) _____ JONAS MEKAS _____

(professional name) _____ SAME _____

(address) _____ 491 BROADWAY _____

_____ NEW YORK, NEW YORK _____

Has been certified as an artist by the New York City
Department of Cultural Affairs solely for the purpose
of eligibility to occupy a legal living-working loft
in the MI-5A and MI-5B Districts or any legal AIR loft
where the zoning permits.

This certification is effective:

from _____ JUNE 25, 1979 _____ to ___ JUNE 25, 1982 _____

Sincerely,

*Henry Geldzahler*

Henry Geldzahler
Commissioner
Department of Cultural Affairs

Good luck!

**Henry Geldzahler**
*Commissioner*

140

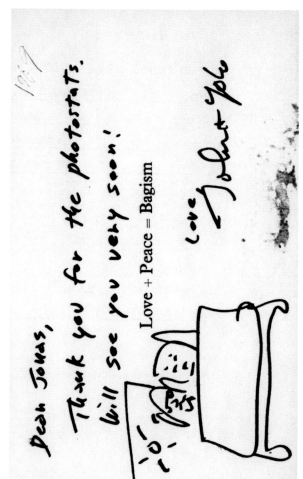

Dear Jonas,

Thank you for the photostats.
Will see you very soon!

Love + Peace = Bagism

love
John + Yoko

## JOHN LENNON AND YOKO ONO'S
## ARRIVAL IN NEW YORK

It was June 1971.

I was living at the Chelsea Hotel at that time.

At midnight the telephone rings. It's Steve Gebhardt. He is with Yoko Ono and John Lennon, who had just landed in New York in their escape from London.

"Do you know a place for Irish coffee? John wants Irish coffee and all places are closed."

I have to tell you that in New York in 1971 you couldn't easily find a good coffee after midnight, not to mention espresso or Irish coffee.

But Steve called the right man. I knew the place. Café Emilio, Sixth Avenue and Third Street.

So we all had some Italian food and John had his Irish coffee. We stayed there for a couple of hours. Yoko and John had to acclimatize to New York. They got relaxed. It was two in the morning by now, and there were only a couple of people.

"Ah, what a good feeling to be in a place where nobody recognizes you," exclaimed John.

So we drank to that.

A time came to leave. A waitress came and handed a little piece of paper to John: "Could you please give an autograph for my daughter?" she timidly asked.

John signed it.

Yes, she knew all the time who he was. But she didn't betray it.

143

The author with Yoko Ono and John Lennon in the Invisible Cinema, Anthology Film Archives' screening room designed by Peter Kubelka, in which each viewer had his/her private seat. One could not see any of the other viewers, one saw only the screen. The theater was in operation 1970–1973, at 425 Lafayette Street. It was demolished when Anthology had to move to 80 Wooster Street.

144

P. Adams Sitney and the author, Anthology Film Archives' office, 1971. Photo: Kenji Kanesaka.

# MY LIFE AT ANTHOLOGY FILM ARCHIVES

February 26, 1975

5 p.m. yesterday. Harry [Smith] calls. Could I lend him two or three hundred, whatever I can? Completely broke. His daily food budget is 50 cents.

Mice are trying to get his birds. $400 is due from NYU but it's not coming. Do I know anybody with money? I say yes, I just remembered—we have $100 in *Film Culture* account. I'll take it out tomorrow & you'll return it to us when you get the NYU money. He says yes. He can't leave hotel for health reasons but he'll send somebody, if not tomorrow then after tomorrow. He's only planning ahead, he still has $109 that he got from the Co-op, but wants to be sure that there is money somewhere after he spends the Co-op money.

2:30 p.m. today. I come back from the bank with money for Harry. A message. Stan called. Also a message from Leslie to call him. I start with Leslie. Gregory just called from Paris. Broke. Hotel not paid, stranded. Could I, could somebody send some money? Poste Restante number so and so, Paris. I say, yes, yes, I'll see if there is any money. I have only $12 in my bank.

3:30 p.m. Leslie calls. Spoke with Stan. Could I call Stan? He's very low, is talking about ending everything, about not making any films, not making any prints, ending everything. I say, "Don't worry, Stan likes to dramatize. He's just overworked." Leslie says he thinks he's overworked but it would help if friends would call him, it would help. Yes, yes, I say, I'll call him as soon as I find a minute's time.

5 p.m. Liza Bear of Avalanche calls (431-6560). Says Jack Smith just wrote her, from Rome. Urgently needs money. Stranded. Went to do a show at Lattico Gallery, something went wrong, performance fell through, no details, but he's stranded, needs $300 for ticket back, and somebody please pay his rent in New York, $60. Could I help Jack, could I do something? Yes, yes, I say, I'll see what I can find, something must be done. I'll call you as soon as I find any money—at least maybe the rent.

P. Adams Sitney and the author during the shooting of
*The Double-Barrelled Detective Story* (1965), a film by Adolfas Mekas.

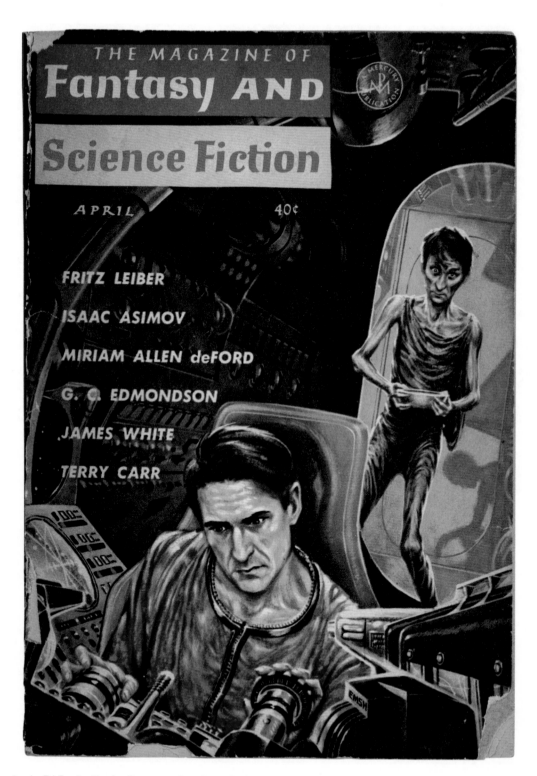

A drawing by Ed Emshwiller for the cover of a science fiction magazine. Adolfas, my brother, is the only person on the space ship who knows how to operate the ship. We are still far away from Earth, our planet, and the food has run out. Since Adolfas is the only chance of us getting back to Earth, I have to feed him with whatever food is still left, while I myself do not eat at all.

9 p.m. Stan calls, at home. "Yes," I say, "Leslie told me you are feeling low. So does Jack Smith stranded in Rome, and so does Harry living on 50 cents a day, and so does Gregory, stranded in Paris, and the other day Sally came to town looking for money, no money for her at Carnegietek. Only James feels OK, I spoke with him yesterday, he's coming for a day next Wednesday, he felt OK." Stan says he's really feeling a little bit better. I say, "Why don't you take it easy for a few weeks? You worked hard enough last fifteen months. Walk through the woods, listen to music, read." Stan says he's feeling better but not good, not well enough to read Henry James. He measures how well he feels by whether he can or cannot read Henry James. It's just that last year's work and all the tax problems, Government vs. Stan the Criminal, got him down. They dropped the criminal prosecution now, he's no longer a criminal, but they are still after Stan the Tax Thief, unpaid taxes on grants—and it will cost Stan, by the end, when it's all through, around $10,000 in lawyer fees. Anyway, he's tired of it all. Tired and low. He doesn't think he can afford making prints of new work, replacement prints; he has become a burden to his family because of his tax problems. Maybe he won't make any prints for three or seven years, he says. Not like Gregory who doesn't want to show his films, no—if anyone is willing to pay for it, let them show them, but he cannot afford to do it himself.

A minute later he calls back: He just came from three weeks of Canada. They are six, ten years behind there; they haven't seen anything. Could we help them? He's preparing an anthology of American avant-garde film for them. Could I give him *Circus*, to Liza Bear of New Cinema? He trusts her. I say, "Yes, of course, if you think so." Oh, Stan, he'll never give up even when he's sick and tired like a dog.

"How is Kenneth? Have you spoken to him lately?" Yes, he's better. Completely broke, but better in spirit, out of his love affair and working, may go to London soon, but not because of Jimmy, Jimmy let him down again. Kenneth had to pay his own plane ticket last time Jimmy got him to come to NY.

Harry Smith, 1975. Photo: Friedl Bondy.

## ON HARRY SMITH

February 13, 1987

We were talking about Al Robbins' death. Harry Smith said, "I am always disappointed when I wake up in the morning and I see I am still here and not in Heaven, Hell, or some other place."

November 1, 1987

Allen [Ginsberg] came. We are trying to set up some kind of fund to help Harry Smith to survive during the next twelve months or so. Harry Smith Fund.

"By the way," said Allen, "last time he stayed with me, he ruined my window. He cut out a hole in the glass so he could stick his mike through it to tape street sounds."

No date, 1992

*From a letter to Allen*

The other day I happened to be invited to participate in a psychic session. This woman—she is known by the name of Angel—is a very well-known psychic. So I said, why not? So this woman says: "Write down the name of a person who was close to you, but now is dead, and I'll contact this person for you." So I wrote down the name of Harry, Harry Smith. This woman takes the piece of paper, holds it in her closed hand, and she begins to giggle and laugh. She goes nuts. She says to me, "I don't know who this person is, but this person is very, very funny. And he wants to tell you that he is somewhere where it's very, very boring and he's anxious to leave that place soon and go to where it's more interesting." As she spoke so, I knew, I had no doubt, that she had contacted the real Harry Smith.

20 September 1972
RD 2 Cherry Valley
N.Y.
13320

Dear Jonas—

Here is a post-dated check for Harry Smith made out to you for $250.00—good November 1, 1972—I'll give a few poetry readings in October end, so money shd. be in bank to cover it by then—I'm broke and in debt now so can't do it smoother.

Nice seeing you the other day. Please invite Trungpa Lama to see some appropriate films sometime—Brakhage, Smith, etc., maybe *Pull My Daisy*. He'll be back some season soon, his secty Ruth in N.Y. phone 929-5549. He shd. be encouraged to get into N.Y. film avant-garde universe, he's not yet familiar with it & wd. like it I think, & learn—

Love, Allen

Since I am on the subject of Harry Smith, and the supernatural, I should tell you another related anecdote...

First I should tell you that in 1987/1988 Harry Smith, the genius musicologist, film-maker, painter, and anthropologist, was working at Anthology Film Archives as an artist in residence.

After Harry's death, some of Anthology's workers kept reporting to me strange occurrences taking place in Anthology's basement where most of Harry's art, music, and anthropological materials are stored. Auguste Varkalis, who followed Harry as our artist in residence, who used to sleep at Anthology, kept reporting to me that he heard the steps of someone walking up and down the stairway leading to the basement. Ralph, my film programmer, eventually refused to go to the basement because several times, when he went there to look for some films, suddenly film cans were flying at him from the shelves.

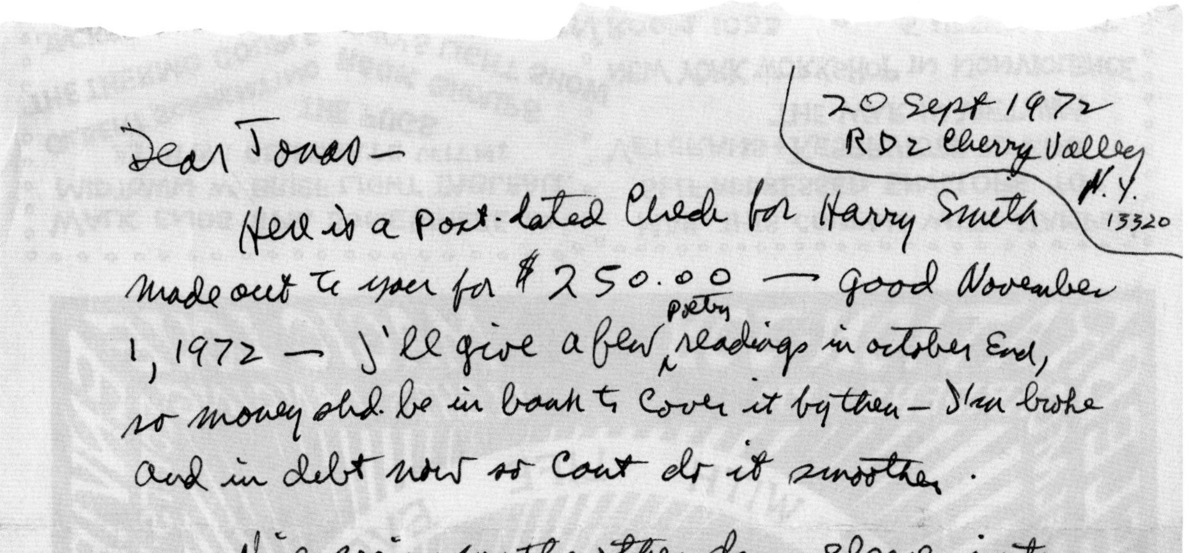

Dear Jonas —

Here is a post-dated Check for Harry Smith
made out to you for $250.00 — good November
1, 1972 — I'll give a few poetry readings in october End,
so money shd. be in bank to cover it by then — I'm broke
and in debt now so cant do it smoother.

Nice seeing you the other day. Please invite
Trungpa Lama to see some appropriate films
sometime — Brakhage, Smith etc, maybe Pull My Daisy.
He'll be back some season soon, his Secty Ruth in N.Y.
phone 929 5549.      He shd. be encouraged to
get into N.Y. film avant guard universe, he's not
yet familiar with it & cd. like it I think, & learn —

Love Allen

20 Sept 1972
RD2 Cherry Valley
N.Y.
13320

153

154

In the basement of Anthology Film Archives.

Since these occurrences continued for some time, we decided that Harry was still hanging around Anthology playing games with us. I have to tell you that Harry Smith had the most inventive sense of humor of anyone I have ever known.

So we discussed this matter with Palubinskas, the priest in charge of the church of Saint Mary of the Gates of Dawn, on the edge of Soho. He agreed to perform a ceremony of exorcism in the basement of Anthology.

Two days before the day of the exorcism ceremony we sat with Auguste at the Mars Bar, Second Avenue and First Street corner, in Manhattan, and we talked about it. And as we talked, it became clear to us that Harry was still hanging around Anthology there in our basement only because he loved us, because he had spent two years with us. He used to come early and work all day in the little room I had given him, and he felt good being with us. So we said, how could we do this to Harry? It wouldn't be nice to try to drive Harry out from the place he loves, in whatever shape or transitory stage of being he was now.

Next day I called Palubinskas and canceled the exorcism ceremony.

I think Harry appreciated our decision because after that day there was never reported to me any strange occurrences taking place in Anthology's basement.

Joseph von Sternberg with Marlene Dietrich. Photo: Anthology Film Archives.

# JOSEPH VON STERNBERG

February 21, 1954

Joseph Von Sternberg was the speaker at today's showing of the Group for Film Study. We invited him to introduce *Salvation Hunters*.

He stood there, at the Irving School auditorium, which we had rented for this occasion. There were some two hundred people. He was neatly dressed and prim, and he kept answering questions that kept coming from the audience, any question. What surprised me was that he seemed to be the only one in the auditorium who disliked *Salvation Hunters*. It was Sternberg himself who said the most cruel, negative words about the film.

Here are some notes I made from Sternberg's remarks:

"I was invited to introduce this film to you, but at the time I made this film, its sole purpose was to introduce myself...

"I tried in this film to slow down the tempo of the film. Instead of fast cutting, my aim was to photograph a thought. At the time I shot it I thought I'll be able to influence the shallowness of the films of that time. But I did not...

"All my work has been more or less the work of a poet. It has, if anything else, some poetic value, particularly in photography. But it doesn't have (in *Salvation Hunters*) any permanent value. It can be understood and appreciated only in relation to its time. This film is more horrible to watch for me than for you. I wouldn't show it myself anymore, but its showing, as you see, is out of my control.

"Its technique, cinematography, compared with other films of that time, is very good, I think. But the film itself is a very amateurish work."

Question from the audience: "What do you mean by permanent value?"

Sternberg: "I mean that a work of art can be appreciated and enjoyed regardless of the time when it was made, like Shakespeare or Dürer. This film can't stand that.

"The film was made with nonprofessionals. There was in it only one professional actor, a star, who worked for $100 a day. He did not accept my check so I paid him in silver and asked him not to come anymore. The girl that acted in this film impressed Chaplin so much that he took her for *Gold Rush*. Some of the other actors too, later.

"At the time I made this film I didn't put in it any symbolic meanings whatsoever."

Question from the audience: "But this film bears the mark of all your films, your style. I mean, the particular symbolism that is in all your films."

Sternberg: "Now I am being informed about it myself."

Question: "Do the horns in the film have any symbolic meaning?"

Sternberg: "No. We rented the studio for $500 a week, and when we came, the horns were there. So we decided to use them in the background. The same with the dredge in the background. When we came, it was there, so we shot it, and the next day it was gone. It wasn't planned.

"To use the machine as the hero of the film was more a photographic contribution or idea, than a directorial one.

"I started as a splicer. I used to splice fifty films a year. So I got used to film."

Question about the inter-titles in the film.

Sternberg: "When Schulberg saw *Salvation Hunters* he thought I was the best subtitle writer in the world and gave me a title writer job. He said the subtitles were so good that they saved him money filming some parts of the story."

## ANNETTE MICHELSON, PETER KUBELKA, AND THE BEGINNINGS OF *OCTOBER* MAGAZINE

I think it was in 1975.

We were in Paris: Annette Michelson, Peter Kubelka and myself.

Annette took us to one of her favorite restaurants. We had something to eat and we had some good wine. Then, Annette, in a voice that, in retrospect, seemed to have a tint of destiny, said:

"I want to tell you I decided to start a new magazine. I want you to read the editorial I wrote for the first issue. I need your reactions."

She took out from her pocket a couple of typed pages and handed them first to me, which I read, then to Peter.

Peter read it with great concentration. Then he fell silent. He filled our glasses with more wine.

Then Peter turned to Annette and uttered three words that I will never forget—I can still hear Peter's voice:

"Don't do it."

I don't have to tell you that Annette went ahead and did it, and when, at the celebration of the hundredth issue of *October* magazine I reminded her of that afternoon in Paris, she laughed. She laughed in her very unique, philosophical Annette Michelson laugh, same way as that afternoon in Paris, in 1975.

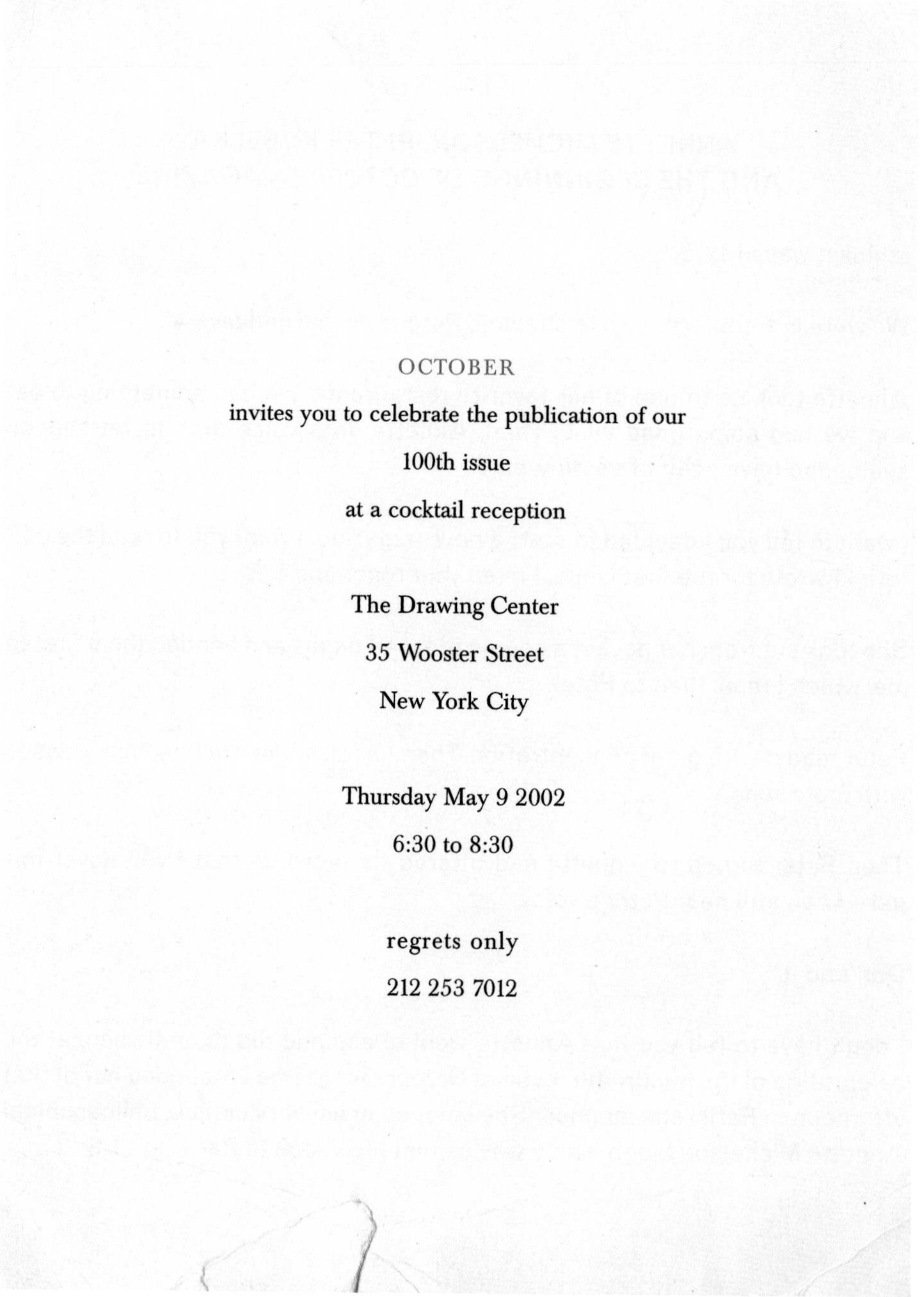

OCTOBER

invites you to celebrate the publication of our

100th issue

at a cocktail reception


The Drawing Center

35 Wooster Street

New York City


Thursday May 9 2002

6:30 to 8:30


regrets only

212 253 7012

OPPOSITE: Peter Kubelka and Annette Michelson, Paris, 1976.

162

Arthur Miller and Marilyn Monroe on the set of *The Misfits* (1961). Photo: Eve Arnold.

# A VISIT TO ARTHUR MILLER

December 4, 1954

Visited Arthur Miller in Brooklyn Heights. The aim: to raise money to pay for the latest issue of *Film Culture* magazine. We still need $500 by next Tuesday. He was very happy about the magazine and said he will try to get money from some people he knows.

We spent a long afternoon talking. He was complaining that nobody wants to stage his plays anymore.

"My plays are taboo now," he said. "They still think that my plays are plays *à la thèse*. I thought that argument was discussed and closed in the early thirties. But I was mistaken. What can you do with people like that?"

He was depressed and angry.

"They can't understand that an artist could be engaged in his times, problems. The best writer, the ideal writer of today, has to be completely detached from social themes. Complete un-engagement. In novels and in theater you see laborious reproductions of every detail as it is in life. Details, but nothing behind them. Emptiness in all the plays you can see on Broadway or elsewhere."

He said he thinks that the only intellectuals are to be found not among the so-called intellectuals or artists, but among the industrialists, manufacturers who know that culture, arts must go together with production. In America, he said, culture is detached from politics. Politics means campaigning, elections, etc., but no cultural, ethical integration. America is where Europe was seventy-five years ago. The Victorian age here has just passed, and after a great confusion in every section there is a great wish for returning to the point of departure, back to Lincoln, Franklin, the Constitution. They can't understand the relativity of history. They are taking it without adapting it to the changing times.

He expressed his great interest in existentialism, especially in Sartre's plays, such as *The Devil and God Almighty*, wondering why nobody has produced it here yet.

163

# MARILYN MONROE AND THE LOVELESS WORLD

February 9, 1961, *The Village Voice*

Marilyn Monroe, the saint of the Nevada Desert. When everything has been said about *The Misfits*, how bad the film is and all that, she still remains there, MM, the saint. And she haunts you, you'll not forget her.

It is MM that is the film. A woman who has known love, has known life, has known men, has been betrayed by all three, but has retained her dream of man, love, and life.

She meets these tough men, Gable, Clift, Wallach, in her search for love and life; she finds love everywhere and she cries for everyone. She is the only beautiful thing in the whole ugly desert, in the whole world, in this whole dump of toughness, atom bomb, death.

Everybody has given up their dreams, all the tough men of the world have become cynics, except MM. And she fights for her dream—for the beautiful, innocent, and free. It is she who fights for love in the world, when the men fight only wars and act tough. Men gave up the world. It is MM that tells the truth in this movie, who accuses, judges, reveals. And it is MM who runs into the middle of the desert and in her helplessness shouts: *"You are all dead, you are all dead!"*—in the most powerful image of the film—and one doesn't know if she is saying those words to Gable and Wallach or to the whole loveless world.

Is MM playing herself or creating a part? Did Miller and Huston create a character or simply re-create MM? Maybe she is even talking her own thoughts, her own life? Doesn't matter much. There is so much truth in her little details, in her reactions to cruelty, to false manliness, nature, life, death, that she is overpowering, one of the most tragic and contemporary characters of modern cinema, and another contribution to The Woman as a Modern Hero in Search of Love (see *Another Sky, The Lovers, Hiroshima, Mon Amour, The Savage Eye*, etc., etc.).

It's strange how cinema, bit by bit, can piece together a character. Cinema is not only beautiful compositions or well-knit stories; cinema is not only visual patterns or play of light. Cinema also creates human characters.

We are always looking for "art," or for good stories, drama, ideas, content in movies—as we are accustomed to in books. Why don't we forget literature and drama and Aristotle! Let's watch the face of man on the screen, the face of MM, as it changes, reacts. No drama, no ideas, but a human face in all its nakedness—something that no other art can do. Let's watch this face, its movements, its shades; it is this face, the face of MM, that is the content and story and idea of the film, that is the whole world, in fact.

# MOVIE JOURNAL: REPORT FROM BELGIUM

By Leslie Trumbull
January 9, 1964, *The Village Voice*

When the smoke began to clear away from the avant-garde scene last week in Knokke-le-Zoute, Belgium, it appeared that American entries in the Third International Experimental Film Competition had achieved two important results. Two films entered by members of the Film-Makers' Cooperative in New York tied for second place in the list of cash prizes (totaling $17,000). Stan Vanderbeek's *Breathdeath* and Gregory Markopoulos's *Twice a Man* each brought $2,000 in prize money for its maker—but for several days it was uncertain whether these and other American contenders would be withdrawn in protest of Belgian censorship laws.

The censorship issue arose over the American entry *Flaming Creatures* by Jack Smith. The all-Belgian selection jury accepted the controversial film but was advised by the Minister of Justice that Belgian law forbade its public screening.

### Mekas Arrives

At this point Jonas Mekas, an American member of the jury, arrived, found festival officials' hands tied by the censorship ruling—and promptly resigned in protest. But this was only his first move. Waving letters and cables from several American film-makers, he threatened to withdraw the entries of Vanderbeek, Markopoulos, Robert Breer, and Stan Brakhage. These and other film-makers reacted angrily to the injection of censorship into a festival described by its organizers as encouraging "free artistic creation and the spirit of research"—and in particular, "those films which attempt to extend the scope of the film as a means of expression."

The festival officials countered Mekas's attack by refusing to accept the withdrawals, leaving the situation in a deadlock until an appeal to the Minister of Justice brought a revised ruling.

Knokke
December 30 th 1963

Dear Jacques Ledoux:
I am handing to you the letters of Stan Brakhage,
Stan Vanderbeek, Robert Breer, and Gregory Markopoulos,
which delegate me to withdraw their films from the Festival. I hope
you'll act accordingly to the wishes of the film-makers.
Our position is as follows:
Unless the decision of the selection committee of the 3rd Intern. Experimental film Competition, which states that the showing of the film
"Flaming Creatures" is "impossible in regard to Belgian laws" is reversed
and the film of Jack Smith treated equally with other films
chosen by the committee as worthy of this Festival — in other
words! unless the censorship is lifted from this festival, the
film "Flaming Creatures" accepted into the Competition and shown
publicly — the films of the above film-makers are being
withdrawn from the Competition.
My own resignation as a judge at the Exposition
I have already handed to you verbally shortly after
my arrival at Knokke.

Jonas Mekas

166

OPPOSITE: The author with Jacques Ledoux during the opening of
Anthology Film Archives, November 30, 1970. Photo: Michael Chikiris.

A compromise was reached: The jury might consider *Flaming Creatures* in competition and screen it privately for that purpose, but no public showings would be allowed. As a result, the Smith entry was awarded the "special prize of the censored film (*film maudit*)" by the selection jury. The Mekas forces were unsatisfied, however, and their protest bandwagon rolled on.

Special screenings of *Flaming Creatures* took place in Mekas's hotel room, attended by European film-makers Jean-Luc Godard, Agnes Varda, Roman Polanski, and Gene Moskowitz of *Variety*, all subject to arrest by the local gendarmerie for attending an illegal screening. Occasional taps at the door, however, announced the arrival of more cineastes, about 40 in all.

### Booth Stormed

At one point the Mekas contingent attempted to take over the projection facilities at the public screenings, armed with a print of *Flaming Creatures*. Though this attack was beaten off by Casino employees and house detectives, who turned off the main electrical supply to the projection booth, the resultant uproar won a further gain for anti-censorship forces.

A representative from the Minister of Justice appeared on stage, promising future action to eliminate or modify the censorship laws. Paris, Berlin, and London papers, whose correspondents held several conferences with the American protest group, carried front-page reports of the crisis in Knokke. A reporter for the London *Financial Times* commented, "The battle currently being raged about *Flaming Creatures* at Knokke will almost certainly have significant reverberations for the future of film censorship."

## BARBARA RUBIN, POLANSKI, FELLINI

From Belgium, Barbara and myself, we proceeded to Paris. There we reconnected with Roman Polanski, whom we had met in Knokke-le-Zoute. One good reason for reconnecting was that Polanski had this little cute car into which, with some imagination, it was possible for four people to squeeze in.

One evening when we were crossing the River Seine, Barbara suddenly asked us to stop and let her and Debby, her New York friend who had joined her in Paris, step out.

"Why," we asked "aren't we going to La Coupole?"

"No," said Barbara. "We want to go swimming in the Seine."

"But that's a bit nuts," we said.

Barbara wasn't the kind of person that you could argue with and win. She just had to do it.

"OK," we said. "Go for a swim! See you at La Coupole!"

At La Coupole we found some of our friends, Louis Marcorelles, David Pascal, Christian Rocheford, and a few others, drinking beer. Polanski, who was a little bit annoyed with Barbara's Seine affair, made a little drawing which I am including here, and Pascal made one of me.

Next morning I left for New York. Barbara and Debby proceeded to Rome.

170

171

Barbara Rubin as imagined by Roman Polanski. Drawn in Paris at La Coupole, January 1964.

It's a long story, but I had somehow become Fellini's guide through New York. And we had this agreement that if any of my friends come to Rome, they should come and have a drink with him, no matter what he was doing.

So, before Barbara and Debby left for Rome, I told them please see Fellini, you must.

What happened next is Barbara and Debby ended up in a Roman jail. I do not remember for what; it was a minor case and they were released in a week or two, with their heads shaven.

They remembered I had told them to see Fellini, so they went to Cinecittà, where Fellini was shooting. I have to find out what he was shooting in early 1964. But he was shooting and he was in the middle of a scene when Barbara and Debby arrived on the set.

It was a few months later that I saw Fellini again in New York. I asked him if Barbara saw him. Yes, he said, they appeared on the set—these two amazing creatures with their heads shaven—and he thought they were just perfect for the scene he was shooting. So he immediately invited them to be in the scene. But no, Barbara said no, she didn't approve of the scene, she didn't want to be in it. And that was it. Barbara didn't want to be in the film; she left. He couldn't persuade her to be in it, he said regretfully.

April 27, '65

Dear Jonas

WE ARE HERE!
SPENT 10 HRS. IN THE AIR WITH BOBBY & JOAN
BIAZ BOTH HAVE SCRIPTS
GOT THRU CUSTOMS
FOUND A PLACE FOR THE NIGHT WITH A
NEWSPAPER "CRITIC OF ARTS" WHO KNOWS THE
BEATLES
UP EARLY BEAUTIFUL MORN TO MOVE INTO
KATE'S APARTMENT IN CHELSEA
WE ARE LIVING IN HERE ANTIQUIOUS?
FLAT AT    28 HEREFORD BLDGS
                OLD CHURCH STREET
                CHELSEA LONDON SW3
                FLAXMAN 7369

All's BEEN LOVELY MAGICAL COINCIDENCES
MARKED BY TOUCH OF MIRACLES!

AS FAR AS SCRIPTS, BEATLES ETC
I HAVE DONE AS MUCH POSSIBLE "NOW"
(BOBBY will GIVE JOHN LENNON THE SCRIPT
& MAKE MUCH TALK)
FOR THEY will NEED TIME PASSAGE &
DAWNING REALIZATION TO experience
THE complete essence OF THE MOVIE
& THEIR OWN AWARENESS
I'M CONTACTING TONY TO SEE WHAT

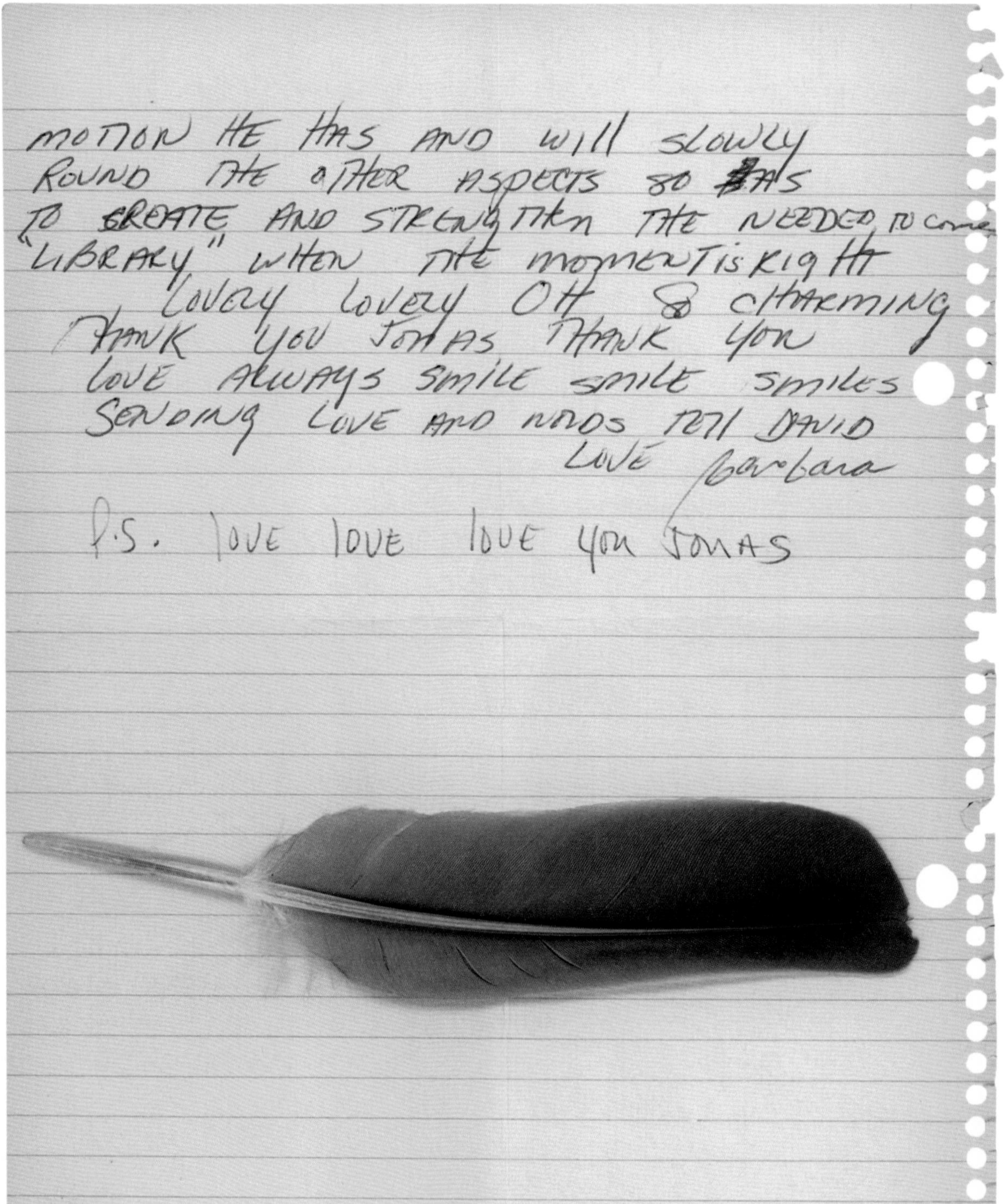

MOTION HE HAS AND WILL SLOWLY
ROUND THE OTHER ASPECTS SO HAS
TO CREATE AND STRENGTHEN THE NEEDED TO COME
"LIBRARY" WHEN THE MOMENT IS RIGHT
        LOVELY LOVELY OH SO CHARMING
THANK YOU JONAS THANK YOU
LOVE ALWAYS SMILE SMILE SMILES
SENDING LOVE AND NODS 1971 DAVID
                LOVE Barbara

P.S. LOVE LOVE LOVE YOU JONAS

174

# LETTER FROM BARBARA RUBIN

April 27, 1965

Dear Jonas,

We are here!

Spent 10 hrs. in the air with Bobby & Joan Baez Both have scripts

Got thru customs

Found a place for the night with a newspaper "critic of arts" who knows
The Beatles

Up early beautiful morn to move into Kate's apartment in Chelsea

We are living in her antiquious? flat at

28 Hereford Bldgs.
Old Church Street
Chelsea London SW3
Flaxman 7369

All's been lovely magical coincidences marked by touch of miracles!

As far as scripts, Beatles, etc. I have done as much possible, "now," (Bobby
will give John Lennon the script & make much talk).

For they will need time passage & dawning realization to experience the complete essence of the movie & their own awareness.

I'm contacting Tony to see what motion he has and will slowly round the other
aspects so as to create and strengthen the needed to come "library" when the
moment is right

Lovely lovely oh so charming thank you Jonas thank you love always smile
smile smiles sending love and words tell David

Love
Barbara

P.S. love love love you Jonas

A, P.S. TO CHRISTMAS ON EARTH & ALL THAT FOLLOWS FROM
THIS VISION, an example in me

It was one week out of being put away
where coincident held Miss Edie Sedgwick & myself
that was June of 1963 & I'd just turned 18
& i met Jonas & he gives me a camera & film & love & interested trust
so i shoot & shoot & shoot & shreak
up over slow & fast down & often all the way around & rewound many
times
the subject, what else could it be, was all about cocks & cunts &
fantasies
that freely expressed our sexual needs & dreaming beliefs
painted on their nude bodies
When we did finally film, though quite open & free
it was the beginning for me to see that fantasies repeat
when there's no love there to weep
but that wasn't enough
so i spent 3 months chopping the hours of film up
into a basket
and then toss and toss
flip and toss
and one by one
Absently enchantedly Destined to splice it together
and separate on to two different reels
and then project one reel half the size
inside the other reel full screen size
and then i showed it
and someone tells me, "my what a good editing job that is indeed!"
& God Bless thee
God Bless you

& Swedish Pancakes in 2 days as Bruce De Foreest said to me, "all
we wanted to say was the camera was borrowed & the film was free,
it's the first movie we ever made & it was pretty good on the
bedroom wall."


SOMEHOW THIS EVENING, FRIDAY, DECEMBER 30, 1966, is our
CHRISTMAS of sorts, held together by some SWEDISH PANCAKES
& HARE KRISHNA
somehow this evening naturally happened
somehow we all hope that it's not too much for you

MERRY CHRISTMAS

176

The author and Barbara Rubin at Cafe Bizarre listening to the Velvet Underground
in probably December 1965. Photo: Adam Ritchie.

178

# FROM THE DIARIES: PETER KUBELKA

When it comes to art, I am very materialistic. Above everything else, I value the uniqueness of a work and the pleasure it gives me. When I see something that is not like anything else I've seen, I get very excited.

When I saw Peter Kubelka's film *Arnulf Rainer* for the first time, I had such an experience. It was at the Third International Experimental Film Exposition in Knokke-le-Zoute, in December 1963. The screen suddenly lit up with energy; everything came to life, and I was elated. It was an incredible celebration of cinema; a hymn to light. Helios. The Greek civilization that produced us had its culmination in *Arnulf Rainer*, in light.

The film ended. I did not want to see anything that followed it. I walked out into the lobby. There I saw a man standing, depressed. I immediately knew it was Kubelka. I knew it from his sadness. I had seen the faces of the people in the auditorium, and they did not appreciate his film at all. The beauty of it, the light of it escaped them.

So we stood there in the lobby, sharing our common sadness about the state of avant-garde film audiences.

That's how Peter and I met.

No date, 1971
London

At the Tate Gallery, Peter leads me to a painting by Piero della Francesca. Three singing angels.

"Look at his colors, look," he said. He was all excited. Ecstatic. "You see, he used colors only from his own region. He used pebbles and stones which he ground up to make his paint, to make his pigments. These stones, these pigments cannot be found anywhere else. He was a regional painter. When I go to Italy, I always drink the wine of the region in which I am staying: It's always the best."

OPPOSITE: Peter Kubelka, Vienna, c. 1963.

June 18, 1974

Peter talks about pissing in all his favorite places—cities, hills, meadows, oceans, and how he thought he does it because he wants to establish a sense of superiority over them, and how he one day went on a hill, overlooking Toulon, his favorite hill, and found an American tank there and was so abhorred to find it there that he did not want to piss there again, and how he then understood that his wanting to piss in all the places he loved was not a manifestation of a wish to establish superiority, but a need to establish a connection with those places in the most intimate terms the way dogs piss in places they like, so he too had this very basic and primitive urge and way of communicating. He no longer wanted to communicate with this hill, where this inhuman cold American war tank was sitting, even if it had been one of his favorite places.

February 6, 1977

180

Peter is in town. Staying with us.

Peter made a date with Ken Jacobs, to eat in Chinatown. He says they are to meet on the corner of Broadway and Canal Street at noon. "Really?" I say, "Don't you know that Ken is always two hours late? It's cold on Canal Street."

Peter laughs, "I told him to call us when he is really ready and standing by the door." We agree that that was a smart move.

It is Sunday morning. Peter is practicing his recorder. We are all ready to go. We are sitting around waiting for Ken's call. Twelve. Twelve fifteen. Twelve thirty. I say that I will call Ken to see what's happening. Nisi answers. Ken comes to the telephone, either sleepy or spaced-out. He seems not to know what time it is. I put Peter on the line. They make a different arrangement: We'll leave now and meet Ken and Florence in the restaurant, the Phoenix restaurant, in Chinatown.

OPPOSITE, FROM LEFT TO RIGHT: Two unidentified musicians, Raimund Abraham, Hermann Nitsch, Arnulf Rainer, Peter Kubelka, c. 1960. Photo: Archiv Sohm.

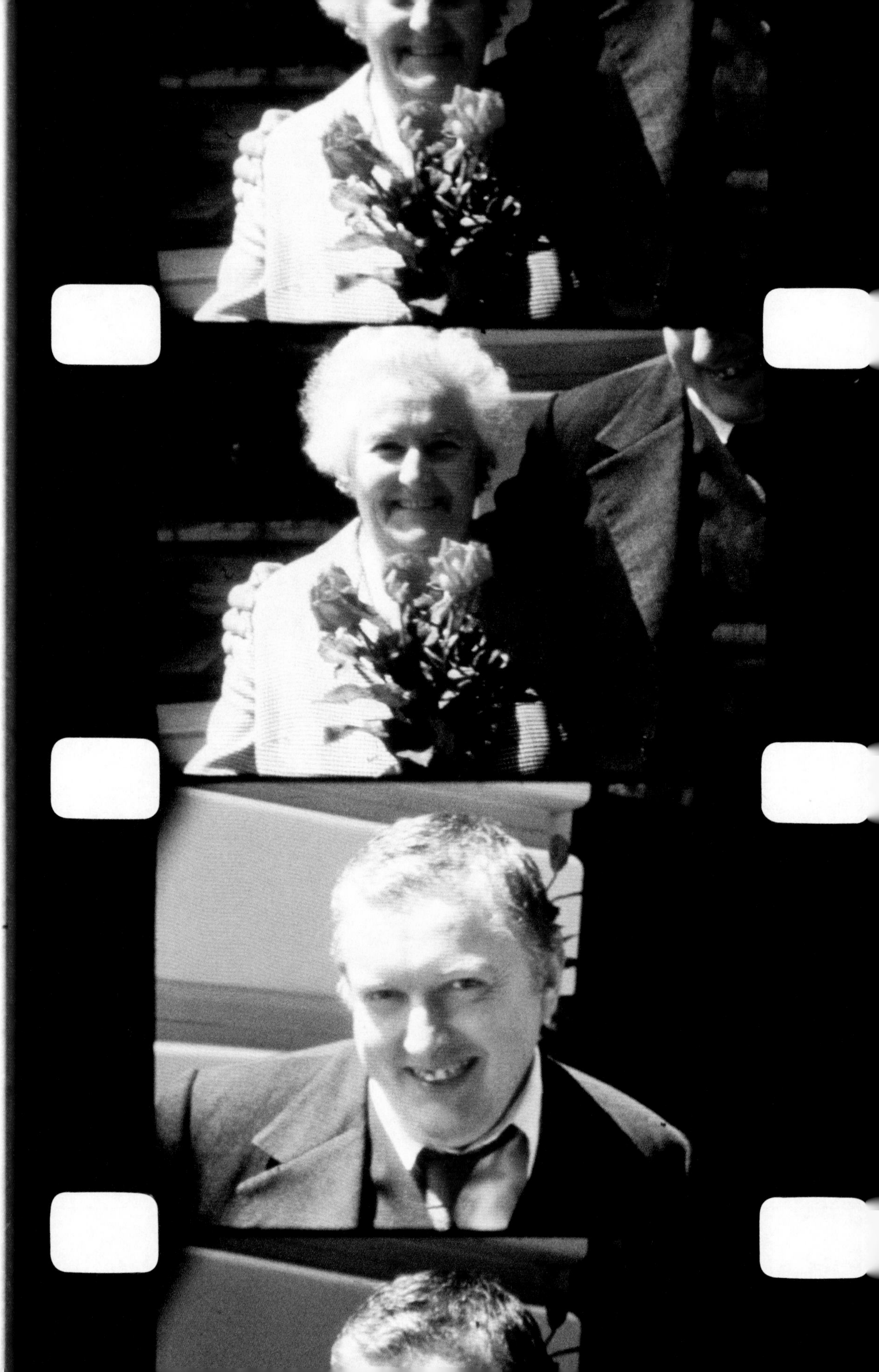

We walk along cold Broadway, and then along Canal Street: Friedl Bondy, the three of us, and Robert Haller, who happened to come by. On the corner of Canal and Mulberry Street, Peter stops and runs into a store. "Where's he going?" I ask.

"He's going to buy some meat to eat while we are walking so we won't be so hungry," informs Friedl.

I am not too crazy about eating meat in the street. We stand there waiting for Peter. It's cold and windy, wet snow. Peter comes back, all excited, with a bunch of some kind of sweet, dry sausages. "Try," he says, "they're very good." We all try them. Delicious. Oona, my four-year-old daughter, eats one, two, five chunks, probably more. We continue walking.

The journey is very slow; immensely slowed by all the vegetable carts in the street. Peter has to stop and survey absolutely every cart, every barrel, every bag. Peter and Hollis get very excited by some long, green vegetables.

While they are digging through the greens, I stand and wait next to a young Chinese woman with a smoking kettle on something that looks like a hamburger wagon. In the kettle: brown baked eggs. I make a joke to Peter: "Hey, look at the Chinese frankfurters!" Peter comes over, peers into the kettle and seems rather enthused. "We must have these," he says. "No," I say, "you might get poisoned or something. Just look at them, they are all broken, brown and yucky." But no, nothing can deter Peter now, he has to have them. "Anyone else want any?" he asks. Infected by Peter's enthusiasm, I decide to try them too. They're fantastic. Peter stands in the street peeling them and we eat, and they are just great. Snow is falling on us.

We continue our walk down Canal Street, and then along Mott Street, walking around, stopping here and there with Peter going up to every store window. We arrive at the Phoenix around two. The Jacobses are there waiting for us: Flo, Azazel and Nisi. Ken is elsewhere, searching for us. "He went again to look for you. We thought you got lost," Flo says. Ken comes back happy to see us.

Just another little walk through Chinatown... Just another day, another lunch together, with Peter and Ken. Nothing much has changed.

183

OPPOSITE: Peter Kubelka with his mother, Vienna, 1975.

April 5, 1980

Peter is telling us how, about five years ago, he went to Sicily when Etna was erupting. He felt a great urge to confront it, to experience raw, uncontrolled nature. He dressed up in his best Sunday suit, necktie and all, packed some prosciutto, loaded his Bolex, left Gertie in town, and drove up Mount Etna as far as he could. When he could not drive any further, he left the car and started walking. Etna was spitting and roaring. At least seven new mouths had opened. Rivers of lava were rolling down the mountain.

Somewhere, midway, towards the last plateau he met a group of scientists who were studying the Etna eruption, world-known scientists. They were walking hurriedly down, dressed in special fireproof suits and masks. They were quite amazed to see Peter walking past them, dressed in his best Sunday suit. They tried to persuade him to give up and return because it was too dangerous to go any further. Peter thanked them and proceeded further.

184

He chose a narrow passage between two lava rivers, a strip in between about 1,000 feet wide. He walked between them. Eventually he reached the final plateau, where it was chilly. Etna continued to spit and roar. The sun was setting behind him. The moon was coming up. He pulled out his prosciutto and decided to have a peaceful undisturbed supper. But the wind ripped the paper with the prosciutto out of his hands and swung it into the air, away, towards Etna's mouth.

He stood there by himself, on top of this mountain, contemplating it. He had confronted this force of nature, felt the nothingness of himself and the eternal power of nature. Peter pulled out his Bolex and began filming.

Later, people in Vienna heard about this event. A TV program wanted him to go back so they could film him. Peter said, "Take me there with a helicopter and set me down on top of Etna, on the plateau, with a fully set table, and you can film me there from the helicopter, eating my dinner in my Sunday suit." So the TV people took him to Etna, with the table and all, but Etna by that time was so wild the helicopter couldn't land. They considered renting a special army helicopter, but they weren't sure they could land it either. They returned to Vienna, the project dropped.

OPPOSITE: Peter Kubelka, Vienna, 1975.

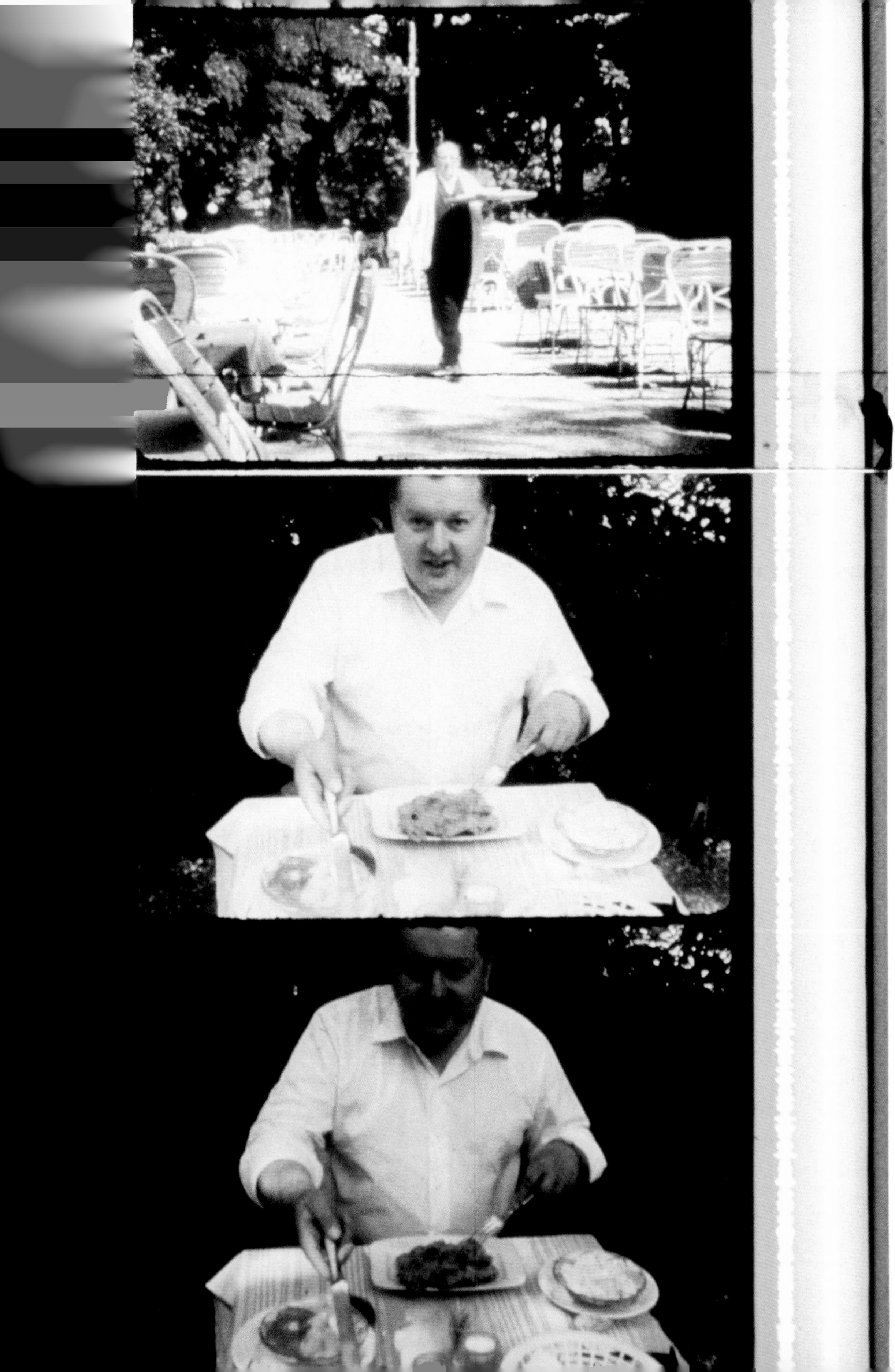

A SEQUENCE OF 21 DISHES MADE

# TO CELEBRATE

THE BAPTISM OF MY GODCHILD

# OONA MEKAS

ON THE 21st OF JUNE 1975

4PM    CHEESE MADE TODAY — BREAD

5PM    SOURCREAMSOUP
ROASTED PORK — RICE — WARM CABBAGESALAD
STEWED APPLES

7.30    TRIPPA

8.30    VEAL BRAIN SOUP
BLANQUETTE OF VEAL — ORZO — SWEET CAROTS
SPINACH IN BROWN BUTTER
CHAUDEAU OF WHITE WINE

11.30   SALAD OF MEAT — ALIOLI — BAKED TOMATOES

1.AM    TESTICLES — PEPERONATA — MUSHROOMSAUCE
SWEET OMELETTE

BY

PETER KUBELKA

October 6, 1985

We visit Annette Michelson in the evening. Peter gets into a long discussion/ argument with a guy from Israel, an art historian, and P. Adams Sitney, regarding Israel. Peter made a statement that Israel is an atheist state where real, conservative, believing Jews are either prosecuted or ignored. A debate over what makes a "real Jew" begins. It comes out that Peter thinks the Hasidim who still wear traditional clothes and perform their traditional rituals are the only true Jews. This starts a big disagreement, which is left unresolved. The discussion then drifts to Stan Brakhage with whom Peter had a conversation a few days ago. He says that Stan told him that nobody likes his films anymore and that in San Francisco, among other places, they boo when his films come on screen. P. Adams reports that Stan has never had fuller houses, that his shows at the Donnell Library and Millennium and even in San Francisco had standing-room only.

Peter then relates what Stan told him on the phone: that he had sent one of his films to a show in San Francisco under an assumed name, where everybody thought it was a terrific film and liked it because they didn't know it was his. P. Adams says it's Stan's fantasy; Stan never did anything like that, we would have heard about it. Peter then says it may be so, but he never takes Stan's words literally. The words to him are like a barometer of the times, indicators of deeper truths that they signal. Stan may be saying total nonsense and he may be an idiot, but beyond all that idiocy lies the essential truth of the situation of the avant-garde film today: a situation in which the field has been taken over by promoters, political activists, students, academicians, etc.

The evening then turns to Gaelic language and poetry, with which Peter is now deeply involved.

Oona (*far right*) in the American Ballet Theatre production of *The Nutcracker*, 1984. Photo: Martha Swope.

Peter Kubelka, Walther Derschmidt and Ulf Derschmidt in New York, March 1989.

JOAN CRAWFORD

January 16, 1963

My dear Jonas Mekas,

How can I ever thank you for making my New Year perfect by your wonderful review of "What Ever Happened to Baby Jane?"

Bless you - and my complete gratitude.

*Joan Crawford*

WESTERN UNION
TELEGRAM

*Send Jonas instead of filing*

W. P. MARSHALL, PRESIDENT          NNA          1201 (4-60)

The filing time shown in the date line on domestic telegrams is LOCAL TIME at point of origin. Time of receipt is LOCAL TIME at point of destination

D2CC 6R DL PD    WUX NEWYORK NY 1147P JAN 8 1962

EDITOR, VILLAGE VOICE        1962 JAN 8 PM II 57

   61 CHRISTOPHER ST SHERIDAN SQUARE NYK

DEAR VV: I SHALL PAPER MY SLEEPING ROOM WITH

RAINBOW-HUED PAPERS WITH FACSIMILIES OF JONAS MEKAS'

REVIEW OF MY FILMS AT THE CHARLES THEATRE TO DAILY

WAKE UP AND FIND HIS BEAUTIFULLY POETIC PROSE STILL

THERE AND TO REMIND ME TO CONTINUE IN A DIRECTION

WHICH UNLOOSENED THIS ECSTATIC VERBIAGE

        MARIE MENKEN

**LA ESTRELLA**

To Jonas
mekas
☆

---

MEMO

♭ ♪ ♪ ♪ ♭
dear Jonas Mekas,

When I was in mexico
I got a Village Voice +
read what you writ about
Harry.

I was so happy I
started crying. I love Harry
just like a father. That
may seem strange but
he has been like a daddy
to me.

I was very proud
and Happy with you
for writing it.

I just got back here

---

MEMO

and Harry looks real
healthy. I woulda writ
you from mexico but there
was a hurricane there +
no phones, mail etc. for
a week.

Every saint still
needs a guardian angel.

Thank you again
♡

patti smith

192

## YEVTUSHENKO

First time I met Yevgeny Yevtushenko was at the 1971 Moscow Film Festival party. I don't know why and how but I found myself remarking on how terrible were all the American movies shown at the festival. And they really were terrible. Yevtushenko listened patiently to my tirade, then he said:

"But you don't realize our situation. You say these movies are horrible. But if you'd know what shit we are given here daily, then you'd say, thank God for these bad American movies."

On that note I had to admit that he was right. I was actually embarrassed by my temporary blindness to the realities of the country I was in. The Soviet Union was still going strong and bad.

OPPOSITE: Mayakovsky Plaza, Moscow, 1971.

194

Postcard from Cindy Sherman, 1996.

## LETTER TO CINDY SHERMAN

August 30, 1995

Dear Cindy,

This past May, I was in Napoli. It was raining, it was raining very badly. I was visiting a friend of mine, Giuseppe Zevola. He lives in a huge loft, top floor of an old building, and the rain was coming down, through the roof, on his paintings and on his books. One book especially attracted my attention, because it was getting very wet. So I picked up the book and began to dry it. I opened it and there was an inscription: To Claude Cahun—André Breton.

That moment my friend, Giuseppe, returned. I showed him the book. "Ah," he exclaimed, "it was good you saved it: It has to go back to Paris, to a Claude Cahun show. I picked up the book right here, in Napoli, in the street, for a few liras."

He told me a lot about Claude Cahun, and I got very interested in her work. This August, I had a chance to be in Paris when a big show, dedicated to her work, took place at the Musée d'Art Moderne de la Ville de Paris, and I was very, very impressed with Claude Cahun's work. I also felt that there was some kind of kinship between her and you. You extended the work she began much further—but she was your younger sister. So I decided to send you this book, as a present, and as a token of my appreciation of your work and your self.

With Love,
Jonas

2/4

196

Dear Jonas,
    Thank you so o
much for the Claude
Cahun book — I've
always been fascinated
by her, but have never
found any catalogs or
books of her work.
    That was such a sweet & generous gesture!
        thanks again —
            Cindy Sherman

Jonas Mekas
Anthology
    Film Archives
32 second Ave.
NYC   10003

# MY DAY (HALF OF IT)

October 11, 1995

6:35 a.m.    I get up, prepare breakfast for Sebastian, and his school lunch bag

7:00 a.m.    I wake up Sebastian

7:30 a.m.    Walk with Seb. to subway, then to Anthology

8:00 a.m.    At Anthology. I feed Maxi, the cat. Look through the newspapers. Fax a letter to Galerie du Jour. I file the Library stuff because the pile on my table is too high

8:45 a.m.    Express delivery guy comes with mail; I fax a letter to CIAK re. Nico film footage

9:00 a.m.    I work on November–December schedule

9:25 a.m.    Call to DoDo. Receive a call from Nat. Endowment for the Arts re our application

9:40 a.m.    I go out for a cappuccino

9:50 a.m.    A guy from Israel drops in, needs info on Tarkovsky, I give him some leads, ten minutes wasted

Kelmen's NY friend Caroline calls 343-9591 about us premiering his film *Fate*

Fabiano calls asks if we could store his films, has an idea about reopening Charles Theater which I find unreal

10:05 a.m.    Back to work on Nov–Dec. schedule

10:20 a.m.    Meeting with Jim, trying to figure out what materials we have on Ed Emshwiller's film *Life Lines* and *Dance Chromatic*

A call from NYU about student internships at Anthology

I call Film Co-op to see what prints of *Dance Chromatic* they have, get involved in an emergency case of a Ken Jacobs film which is not back from rental on time

Stan Vanderbeek and Gerald O'Grady, c. 1975.

Peter Kubelka, Raimund Abraham and the author in front of Anthology Film Archives, corner of Second Street and Second Avenue, New York, 1988. Photo: Hollis Melton.

10:35 a.m.   Working on Gallery of Toronto request (Shedlin)

10:40 a.m.   Conference with Matt & Jim about acoustics in our upstairs theater & speakers—BAD STORY! One speaker must be replaced.

10:50 a.m.   Back to work on the Toronto request...

11:00 a.m.   Conference and review of morning with Haller

11:05 a.m.   The guy from Hamburg visits, made a film on Vertov brothers

11:10 a.m.   Kaplan Fd, Bill Callahee, calls re. our loan

             Charles Levine calls about depositing his films with Anthology

11:15 a.m.   Julius arrives. We talk about the downfall & disintegration of Robert Wilson... at BAM...

11:30 a.m.   I continue work on Nov. Dec. schedule. Search for photos. A call from Anja Czioska

12:35 p.m.   Fax to Galerie du Jour

1:00 p.m.   Half an hour wasted because Nickelodeon TV didn't show up but 100 school kids did and I had to entertain them

1:25 p.m.   Working in the film vault which is a chaos

1:30 p.m.   I go home, to grab something to eat

Here I give up on my notes of the day. Too time-consuming. This was an experiment. I wanted to have a list of things I do on my usual day at Anthology. So you have some idea...

The author with his daughter, Oona, c. 1998. Photo: Arunas Kulikauskas.

The author with Dustin Hoffman and the young Sebastian Mekas.

## JULY 4, 1995, NEW YORK

10:00 a.m.: It's still very quiet...

Only occasionally small firecrackers can be heard in the Italian section of the city, right east of us. It's loud enough for our cats to run and hide under the stove.

I am reading Oona's essay on television. It begins with a quote:

"Instances of people harmed by television will not be found in averages or statistics but in hospitals and prisons."

> — Harry J. Skornia, past President of National Association of Educational Broadcasters, 1965.

12:00: I walk to Anthology Film Archives. A very fine day. Streets are empty. Half of the people of New York leave town during this weekend, the other two million go to the beaches. So it's very empty, beautifully empty. I like New York on days like this. I walk through the empty streets flooded with summer light and heat and I am in ecstasy. I feel like all my sins have been washed away.

2:00 p.m.: I am back home. *Stitch* team arrives, dragging heavy bags full of cameras... Outside is getting noisier. We have some sake, and some wine. What's-his-name is not drunk, he is mad: He is totally immersed in his camera world. He disappeared in our messy apartment, snapping, snapping. I like crazy people like that. I am just like that myself. Either you are totally dedicated to something or you are not.

"Let's go out and see the city," I say. So we all go out and walk through the Soho streets, then we turn east, towards Little Italy. Not too many people. It's getting hot, so we stop at Milano's bar for a beer. The bar is empty, only some lonely elderly people who hate beaches and have no friends out of town to visit, sit and sip beer, watching TV. It's a little bit depressing but we act bravely. What's-his-name snaps more pictures. I get excited about filming beer glasses. It's an old bar; it used to be a bum's bar, but now it's a journalists' and artists' bar—that is, on regular days. Today, however, is not a regular day: Today is July 4th. So, everybody's somewhere else, with only these old people here and the *Stitch* crew.

OPPOSITE: Robert Frank on Bleecker Street, c. 2000. Photo: Peter Sempel.

We leave Milano and turn into Bleecker Street. We pass by house number 7. "Let's see if Robert Frank is home," I say. I bang on the door, then I shout: "ROBERTO! ROBERTO!" Nothing happens. Then what's-his-name points at the doorbell and says, "Why not buzz him?" and sure, yes, there is the damn doorbell, so I buzz, and Robert comes down, good sweet Robert, and we agree to have dinner next weekend; he knows a good place somewhere in Brooklyn. We joke for a while, then we say goodbye and proceed further east, to the corner of Second Avenue and Second Street, to Anthology Film Archives. It stands there very lonely and empty today. Only Maxi, the cat, is there, to greet us... So we talk to the cat, take some pictures, I pick up some faxes that had just come: one from Ulrich Gregor, Berlin, another from Giuseppe, Napoli, about my trip to Lithuania, in August. Then we continue east. Not much of the July 4th here, we say. Maybe we should have gone downtown, to Battery Park where you can see Statue of Liberty. There must be thousands of people there, celebrating July 4th... We made a mistake to go to the East Side... "Ah, where is the real America?" I said. But the East Side is also America. Ah, there are so many Americas... there are so many Japans... so many Lithuanias... Here, on the Lower East Side, Loisaida, there is an America here that exists outside of July 4th... They have never heard of July 4th, these streets covered with dirt and junk, flea markets full of tchotchkes that nobody wants to buy. Ah, no celebration here today. So we stop at Sophie's bar, on East Fifth Street, where usually, evenings, I sit and sing with my young Lithuanian friends, all new immigrants, but even Sophie's was empty today: Only a few local people were sipping beer and a guy was playing pool, all by himself. "Are you an immigrant?" asked the bartender. "No," I say. "I am not. United Nations dropped me here, I never wanted to come here, I was simply dropped here." "What do you think of America?" "I think nothing about America because I don't know America. I know only New York and I love New York. Especially on days like this." "You must be joking." "No, I am not," I say. "People are no good, the air is better when they go away."

204

The author during the filming of Robert Frank's *The Sin of Jesus*, 1960.

The author and Nagisa Oshima at the art auction to benefit
Anthology Film Archives, October 21, 1983. Photo: Akiko Iimura.

Anthology Film Archives' main auditorium space before it was transformed into a film theater.
The crew of Susanne Vega shooting her first music video, 1988. Photo: Hollis Melton.

206

The author with Claire Bloom, 1993. Photo: Arunas Kulikauskas.

We decide to visit Julius Ziz, my Lithuanian friend. He just got his first apart-ment, in Brooklyn. He came to New York two years ago, but he always lived in friends' places. He is one of Lithuania's best film-makers and playwrights. He is twenty-four, and when I told him that Eisenstein was already making *Potemkin* at twenty-four, he said, without blinking, "But I at twenty-four made my first Three-Image film." Which is true: He has just invented a new form of cinema, a form that consists of only three images, something that could be com-pared only to the Japanese haiku form of poetry. I like his work very much. In any case, two days ago he got his first apartment in Williamsburg, Brooklyn, where I myself spent my first two years of my "American" life. So we had to visit him.

The taxi dropped us practically in no-man's-land. We thought we were close but we soon discovered we were some two miles away from where Julius lived. Brooklyn is big and confusing. Thomas Wolfe wrote a short story called "Only the Dead Know Brooklyn," a beautiful short story. So there we were, in dead-man's-land. We did not know where we were. So we said, "Let's walk; we'll see more."

We were surprised that here, in the heart of Brooklyn, suddenly there were glimpses of July 4th celebration. There were people, entire families having parties in the middle of the streets, tables loaded with food and drinks, and they all looked perfectly happy. So we took some pictures, and nobody minded us at all—they waved and laughed, they were happy. Later, as we continued walking, I was thinking, I remembered my old days in Brooklyn, and it seemed that every weekend people here were having parties like this, July 4th or no July 4th... Still, it was good to see people having a good time.

Two miles became very, very long, and it was hot. We were practically pooped out by the time we reached 1012 Manhattan Avenue, Brooklyn, Greenpoint, and we all collapsed on the floor, in the new home of Julius and Carrie, his girl-friend. I say "on the floor" because Julius decided not to have any furniture in his apartment, not even tables, and no telephone, nothing. He is going through the ecstatic idealist period of his life, and all Gods are with him. Which means he is a revolutionary... He wants to keep his life and his room pure, bless him. And, luckily for all of us, he had prepared a little feast for us, poor as he is, with cheeses and wine and bread and even caviar... So we refreshed ourselves, and Julius said, "Now we have to sing." Julius and I sang a little folk song about beer, but what's-his-name said he could not remember any songs right now; maybe later. Julius said, it's OK—you don't have to sing, because you take good pictures.

9:15 p.m.: This is the evening for the traditional July 4th fireworks. We all gathered on the roof of 491 Broadway, twelve stories high, a good view, and we watched the fireworks. They were noisy, and there were a lot of them: big ones on the East River, coming from the boats there, and little ones, but very noisy, from the Italian neighborhood right below. "I remember they used to be much better," said Oona, now twenty years old. "Or maybe it's my memory, childhood memories?" I was thinking about our two cats. They must be hiding under the bed now, probably, poor things.

11:00 p.m.: Everybody departed. Outside it's still very noisy. I am trying to clean up my table, what a mess, what a mess. My eye catches a clipping from a paper. I cut it out, yesterday. It's about Cioran, the French philosopher; he just died. The article lists some of the titles of his books, such as *The Fall into Time*, *The Temptation to Exist*. He also wrote an essay called "The Sources of Emptiness." He never signed his name in full. He was known only as "EM." I have to look up his books. That's my pledge for July 4th. Outside is night, New York night. Somewhere, further there, is America, World, and the Russian and American cosmonauts, far above this Earth. They're supposed to return back, next week, back to Earth. But I have never been on Earth yet, not really. Someday I would like to touch this planet Earth with my bare feet, not just with the camera. Or is my camera my Feet? Gozo, is your pen your Feet? Maybe. Who cares.

## MEETING TIMOTHY LEARY

I was invited to spend the weekend of July 4th, 1965, in Millbrook, at Timothy Leary's place. I had some friends there that weekend. I had been working very hard all week and I thought a weekend in the country would do me good.

So I did a lot of walking around the fields and did a lot of quiet reading. By pure chance, I picked up and got very engrossed in a book about the life and work of Meher Baba someone had left on the table. Since some of my New York friends were sort of gaga about Meher Baba, and considered him their mystic guru, I thought I should inform myself about him. I was surprised to find out something very different from what my New York friends had told me about him. I found that Meher Baba was actually a very serious doctor, like Schweitzer, who specialized in mental illnesses and was running several very successful hospitals in India. There was nothing "guru" about this.

But that's not what I wanted to tell you about this trip. What I wanted to tell you is the following:

The third day of my stay in Millbrook, or rather my third day of walking and reading, Timothy Leary invited me for a walk.

We walked into the fields, quite silently, just a word or two commenting on nature. Then we came to a little brook and a little bridge. Tim stopped on the bridge and we both contemplated the quietly running waters.

Tim was the first to speak.

"Look," he said, "I have been watching you these three days. All your friends here are really having a great time. If you want to try LSD, this is the place— I am here and Richard Alpert [later known as Baba Ram Dass] is here too, to supervise and help. But you seem not to be interested in it. You are only reading and walking."

I listened and contemplated what he said. Then I said:

210

"Tim, I have tried this and that in my life. For experience and knowledge. I am not innocent. But all the drugs that I've tried were always a disappointment, a letdown. None gave me a lift as unforgettable and as mind-changing as when I first read Rimbaud."

Tim said nothing.

We stood on the bridge silently, for a long time. Then Tim turned towards the mansion and we both walked back, silently, all the way. Tim didn't say a word to me during the rest of my stay in Millbrook.

I didn't feel like telling Tim that I had already taken LSD. I took it with Barbara Rubin, a year or so earlier. But I wanted it to remain a one-time experience.

OPPOSITE: Timothy Leary's working studio, July 1965.

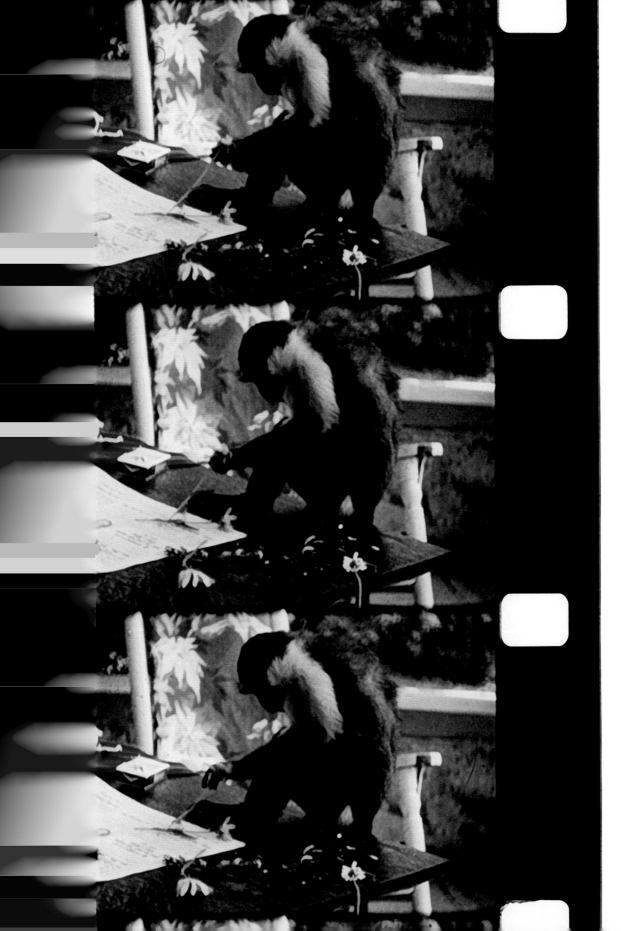

211

Irene Selznick, from an old movie magazine.

# AN EVENING WITH IRENE SELZNICK

## Part One

Julian Schnabel had an opening at Mary Boone's. After the opening Mary threw a party for Julian and guests. We are in April 3, 1983.

I was seated next to Irene Selznick.

We all ate and drank and it was a very fine and happy occasion.

Somewhere in the middle of this happy occasion, Irene turns to me and in a very concerned voice says:

"I think I am about to get pneumonia."

"How come?" I ask.

"Don't you feel anything? Put your foot next to mine."

I did as instructed. Immediately I felt an icy cold stream coming up my leg.

I crouched under the table and saw an apple-size hole in the floor right under Irene's legs. Obviously, under this room in which we were having this great dinner there was an empty, unheated space. This being winter and a very cold day, the cold air from underneath decided to come our way and up Irene's leg.

Suddenly a gentleman woke up in me:

"Dear Irene," I said, "do not worry: I'll put my foot on that hole."

And so I did. And I kept my foot on it the whole evening. I suffered, but I didn't catch pneumonia. Mrs. Selznick thanked me at the end of the evening and I felt like I had done something good that day.

## Part Two

In the summer of 1979, Anthology purchased the Second Avenue and Second Street corner courthouse building where we are now. The building was in horrible shape. I needed a lot of money to fix it up. The renovation and transformation of it into a film museum, I was told, would come to over $200,000 (eventually it cost us $1,750,000...). One of the first people I called was Danny Selznick, whom I had already known from before. "Come," I said, "take a look at the building. I need help. Maybe you can get me in touch with some money people. After all, I saved the life of your mother." And I told him the Schnabel party story.

So he came. I gave him a tour of the building, or rather the structure that once had been a building. At the end of the tour, he stopped and simply said:

"Forget it. Give it up. This is hopeless."

We had a drink. I thanked him for coming and we parted.

I invited Danny again some ten years later, for the October 12, 1989 opening of Anthology's new home.

He came. He was very apologetic when he saw that the project he had declared hopeless was being celebrated. So we had a drink for the occasion. And we are still friends.

# NOTES ON ST. TERESA DE ÁVILA

A letter to P. Adams and Julie Sitney

July 1, 1967

I was told that the Italian mailmen are on strike. I hope this letter will reach you this year (what year?).

We are somewhere in New Jersey, in a very lyrical green place, just after the rain, and there is Thoreau's *Walden* on the table, someone has been reading it, and we have been shooting for the last five days Adolfas' movie. I haven't seen much of New York since I came back.

As you know, I proceeded from Cassis to Madrid. Arrived there Tuesday evening, and slept in a small place, somewhere in Madrid, and had a strange dream. Usually my dreams are very simple, down to earth, farmer's dreams. I have no "strange" dreams, no symbolism, no surrealism. But this time I dreamt I was trying to tame a DRAGON. I was riding it, and I was in complete mastery, I had no fear of any kind and someone was telling me that in the old days they used to kill dragons, but that today we should try to make the dragon work for us, we shouldn't kill the dragon, and that my (and our) function really is to teach people how to make the dragon work for us. WORK, WORK, WORK, was the message given to me by someone, WORK WITH PEOPLE. I know only very little about the ancient symbolism, really, about the subconscious meanings of dragons. I told my dream to Richard [Foreman] (& Amy) and Kelman and Storm [de Hirsch] and I got different interpretations. Dragon as Europe (Old Continent); Dragon as Wisdom (Storm), etc.

Next day, very early, at seven o'clock, I took a train to Ávila. We crossed the craggy, stony hills and mountains (Ávila is at the height of 9,000 feet), the landscape rained with stones, and after a three hour ride there it was, it said: ÁVILA. I had with me only my camera bag, I left all other belongings at the airport, so I swung it across the shoulder and proceeded to walk into town. The day was clear and blue and it was very hot. I tried to find a map of the town, but nobody had one. And since my Spanish was practically nil, I decided to rely purely on chance, intuition, and the guidance of St. Teresa. I immediately found myself in a beautiful square full of blue wild flowers, and I picked up two of these blue flowers and I put them into my camera bag. (Later I discovered that there were roses and roses around the houses, further in the town.) There were two churches, two very old churches around the square and there were children playing around them and I took a few frames of them, although I didn't go into the churches. I proceeded, walking deeper into the town, and soon I came before the gates of Alcazar, one of the many gates in the walls that surround Ávila's heart. I saw no tourists, and practically no cars, only the donkeys loaded with baskets of bread stood on the sidewalks, and the faces of the people were good and there was a feeling that I was in a different century. The rest of the world had disappeared somewhere behind that railroad station and those hills and the fields—I was completely somewhere else. I hadn't eaten since I had left Cassis, thirty hours ago, and I felt I shouldn't. I felt I shouldn't speak to anyone or ask for anything from anybody, that whatever there was for me in this city it will come to me by itself. And when I asked someone where St. Teresa's house was the man didn't know it either, and he told me to continue going. Soon I found myself in front of the Cathedral of Ávila, and it was completely empty. It was still too early for the tourists if there were any, and I walked in and as I stood there looking around, a very, very old eleventh-century church, I saw a small note which said to the effect (it was in Spanish, of course) that here, it was in front of this little altar, that Santa Teresa de Jesus was first visited by St. Mary. So I took out the two blue flowers from my camera bag and I put them on the altar, beside a few roses that someone had placed there, and I sat on the bench for a little while resting, giving my regards to St. Teresa and to St. Mary from all the avant-garde film-makers of New York, and from both of you who couldn't be here.

As I then continued my journey through the town, I came to another church. In truth, it was a pretty drab "modern" church, and I walked in, and it was a church built upon the spot where St. Teresa was born. There was a room with a statue of St. Teresa; it was a small room, exactly (a note said) on the spot where Santa Teresa was born. It was one of the most silent spots I have ever been. In fact, it was so silent, so silent, that the silence became like matter, you could go deep into it, and there was no end—it was leading me into somewhere very, very deep, very deep. Again, the room was completely empty, I was the only visitor there, and I sat in the room for a long while, with an unmistakable feeling of the presence of the Saint in the room, and I didn't know what to do or what to say although I knew St. Teresa was there. So I proceeded further.

I walked out through the gates of St. Teresa. I left the heart of the old Ávila and descended into the tiny streets of the suburbs of Ávila most of which in the days of St. Teresa was just a plain field but which now is covered with tiny streets that run down the steep hill and into the fields. On my way down the hill I saw a girl by a house that was practically covered with roses. I asked her for two roses, and she gave me them, and I continued further down the hill to where I guessed the old convent of St. Teresa stood, the one she built secretly and with great difficulty, her first one—and when I arrived, the gates were closed. I walked around it, to the other side, and I found a small door, used by workers, so I walked into the courtyard. I saw a nun walking in, so I followed her and I found myself in a long dining hall, in which there was nobody, not a soul, but there was a long table where the nuns, it seemed so, ate. At the end of the room there was another table, a small one, and since I didn't want to go

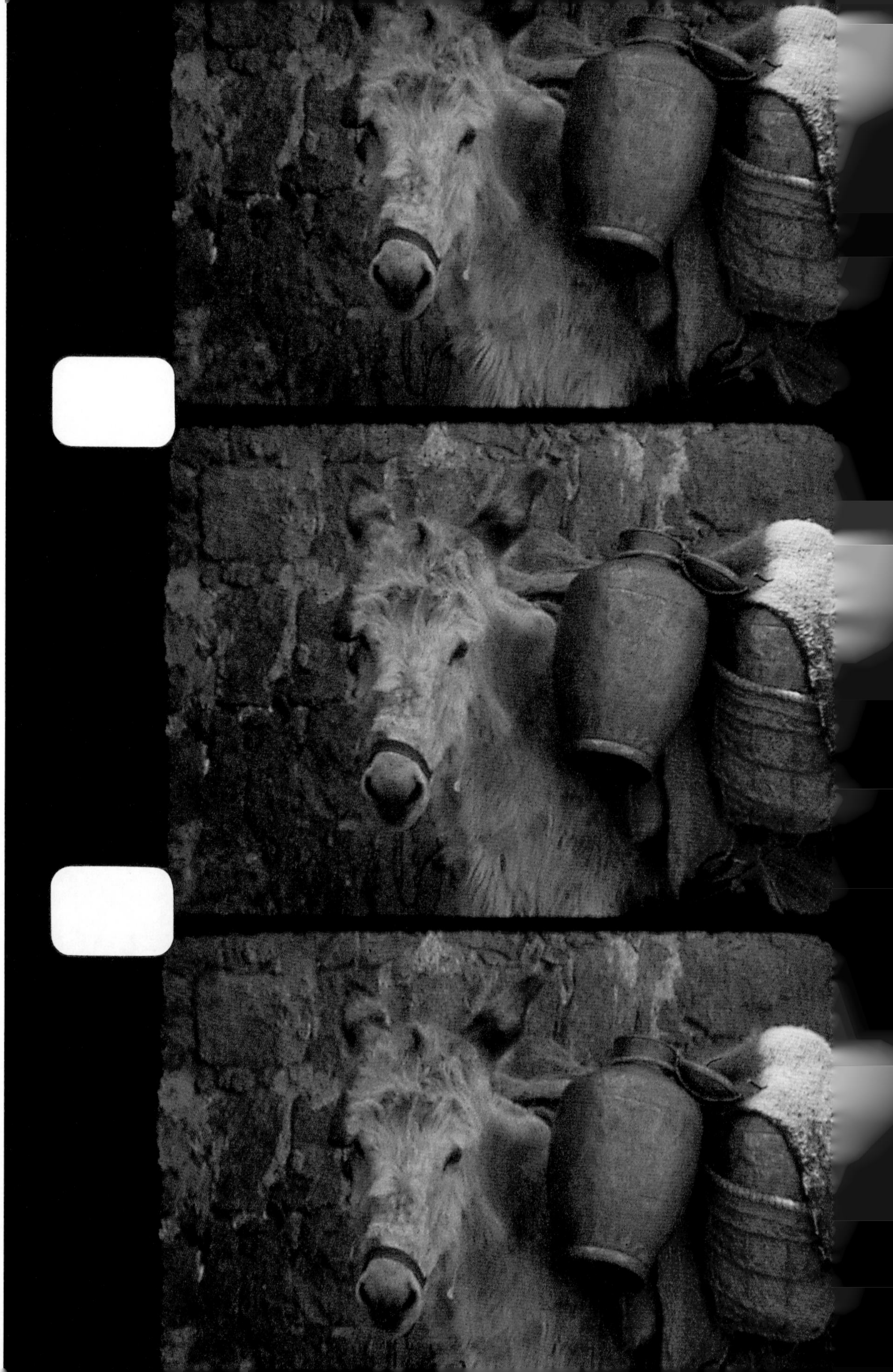

further and disturb the good nuns, I placed the two roses on the little table, and I walked out of the convent and out of the courtyard, the same way I came in, and soon I was in the fields where the rye was in full growth, full of red poppies and blue flowers the name of which I don't recall in English but in Lithuanian they are called "Rugiagėlės," the "rye flowers." The fields were full of sun and heat. By now I had walked for several hours and I was hungry and thirsty but the whole field, the entire slope was like the essence of summer. Really, it was also the essence of my own childhood, so I stood there looking at the fields and breathing the smell, the whiteness, and the greenness of the rye-fields.

I kept climbing up the hill, and kept walking along the wall surrounding Ávila. The hot white dust of the sandy field covered my feet and I was getting dizzy from the brightness and Ávila. But I felt I had to continue walking. I went back to the Saint's birth chapel, and I sat in the solitude and rested for another while. I thought I was all alone. But I wasn't. There was a girl in the corner of the chapel, sixteen or seventeen, kneeling. I could see her face, it was a very sad and intense face and a very beautiful face and our eyes met for a second and I was again alone in the chapel.

I continued walking the streets of Ávila the rest of the afternoon and evening. I felt like retracing, like crossing every street that St. Teresa had walked, I was walking the streets for her, again, crisscrossing the traces left by the Saint. I came upon a little plaza, called Plazuela de las Vacas—the little plaza of the cows—it was the old field where the cows, the cows plowed the field by themselves while the farmer, St. Teresa's friend, prayed in the church with the Saint. Now the field was a plaza with a tiny monastery on the side and little houses and streets all around it. The plazuela was full of children and I sat there for a good hour, surrounded by children, click-clacking my Bolex, and I had never seen anywhere such beautiful children, they were like angels. It was one of the things that amazed me in Ávila, the children, how angel-like they looked, the children of Ávila.

I felt here no presence of the sadness of the Western Civilization. The town was still in another century, the faces, the eyes of the people, the streets were in another century, and there was something very noble and serious about their countenance. Eternity was hovering over the city. While I was walking down the hill, an elderly woman with two children joined me for a few streets, and she kept saying "calore," which I understood meant HEAT, heat and I said, "Sì, sì, calore, calore," and the children laughed. The woman was dressed all in black, very beautiful black (the beauty of the black was another thing that struck me in Ávila—before I never really believed that black could be so alive and so beautiful) and her face was like you see only in some old books or some of the faces that I saw later, next morning, in the early Spanish paintings, and in Goya, at El Prado.

The evening came and I filmed the setting of the sun as it slowly sank behind the gates of Alcazar and behind the walls. I went back to the place where St. Mary appeared to St. Teresa de Jesus, and next to the cathedral I found a third-rate hotel called Roma and I took a room for the night. Then I went back into town. I stood in front of a small restaurant, completely tired, trying to make up my mind: to have a glass of wine or not? And as I stood so, looking at my feet and the dust on my shoes, looking back at the day, I kept asking myself: Why did I really walk and walk and walk like that? I probably walked every street of Ávila and I walked around the town twice, and all the fields around Ávila. I didn't exactly notice it, when I did it, but it all came into consciousness now, as I stood there, and I had no explanation and it didn't make much sense. There must be a meaning in all of this, I thought. And as I stood there, thinking like that, a small dog came from somewhere and started licking my feet and the dust from my shoes, a little dog, and he licked off all the dust of my shoes, and I didn't move. I took this as a message from St. Teresa. I felt that St. Teresa had sent this little dog, as if she was thanking me for my walking, for all the streets that I walked for her, and she was taking back the dust from my shoes although I didn't deserve it at all, because it wasn't me who was really walking the streets of Ávila—I was totally unconscious of it—somebody else was walking them and this dust, I had a feeling that this dust was a closer bond between us than anything else I could have done.

So I went back to the hotel and I slept in peace and I dreamt nothing, at least not that I know of.

220

I left Ávila at six in the morning. The entire city was sleeping. The streets were completely empty at dawn. I was in the Church of the Dawn, alone. I was walking towards the gates of the city, and my steps were making a sound that seemed to echo across the entire city—the city was so silent. I was walking with one thousand feet, the stone pavement went *clink clink clink*, a sharp clinky stone bell sound, as I walked behind the gates of Alcazar, with my camera bag on my shoulder, from one end of the city to the other, to the East, where the railroad station stood. The train was just pulling into the station so I jumped on and then I went to the window to look at Ávila, I leaned out, but it wasn't there. I looked but I couldn't see it—Ávila was behind us, directly behind the train line, in time and in space, all I could see was the rising sun, so I took my camera out of the bag and I started filming the sun—*click clack click*—as it was slowly rising above the stony landscape of Castile.

I should add here a footnote to my Ávila trip. At JFK Airport, upon my arrival in New York, late the same day—after spending seven hours at El Prado—the customs officials seized all the film I had with me, all my New York diaries, and all my undeveloped film shot in Italy, Vienna and Cassis. They snooped through all my luggage and even through my papers, and I was getting all angry and pepped up about it—some welcome home, I thought. Only next morning, at home, when emptying my suitcases and bags, I discovered that the custom men had overlooked two rolls of film. After looking closer, I discovered that those were the two rolls that I had shot in Ávila... And as I looked at them, with some amazement, thinking about the amazing coincidence, suddenly the room was filled with the smell of roses—a brief gust of roses, very, very strong—and it lasted a few seconds, and then it was gone.

142 Columbia Heights
Brooklyn, New York 11201


May 20, 1968


Dear Jonas:

       Your letter was fine and generous and splendid as you
always are with your open reception, nay, your incredible
sensitivity to what is new and valid in everyone's work.  And I
hope the picture is as good as you say it is--there are times when
I think it is.  You know I never told you this but one of the ten
reasons why I got into making films has been reading your columns
over the years and as a result slowly connecting to some of the
ideas--for I missed many of them--in avant garde film which loosened
me up.  So this is not only to say that I will be quick to call on
you if there's need, but that I look forward to us finally having
a conversation some day, not an easy matter for either of us, for
so many conversations are disappointments, but maybel we'll have
the opportunity to take a crack at it.  Will you be on the Cape
this summer?  If so, please come by to visit.   The phone number
is 487-9325, and if not, I'm sure we'll see each other in the fall
on that movie board of which we're both, bless us, members.

223

                        Yours and best,

                        *Norman*

---

224

# BARBARA RUBIN

December 18, 1980

Gordon Ball called to confirm Barbara Rubin's death, somewhere in the south of France. Bracha Barsacon, that was her married name when she died giving birth to a child. 50 Montée de la Reine Victoria, Aix-les-Bains. Something like that. I got the address from Cassandra in her fancy handwriting, hard to read.

Goodbye Barbara. I owe you a lot. And so do many other people. I cannot imagine New York's sixties film and poetry scene without you. You breezed in like a mysterious messenger. You urged us, you scolded us, you pushed us, you kept us together, you provoked us, you challenged us, and you argued and you argued and you argued. And you were everywhere. You moved from Jack Smith to Genet to the Beatles to Ginsberg to Bob Dylan, to Burroughs to Harry Smith to Lou Reed to Lenny Bruce to James Baldwin to to to... Your energy was inexhaustible; your belief and faith in us and in what we were doing was absolute.

I met Barbara in the spring of 1963. She was seventeen. She died seventeen years later, at the age of thirty-four.

One evening after a show at the Gramercy Arts Theater, where the Film-Makers' Cooperative held its film screenings, where films such as Markopoulos' *Twice a Man*, Warhol's *Sleep*, Jack Smith's *Flaming Creatures* and Kenneth Anger's *Scorpio Rising* were premiered, a man by the name of William Rubin approached me and asked me whether I needed some assistance at the Cooperative. He said he had a niece who loved movies and she was just released from a correctional house, one of those places where they put teenagers when their parents cannot deal with them, teenagers gone totally "wrong"... Barbara had run away from her parents, got into drugs, ended up in the correctional house. But she was OK now, he said, and the police had decided to let her go home with the condition that she'd take a "regular" job to occupy her mind and time. I told him that she should come to the Co-op on Monday.

She came. Frail, very young, totally scared, and totally silent. She was still in a stupor. She did everything I asked her to do but she said no word. Maybe she thought she was sent to some extension of the correctional house... She only watched, listened, nodded and, sometimes, smiled weakly. She was very, very sensitive, and very, very responsive. But she said no word.

Several weeks passed like that. David Brooks, who was the main worker at the Co-op at that time, kept asking me, wondering why I was employing this simpleton. He thought she was a totally dumb suburb kid—she was from Cambria Heights, Queens. He himself, eighteen at the time, was a man of the world who knew all the jazz places and knew where to get pot and etc. and etc. When he smoked pot he did it hiding, in order not to shock Barbara.

This, as I said, went for several weeks. The Film-Makers' Cooperative, located in my loft, in those days was a meeting ground for a lot of different people. You could bump into Warhol (if you knew how he looked—I didn't for months), Ginsberg, Jack Smith, Harry Smith, Jeffrey Joffen, Ron Rice, Ken Jacobs, Taylor Mead, Bob Kaufman, Robert Frank, Burroughs, and Andrew Sarris, and Peter Bogdanovich and Parker Tyler, and George Maciunas, and teenager P. Adams Sitney, this being also the editorial office of *Film Culture* magazine. And on some evenings you could even hear Salvador Dalí's cane, climbing up to the third floor of 414 Park Avenue South. It was my loft, but the Co-op had taken over it.

OPPOSITE: Barbara Rubin and the author, Central Park, New York, 1962.

227

The Underground will present a festival of movies, slides, film
loops, jazz, rock, et al. The artists, led by Barbara Rubin, plan to
topple the current concept of theatre and movie house by placing the
musicians in the middle of five screens (one on the floor!) and seating
the audience on large palettes instead of the conventional rows of seats.
Featured are top jazz saxophonist Gato Barbieri and his quintet and the
exciting new rock sound The Free Spirits, plus films by leading underground movie-makers; among them Andy Warhol (responsible for "The Chelsea
Girls"), Jack Smith, Ed Emshwiller, Jonas Mekas, and Miss Rubin.
It's all part of the radical new programs being presented at the
Film-Makers' Cinematheque, 125 W. 41, under the title "Catepillar
Changes". There will be shows nightly at 8 p.m. from Saturday, Feb. 18th,
thru March 2nd. Tickets, priced at $2, will go on sale each evening
one hour before the performance.
On Saturday, Feb. 25th, there will be a special matinee (the
"kiddie" show), from 2 to 6 p.m., for which admission will be free.
(Attendance is limited to 200.)

For further information, call 564-3818 after 3 p.m.

228

TO THE PRESS
ON FEB. 18th to MARCH 2nd at the CINEMATHEQUE 125 west 41st STREET
FROM 8PM ON WE ARE HAVING NEW YORK'S FIRST UNITED ACIDHEADSPEED RELIEF
FUN BALL & GLITTER PARADE. IN THE DENTAL DESTRUCTION OF THE CHAIRS
A MASS MENTAL CONCENTRATION AGAINST FURNITURE INSTIGATED BY THEIR
PRESENCE BY ANGUS MACLISE & THE VELVET UNDERGROUND WITH THE CONTRIBUTIONS
OF THEIR MOVIES, SLIDES, LOOPS, PROJECTORS, & MADNESS OF HARRY SMITH
ANDY WARHOL RAY WISNIEWSKI JONAS MEKAS TED GERHKE STEWART REED GORDON
BALL LOUIS BRIGANTE KEN JACOBS FRED WELLINGTON MATT HOFFMAN DICK PRESTON
JOHN CAVANAUGH JACK SMITH PIERO HELICZER SUSANNAH CAMPBELL BOBBY NEUWIRTH
DAVID THURMAN AMY TAUBIN RICHARD FORMAN GERARD MALANGA STORM DE HIRSCH
WEE GEE ANDY NOREN SHIRLEY CLARKE JUD YALKUT PENNEBAKER DAVID HOFF DON
SNYDER JERRY JOFFEN MARIE MENKEN JIM MULLINS ED EMSHWILLER STAN VANDERBEEK
HOHN HAWKINS ROBERT BREER JERRY HYLER WILLARD MAAS DAVID BROOKS BARBARA
RUBIN PLUS IN PERSON THE MUSIC OF GATO BARBIERI QUINTET & THE FREE SPIRITS
& JUST ABOUT ANYONE ELSE YOU CAN THINK OF FOR 12 DAYS IN THE MASS LOVE
CONTEST "SMOTHER ME". WE EXTEND AN INVITATION TO YOU GLADLY THOUGH I
SINCE OUR LAST MEETING AT THE EVENING OF NAM JUNE PAIK & CHARLOTTE
MOORMAN WE WILL HAVE TO MAINTAIN BETTER THE er THE ER OF THE BUILDING
& THE FIRE & THE LICENSE DEPARTMENTS SUGGESTIONS THOUGH AGAIN WE CAN
NOT GUARANTEE WE WILL COMPLETE THIS SHOW EITHER. & PLEASE BRING YOUR
WIFE GIRLFRIEND CHILDREN FRIENDS & ALL TO OUR MATINEE PERFORMANCE ON
FEB. 25 th STARTING AT 2 pm love & kisses   ALL OF US

I don't know how it came about, but David Brooks or someone else got involved in a hot discussion on the subject of the new generation, and David, who, as I said, was eighteen, said something that Barbara didn't like. I do not remember what he said, but it was enough to break Barbara's silence. No, she didn't speak: She came out like a spitfire. Like a painful stammering torrent of words long held back. Her speaking always had these almost painful hesitations, as if there were so many words on her mind that she didn't know which ones to choose. So she called David and everybody else there "full of shit" and proceeded to inform us all on the subjects of teenagers, drugs, parents, etc., and made us all sit open-mouthed and listen to her because she knew what she was talking about; she knew it all firsthand. And from there on, it was Barbara who spoke and we were silent. Or we argued. Ginsberg, Burroughs, Voznesenski, Dylan—she argued with them all and gave her idealism to them all. Dylan, she helped him to come back to life after the motorcycle crash. Dylan was also one of the last people she saw before leaving for France. We had a drink together across from Anthology, 425 Lafayette. She was always busy, always making peace between the various factions of the underground art community. We were all bad children to her, not really doing our duties fully, not serving humanity enough, too much in our egos, not serving our art enough, or God, or ourselves. I think she was the most idealistic human I had ever met.

And, of course, there was her own film-making, her own very special, swinging, shaking, swishing, flashing Bolex style, with innumerable superimpositions, no matter from which end, upside-down, or right or left. And all those unrealized huge projects, scenarios ("Christmas on Earth Revisited"), starring practically everybody from Lenny Bruce to Brando. And there was *Christmas on Earth*, the film, her masterwork which she gave me before leaving for Europe and asked me not to show it while she was alive. And then there was Lou Reed and the Velvet Underground, which I know would never have been what it became if not for Barbara, who brought Andy and the Velvets together.

And then one day she left us.

And she never came back.

Ah, Barbara you left us, like Rimbaud. You disappeared into the sands of some spiritual Africa, never to come back.

OPPOSITE: Poster for Barbara Rubin's mixed-media extravaganza at the Film-Makers' Cinematheque, Spring 1966. Designed by Barbara Rubin and friends, printed by George Maciunas.

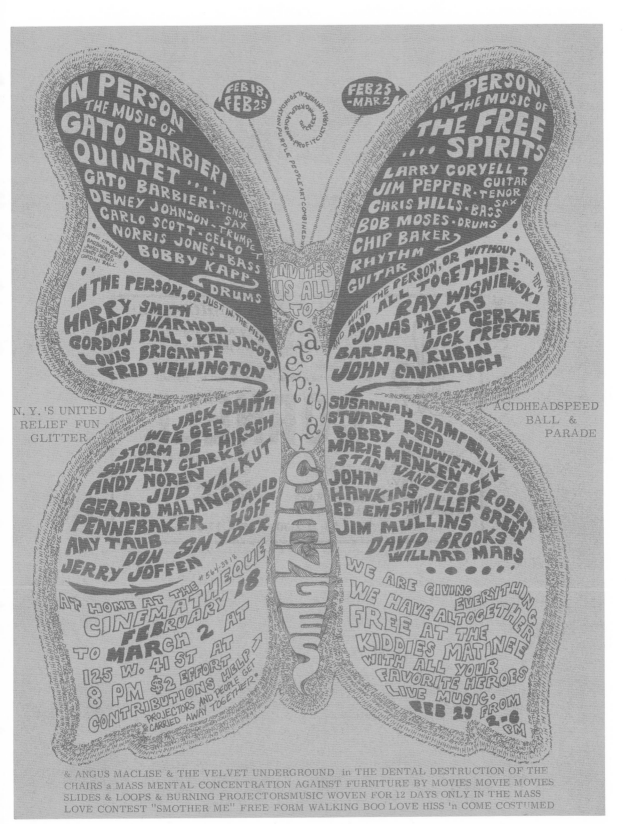

& ANGUS MACLISE & THE VELVET UNDERGROUND in THE DENTAL DESTRUCTION OF THE CHAIRS a MASS MENTAL CONCENTRATION AGAINST FURNITURE BY MOVIES MOVIE MOVIES SLIDES & LOOPS & BURNING PROJECTORSMUSIC WOVEN FOR 12 DAYS ONLY IN THE MASS LOVE CONTEST "SMOTHER ME" FREE FORM WALKING BOO LOVE HISS 'n COME COSTUMED

232

FILM-MAKER'S SHOWCASE

at the Gramercy Arts Theatre,
138 E. 27th St. (near Lex.)

The complete films and works-in-progress
of the distinguished "Object" maker, JOSEPH

# CORNELL

NYMPHLIGHT
A FABLE FOR FOUNTAINS
THE AVIARY
A COLLAGE OF ROSE HOBART
A CENTURY OF JUNE

Plus one film each by
BREER
BRAKHAGE &
MENKEN

MONDAY, Nov. 25 at 7:30, 9:15 & 11:00 p.m.

October 21, 1963 V.Voice

## JOSEPH CORNELL FILM SHOW
## AND HERMANN NITSCH

It was November 1963. I lived in a small third-floor loft on 414 Park Avenue South, between 28th and 29th Streets, just across from the Belmore Cafeteria. The cafeteria was known as a taxi-driver night stop. It was quite spacious. And it had a very decent and cheap taxi-driver's night meal selection. And it was open all night. And since my loft had become a place of nightly shows and gatherings where you could meet everybody from Allen Ginsberg, Harry Smith, Salvador Dalí to Parker Tyler and Warhol himself, Belmore was where they ended up for a cheap sandwich. Some used to come from further downtown, like Rauschenberg and Larry Rivers. You could see them at the Belmore after all the downtown places had closed.

So much for the Belmore Cafeteria.

So here I was, in my 414 Park Avenue South place. It was afternoon and I was alone. I had just bought a pocket radio. So I turned it on to check it. The first thing I heard was a voice telling that John F. Kennedy had just been shot in Dallas. I could not believe my ears. Here I am, turning on the first radio I had ever bought in my life, and this guy is coming in with this kind of news!

I had to sit down.

There was another reason for my need to sit down.

Suddenly I remembered that I had planned a one-man show of Joseph Cornell films at the Gramercy Arts Theater for the next day. I had worked hard to arrange this retrospective of his films and I had already heard how sensitive Cornell was about events like this, and I had not met him yet at that time.

Now, as I sat there slumped in my chair, I had a feeling that there would be a complication with the show. And I also knew that there would be a telephone call very soon.

So I sat and I waited. And I wasn't wrong. The call came some fifteen minutes later.

The message was very simple.

"Should we still do it?" the voice said. A voice slow, and low, and questioning.

There was a long silence on my part. For a moment, for a long moment, I was waiting for the angels to tell me what to do, what to say. Then I composed myself and said something like this:

"Yes, Joseph. It's a horrible thing that has happened. Horrible. But don't you think that maybe that makes it even more important for us to show something beautiful, to counteract what happened? What do you think...?"

I was trying to be rational and think it out. I took time and spoke almost as slowly and low-voiced as Cornell; I was caught in his rhythm of speech and thought.

Now there was a long, long silence at the other end. Cornell was thinking. Then a voice came, very brief and to the point:

"Maybe you are right. Maybe we should go ahead with the show."

That's how Cornell's first one-man film show in New York took place.

I have to tell you, I must tell you another somehow related incident that suddenly comes to my mind.

In 1968 I brought Hermann Nitsch, the Viennese actionist/performer to the University of Cincinnati. For those of you who may not know the work of Nitsch, I have to tell you that it's a pretty bloody affair. His Orgies Mysteries Theater involves symbolic slaughter of lambs and there is a lot of blood and guts involved in it. It's all very ritualistic and basic theater, far beyond Artaud. His performances have provoked violent reactions, even jail, as all great theater does.

So here we are, in Cincinnati. We drove out into the suburbs and bought some freshly slaughtered animals and some buckets of blood.

And I am particularly mindful of what you once wrote in the VOICE.

Again, it would facilitate matters for me in my semi-retirement if Mr. Sitney would contact me.

Thanking you again for your fine lines.

Sincerely yours,

Fl. 8-9099

Joseph Cornell

Dear Jonas Mekas,

I have called the office a couple of times hoping to catch Mr. S.— Very in case Sitney he might have the time +

235

inclination to visit again with regard to the proposal in your letter of July 10.

Thank you for your most thoughtful and elaborate sending. I do not feel that my efforts in film-making are really deserving of all that you have written but I do regret that I never had the experience + wherewithal to make them so deserving.

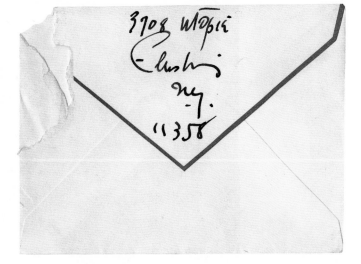

3708 Utopia
Flushing
N.Y.
11358

236

Hermann had completed all the necessary preparations for the performance. He had the main auditorium of the university at his disposal. So now, everything ready, he was walking back and forth, back and forth, as he usually does before his performances, concentrating and being nervous at the same time.

It was at this time that somebody walked into the auditorium—the people were already gathering—and announced that Martin Luther King had just been shot.

Hermann and myself, we slumped down into the seats. And so did Steve Gebhardt, who had persuaded the university to have this event.

I remembered Joseph Cornell, J. F. Kennedy. The same again... This horrible news, again.

Eventually we got a grip on ourselves and began to discuss what to do. The performance could really be taken in a wrong way. Something had to be done. So I brought in the Joseph Cornell case to help us. Why don't we dedicate this performance to Martin Luther King, I suggested, to all the slaughtered lambs of humanity. It's a bloody tribute, yes, but when seen as a tribute, the performance will be perceived completely differently. It will become a tribute.

And that was what Hermann did. He came in front of the audience and dedicated the performance to Martin Luther King and all the innocents who were slaughtered for the advance of civilization. There was a feeling in the audience, after his dedication, a certain electricity that filled the place and made it all work just right.

Immediately after Hermann's dedication, I had to rush to the train; I had to leave for New York that night. I slumped into my seat and stared through the window of the running train still not believing how bloody is the world we live in.

OPPOSITE: Hermann Nitsch in Prinzendorf, 1971, just after acquiring an old monastery building for his Orgies Mysteries Theater.

The house of Joseph Cornell, on 37-08 Utopia Parkway, Queens, New York, in 2002. Photo: Arunas Kulikauskas.

## VISITING CORNELL

September 23, 1971

Linda, Cassandra, P. Adams—we visited Joseph Cornell today. Front lawn was full of leaves. Already autumn!

"How did you spend your summer?" asked P. Adams.

"It was bad; it was very hot," said Cornell. "But it was very, very fine. I like what the heat brings out in one. It brings out things that otherwise wouldn't come out. I did much this summer."

Eh, Cornell, I thought. A magician will turn anything to his benefit. Heat or cold, joy or misery—everything can be magic, everything becomes magic in his hands.

We went down into the cellar. It was more full of things than the last time, last winter. He was all dressed up—for the girls. And he made tea for us, and also some hot potato chips, and cheese, and we spent a very fine autumn afternoon.

Oh, we spoke a little about Maeterlinck. "Do you know that Maeterlinck lived in New York during the Second World War?" Cornell asked. No. We didn't and we were quite surprised. I thought Maeterlinck lived so long, long ago...

It was time to depart. The leaves went *tsch-tsch* under our feet, very magically, on 37-08 Utopia Parkway.

Dumpling evening on 80 Wooster Street, June 19, 1971.

## DUMPLINGS OF GEORGE MACIUNAS

June 19, 1971

George had one of his dumpling parties yesterday. John and Yoko, Andy came, my brother. We all tried to eat those dumplings but they were, in my opinion, the worst dumplings I ever ate—or rather, tried to eat. George likes everything artificial; he makes his dumplings from prepared dough. Same as when he drinks milk made only from milk powder, and makes his scrambled eggs only from egg powder.

But George likes his dumplings, and stuffs himself belly-full.

So we fool around—everybody has a good time, and that includes George's dog. George complains that he got his dog to protect him from intruders, but the stupid dog, he says, likes everybody. But he likes his dog anyway.

A polaroid by John Lennon.

244

A polaroid by John Lennon.

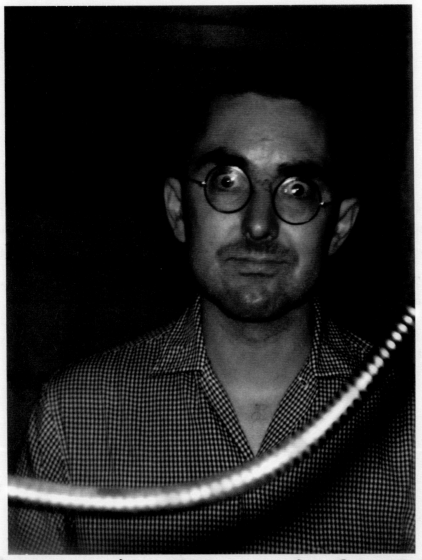

A polaroid by John Lennon.

About protection: When George says protection he means police and building inspectors. They are after him for organizing artists' cooperatives. They are illegal, they say. George says several times they tried to break through his door. So now he has sharp knives covering his 80 Wooster Street basement door. In addition to that he cut a hole in the ceiling leading to the Cinematheque theater floor, a hole large enough to push his thin body through, but no cops, who are known for their bulkiness, would ever pass through. In short, he had devised an additional escape route. Once he is up in the Cinematheque he can just walk out while the cops are still trying to break his door. He finds it all very funny.

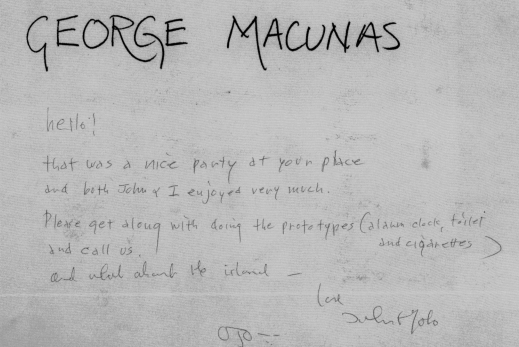

248

## PORTRAIT OF CARL THEODOR DREYER

September 17, 1965

Filmed Carl Th. Dreyer, at his hotel. Cold morning, crossed Central Park, filmed some trees. Dreyer, I met him after his film at the New York Film Festival. I said, I would like to make a film portrait of you. He got very interested. So we agreed to meet early at the hotel he was staying at: He is very busy, he said, it was the only free time.

The sun was streaming through the window. "What do you want me to do?" he said. I said, "Nothing. Just sit there as you are." And I made a few shots, close-up, side, front, different takes. I hope it will come out. He was very intrigued, and asked many questions about what I was doing. So I had to tell him about what is happening in the film avant-garde. He found it all very interesting; he kept repeating, "Interesting possibilities."

OPPOSITE: Carl Th. Dreyer, September 17, 1966.

קרן קימת לישראל

KEREN KAJEMET LEISRAEL TRÆ-FOND
*genplanter skovene på Israels bjergskråninger til*
*minde om Theodor Herzl, zionismens grundlægger.*

With many good wishes

for Christmas and

the coming year

1959

*With sincere greetings*

*Carl Th. Dreyer.*

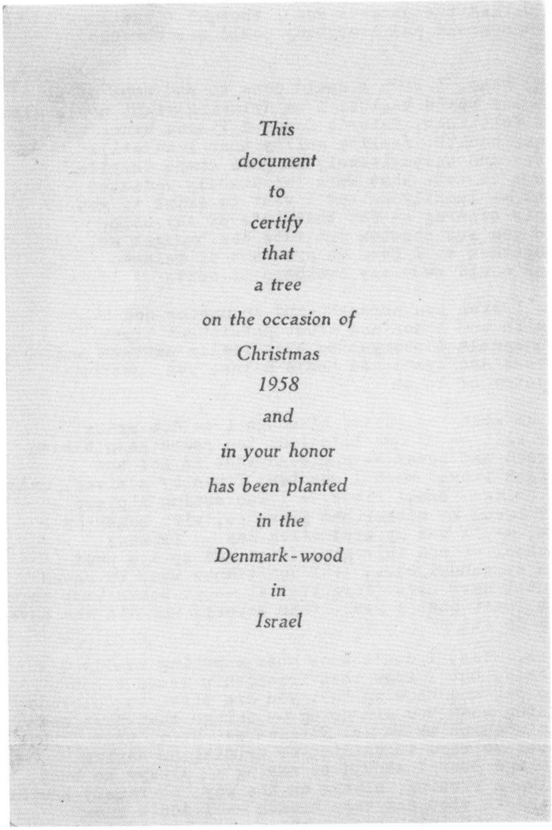

*This*
*document*
*to*
*certify*
*that*
*a tree*
*on the occasion of*
*Christmas*
*1958*
*and*
*in your honor*
*has been planted*
*in the*
*Denmark - wood*
*in*
*Israel*

*June 27 2002*

## Dear Stan:

A huge rain storm just passed by. Thundering
heavily. Disturbing my cats. Some old music
on radio, don't know what but very pleasant.
Pleasant when you are cooking something for your
supper, like me, some potatoes with sour-
kraut... That primitive... I just had a crave
for it.

Haller calls. Tells in a concerned voice all about
your troubles.
Ah, that word, chemotherapy...
How many of my friends had to deal with it...
Susan. George. Annette. I have been lucky
sofar, cross your fingers. I just had some
straight radiation stuff -- but even so
I walked the streets and I thought I was
transparent and everybody could see through
me.

Ah, Stan, I wish I could pass to you some of my
farmer boy's health. I am drinking right now a glass
of Veltliner, Peter's favored Vienna wine, to
your health, feeling guilty that I am still
here and comparitavely in good shape despite
some threats that were immediately radiated
out -- luckily -- but I want to drink to you
this evening -- not that it's of any help
to you but somehow the fate has brought us
together so I feel we are sort of related
one could even say brothers of sorts

so I wish you strength and endurance and
faith and humor and trust persistent trust
in angels & everything that really matters and
frees and opens and heals & yes, yes, poetry
poetry of being

I am with you, Stan, although I seldom write
or call -- my own life last ten years hasn't been
bread and honey -- and even that is not the
right image: when I was ten, I was by a river, under
a bridge, small river -- I was eating a piece
of bread my mother had given me, with honey on
it, -- it was my graduation day -- Primary
School -- and this girl comes and sprays sand
on my sandwich... -- I don't know what it means
but I have never forgotten it -- it comes back to me
at least once a year, this memory: why did she have
to do it!

Yes, Stan, I don't know what anything really
means, but I know that friendship means a lot
to me, and knowing that you are there in Colorado
doing what you are doing -- things that have meant
so much to me -- ah, forgive me, Stan, that I have
been so rare in calling or writing or saying
things that I should be saying -- always so busy,
always running, always on the way, so rarely having
time to stop and take breath -- I don't know
why I got into this -- but that's how my life
has been -- so forgive me, Stan,

Anyway -- I think you should go out and have a
Bushmill or something and no matter what
pep up & boost & drown it all and I wish I could
be there now with you to keep you company and
drink with you -- because Robert he said you feel
very low and are abt to give on chemotherapy &
leave it all to angels  -- /up

whatever happens, whatever is the decision,
I am with you this evening -- this rainy thundering
and very very hot evenining writing you this
long line letter with a glass of Veltliner next
to me which means I am thinking also about Peter
and P.Adams besides you -- which means, the present
is mitigated -- as Peter would say -- with the
past.

We are all still here, separately but
together --

Stan Brakhage, Telluride, 1981. Photo: Hollis Melton.

Stan Brakhage, 1974. Photo: Friedl Bondy.

Stan Brakhage, the author, and P. Adams Sitney at the Film-Makers' Cooperative, 414 Park Avenue South, 1963.

July 4, 2002

Dear Jonas,

No need to forgive anything, Jonas — somehow you've always BEEN there for me and for all in film: I've given my life (as have you) to care for... as you are and do beautifully (clear in your letter) right now.

I'm sorry I cannot answer at comparable length: I have limits to my strength. When I do get a "feeling better" time I either spend it with Marilyn and the boys or I go to my desk where I am slowly putting together film I've been working on for 2½ years — hand-painted

but also complexly step printed
(with help of Mary Beth Reed).
The Painting I had recently been
doing (maybe a second-a-
day) I'd thought was called
"Dance of Death"; but I just
this week realized it is ALL
part of "Ponds For The
Wells of Heaven" — a title
I borrow from Tchelitchew
(and then from K. Patchen's
best book of poetry); thus
I have MUCH to live at-
large: if I succeed, this
will be the 4th Part of
the now-called "Vancouver
Island Trilogy".
So, I go on, as best I can

I write all this (rather than discourse on my illness and/or hard-times) because I know you'll care to have all this information. I want to pleasure you with NEWS from the world of assholes.

I'm sorry I worried Haller so much. Please share this with him... to maybe cheer him up, too.

It is all hardest on Marilyn and the boys. I, at least, have "Panals" unrolling in my spirit-scape. Hopefully they'll also have some such canopy over life's storms and...

Blessings, Stan

# AT THE FACTORY

April 25, 1965

Andy's farewell party (he is going to Paris, for his show). It was sad to see Montgomery Clift, Judy Garland, and a few others from the Hollywood crowd, all good people, but sad and lonely at the Factory. They disappeared among the new, underground "stars" in Andy's loft. They were standing on the side; nobody even wanted to talk with them. Clift was drunk. Only Tennessee Williams seemed to be having a good time, dancing and prancing with the nymphets and having fun, surrounded by his boys. He came to Andy's studio for the first time a month or so ago. I met him that evening, and he was as sad looking as Clift, that evening, staring with blank eyes into the space with an empty glass in hand. Since then he has been coming frequently. I saw him also Friday night, watching *Vinyl* and enjoying himself, not giving a damn anymore about who he was, I mean, the fame and all, and nobody seemed to be bothering him with stupid questions here.

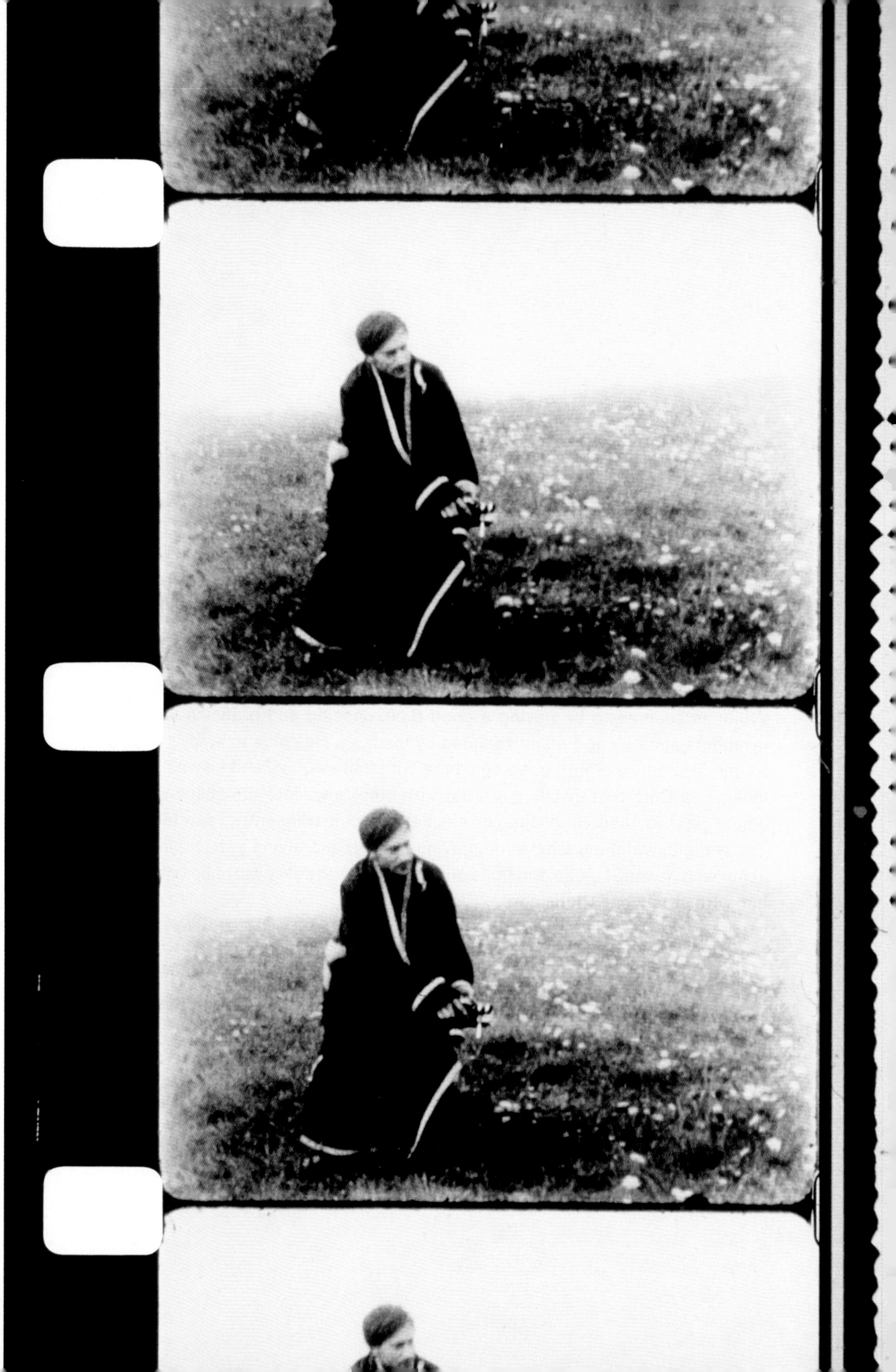

# A SCREENING OF
## *FLAMING CREATURES* IN VERMONT

I do not remember how it really came about, but it happened that in 1964, the Robert Flaherty Film Seminar that took place in Vermont every year had invited me to come and screen Jack Smith's film *Flaming Creatures* as a special event of the Seminar. Earlier that year I was arrested in New York for screening it. So I figured they wanted to find out what the fuss was all about. I agreed to come.

Our little gang, consisting of Barbara Rubin, her friend Debbie, Ken Jacobs and Flo Jacobs—both of whom were also arrested that same evening with myself—we drove to Brattleboro, Vermont, with a print of *Flaming Creatures*.

The screening was announced for 10:30 p.m. We, New York City folks, we thought that was a perfectly good time for closing an evening with a movie.

We arrived on time—actually half an hour early. We drove into the Seminar grounds and we were a little bit surprised to find it totally empty. As we were wandering about it, someone came to us from the half darkness. I recognized the man: It was Louis Marcorelles, my good friend from *Le Monde*, Paris. "Where is everybody?" I asked. "They are sleeping," said Marcorelles.

At that point, a young man appeared from the dark and introduced himself as a man in charge of the screenings. He asked us not to be so loud, people were sleeping. "How come?" I said. "What about our show?" So the guy says, "This being the country, the sleeping time at the Seminar is ten o'clock." "But our screening was scheduled for 10:30," I say. "How come?" "Oh," says the guy, "we told everybody about the screening. We put it on 10:30 slot because of the controversial nature of the movie. We have the projectionist ready for you." "But we have nobody here to see it," I say. "I want to see it," said Marcorelles. "I came specially for it from Paris."

OPPOSITE: From the 1964 Flaherty Seminar footage in *Lost, Lost, Lost* (1976).

"Let's screen it!" we all said enthusiastically. And so we did. For Louis Marcorelles.

It was a cold night in Vermont.

After the screening we were ready to crash. So we asked our host to take us to our rooms. "No," says the guy. "All rooms have been filled. Sorry, guys."

"OK, sorry to hear that," we said. "We'll be OK. Don't worry about us."

We managed. Some of us slept in our beat-up van. I slept among brooms and pails in an abandoned open country truck I found on the grounds.

No, we didn't sleep well that night.

We all got up early.

We were surprised to see a Vermont morning emerge over the landscape. It was beautiful. It was very peaceful and serene. We stood there, still half-asleep, looking at the morning, almost in ecstasy. Then Ken and myself, we pulled out our cameras and we began to film. We had to do it, we had to film; we were filled with the ecstasy of cinema. We felt we were the monks of the order of Cinema.

Then we got into our beat-up van and we began our journey back to New York. We looked at the Seminar houses: Everybody was still sleeping. We thought we had a most perfect screening. We drove singing, happy, as the day was opening around us, a beautiful Vermont day.

OPPOSITE: Louis Marcorelles and Peter Kubelka, Paris, c. 1970.

Ken Jacobs, Flaherty Seminar, 1964.

MURRAY HILL 8-3600

CABLE: "ARNGRANT"

March 16, 1964

Mr. Ephraim London
1 East 44th Street
New York 17, New York

Re: "Flaming Creatures"

Dear Mr. London:

In answer to a letter received from your client Mr.
Mekas in connection with the above film, Mr. Dali advises me
that his attitude is in essence as follows:

"Dear Mr. Mekas,

I am absolutely against your idea that 'Flaming
Creatures' is adequate for everybody to see. As in
the most perfect Greek civilization of Praxiteles
Period (Initiation of Divine Mysteries of Eleusis),
some erotic secrets or even geometrical solutions
were reserved for a few only. And as the atomic
bomb is the result of such secrets it was right to keep
it from everybody.

Nevertheless I consider 'Flaming Creatures'
a work of art and an excellent mystical erotic creation.

Salvador Dali"

Very truly yours,

*Arnold M. Grant*

ARNOLD M. GRANT

AMG:ejh

265

266

## ON FÁTIMA, TO MY FRIENDS

September 11, 1994

Something about a mini-pilgrimage to Fátima.

This September I had an occasion to spend two weeks in Portugal, as a guest of the International Film Festival of Figueira da Foz, some two hundred kilometers north of Lisbon. I was very generously received there by the festival, media, and the city of Figueira da Foz, whose mayor gave me Honorary Citizenship...

I was supposed to fly back to New York, 2 p.m. on the 10th of September, from Lisbon. A day before I had to leave, I found out that the road to Lisbon passed two very important places: the Monastery of Batalha, and Fátima.

I managed to persuade my hosts to start our journey to Lisbon very early in the morning, so that I would have time to stop briefly at each of the two places and still make the plane. Telling the truth, it did not take much persuasion: I discovered that the director of the festival, José Vieira Marques, had spent the earlier part of his life as a priest, and was still a devoted Christian; secondly, I was the only one from all the festival guests who had expressed such a wish. So he was very excited and happy to help me. He actually asked his sister to be my guide.

The Monastery of Batalha was built at the end of the fourteenth century to commemorate Portugal's liberation from Spain. It's a structure of exceptional beauty, one of the great moments of sacred architecture of Europe. Anyone who travels through Portugal should plan the travel so as not to miss the Monastery of Batalha. By the way: This beautiful monastery/cathedral was designed by Master Afonso Domingues who, I was told, was very, very old and practically 100 percent blind at the time he designed it! That tells a lot about where the great things come from!

The cathedral was never really completed. One part of it looks very much like the other never-completed moment of great architecture, Gaudí's Sagrada Família in Barcelona.

Fátima is only some fifteen minutes' drive from Master Domingues' masterwork.

As we were approaching Fátima, I scanned the landscape. The steep high hill-sides were looming around the area. Olive tree landscape. Suddenly I had a feeling I was entering a very, very old part of this Earth. There was something very old and eternal about it. Not just peaceful, or some other similar feeling that you get when you are in a wide, country nature. No. I felt some kind of deep, primordial eternity. And although the place itself was on a slight elevation, I felt I was descending deeper and deeper... and not going up. In retrospect, I find this a very unique experience.

The place where the Virgin Mary of Fátima first appeared on May 13, 1917, and which was then just a pasture, now, this Saturday, at 10:30 a.m.—as I was approaching it—looked just like any other famous tourist place. A lot of tourist buses, cars, crowds, tchachka shops. I approached the Chapel of Apparitions, built on the spot where the Virgin Mary first appeared. In the center of it there was a crude altar structure and four priests were chanting under a statue of the Virgin Mary. A large, thick crowd of people surrounded the altar—the closest I could get to it was some thirty feet. The crowd was a typical tourist crowd. The people who I thought were there out of a real need—many approaching the Holy Place on their knees, coming on their knees from far distances— people, mothers with sick children, young girls with visible wounds and bandaged legs, and etc. and etc.—they could not get close to the altar, they couldn't cut through the tourist circle, so they walked on their knees around the chapel. And no, they didn't walk through the soft, warm dust of this Earth, no: The entire area surrounding the Chapel was paved. Hard cement covered the entire area where the grass used to grow, and flowers, and the bugs crawled... The pilgrims sought the Virgin Mary, and trampled to dust every-thing else that was alive, in their way... I searched for the azinheira tree under which the Virgin Mary appeared to the three shepherd children. There was no tree. Where the tree used to grow, now there was an altar and the white gyp-sum statue of the Virgin Mary. And the four priests. I asked what happened to the tree. They cut it down, I was told. The pilgrims took all its leaves away, leaf by leaf. They took its bark. They took its branches. When there was practically nothing left of the tree, they cut it down...

I was informed that the tree that I saw standing some fifty feet away, to the right of the chapel, was identical with the tree under which the Virgin Mary appeared. So I went to it and stood looking at it. An old green happy tree, very happy to be alive... I filmed it and the tree thanked me for the attention. Nobody else was there, and the tree was very happy about that...

I felt I should ignore all the distractions of civilization and just be there, just me and the place. And I tried. I closed my eyes trying to block out the tourists and the ugliness of the structure built to house the Miracle place—but it was very, very difficult. I felt a frustration deep inside. Then I discovered that by walking around the chapel, by walking to the back end of it, I could come closer to the place where the tree used to stand. Actually, I discovered this by simply following the knee-walking pilgrims, and they were not tourists, they were just people. And there we were in silence, away from all the tourists, with only the smell of hundreds of burning candles in the air. And I still had that feeling of being very deep and very close to something very ancient and very basic. For some irrational reason I craved, as did all these knee-walking pilgrims, to be as close as possible to the place where the tree used to stand. And the closer we came to it, the stronger we felt it, the more it attracted us. That miraculous spot.

269

Since I had only one hour to spend in Fátima, I had to leave. Again I looked at the hills, red clay earth, olive trees—I think they were olive trees, although they could have been some other similar-looking trees—and said goodbye to Fátima. By the way, I was told that one of the three shepherd children who witnessed the miracle, Lúcia dos Santos, is still alive. She lives in Coimbra as a Carmelite nun. The other two children, Francisco and Jacinta Marto, died in 1919 and 1920 of influenza.

A brief advice to those of you who may want to visit Fátima: You should try to arrive very early, maybe 7 a.m., or very late, when the tourists leave. Avoid weekends. Also, avoid May and October, the months that attract the most visitors and pilgrims. Money? Everything costs about one half less than in the United States.

To close: I am still thinking about my mini-pilgrimage to Fátima. The story has only begun.

P.S.

I cannot resist here from telling you about an occurrence that took place in February of 2005, many years later, an event that is connected to the story above.

I was having a small meal at Pink Pony, a café on Ludlow Street, downtown New York. As I was eating, I picked up a newspaper from the counter. In it, there was a picture of the Fátima children and it said that Lúcia dos Santos, the last of the three Fátima children, had just died.

A friend joined me at the table. We spent a long time talking about Fátima, and my pilgrimage to there. Later we left Pink Pony and walked into the windy, cold street. Since it happened to be an unusually cold day, that morning I had decided to exchange my light summer jacket for a warmer corduroy jacket. I do not know for what reason—probably the cold made me do it—I stuck my hand into one of the pockets. I felt something in it. To my surprise, it was a small rosary that the sister of José Vieira Marques had bought and given to me as a present at Fátima and which I had placed in my pocket. As it happened, I had not worn that jacket since the trip, it had been hanging in my closet all those years until that morning.

You can call it an amazing coincidence.

But I know it was not a coincidence.

Herman Weinberg (*at right*) with Fritz Lang. Photo: Anthology Film Archives.

## MY INTERVIEW WITH FRITZ LANG
## AND HARVEY KEITEL'S FIRST JOB

Here is a horror story. The only one, I think, that Fritz Lang was really involved in. I think it was 1958. Or 1959. Fritz Lang was in town. Herman Weinberg, my brother Adolfas, and myself, we decided this was the chance to do the ultimate interview with Fritz for *Film Culture* magazine, of which we were the editors. Herman had met Fritz Lang several times before; they were good friends, and had continuous and lengthy exchanges by mail.

So we all got together. Fritz was in a very good, jovial mood. We settled down in a quiet lobby of a hotel. I do not remember its name, but it was some-where in the West 70s—Herman lived on West 71st Street—and we had a lot of drinks and we talked and we talked and we talked. Usually, in those days, as is my habit even today, I taped all my conversations. But for this special occasion, upon Herman's advice, I think, we engaged a stenographer. She was the daughter of a renowned professor of geography and had just graduated from a stenography school. She dutifully and professionally took down on her pad everything that was said. And there was a lot said. Our interview lasted some four or five hours. Herman knew Lang's work very well and he had many questions, and Fritz, after a few drinks, could not be stopped from talking. I asked questions too, and so did Adolfas, because we admired his work. It was an amazing evening. An amazing, classic interview.

Then we ate, and then we had more to drink, and then we all went home very, very happy.

In the morning I woke up, still happy. Telephone rang. It was our stenographer.

"It was a terrific evening," I said, "how many pages you got?" A long silence. A long depressing silence. Then a meek voice came:

"Jonas, I am very, very sorry. But I have to tell you that at home, I discovered that I had left my pad on the subway…"

I sank into the chair. Probably I went pale too.

During the coming months and years I had several other occasions to be in the same room with Fritz Lang. I always managed to be on the opposite side of the room, from fear that he may ask me about the interview. I think this was the most horrible experience of my journalistic life. And whenever I hear the word "stenographer," I still cringe.

This brings me to another anecdote involving stenography.

The occasion: Premiere opening of Angelopoulos' *Ulysses Gaze* at Anthology Film Archives on the corner of Manhattan's Second Avenue and Second Street. It was in 1979 that we had purchased that building from the city of New York, a dilapidated courthouse building. It had been vacant for a couple of decades. So we fixed it up and made it into our main exhibition space. So now we were premiering Angelopoulos' movie and we had a big crowd and we were waiting for the star of the movie, Harvey Keitel, to arrive.

Harvey arrived, as he should, and walked in. He walked in and suddenly stopped and his face went almost pale, and I could almost see a tint of horror in it.

"Anything wrong?" I managed to ask.

Harvey Keitel and Daphna Kastner, downtown Manhattan.

**Q 334057**

SUMMONS

# CITY MAGISTRATES' COURT OF THE CITY OF NEW YORK

CITY OF NEW YORK

COUNTY OF NEW YORK

LOWER MAN. DISTRICT MAGISTRATES' COURT, Borough of

### In the Name of the People of the State of New York

To _Adolfas Mekas_

Complaint having been made this day by _A. Koeting_

that you did commit the offense of

_VIO. 1292-A-P. L. (res ck $60)_

276

YOU ARE HEREBY SUMMONED to appear before me, or any City Magistrate holding this Court,

at No. _2ND. STREET & 2ND. AVENUE_

on the _4_ day of _November_, 19__, at _10_ o'clock _P_ M.,

to the end that an investigation may be made of said complaint.

AND UPON YOUR FAILURE to appear at the time and place herein mentioned a WARRANT

may be issued for your arrest for the crime or offense charged.

Dated, this _____ day of _OCT 14 1954_, 19__

Officer on Post Please Assist.

_PAUL BALSAM_                    *City Magistrate*

"Wrong? I recognize this place! I recognize this place! This is where I worked as a court stenographer. It was my first job. I have horrible memories from working here."

I had forgotten that this building was still an active courthouse until circa 1961. Some very well-known judges, such as Senator Javits, worked here.

One more anecdote connected with this building.

In late 1954, my brother Adolfas and myself, we brought out the first issue of *Film Culture* magazine. We had no money to pay the printer. But we had heard that there was a Franciscan monastery in Brooklyn that had a printing shop. So we went to see them and managed to persuade them, these people of God, to print the first issue on a postponed-payment basis, hoping that once the magazine is out everybody will be so excited about it that we won't have any problems finding money to pay the printer.

But things didn't go the way we dreamed. We found no money. So the Franciscan monks sued us. I called them and I tried to argue with them, saying, "Ah, you people of God, how could you do this to us, we are like you, doing God's work." But none of my arguments worked. My brother Adolfas had to go to face the judge and make payment arrangements.

Only recently, while going through my old papers—I never throw anything out—I found the original summons to appear in the court. The courthouse was the same building in which Anthology Film Archives is now!

278

Some of the ground floor prison cells where the Maya Deren Theatre is now.
There were fourteen prison cells in the building. Photo: Hollis Melton.

Anthology Film Archives, corner of Second Avenue and Second Street, New York, 1995. Photo: Hollis Melton.

280

## GREGORY MARKOPOULOS
## AND HIS PHOTOGRAPHS

Here is a librarian's horror story... I would like to be funny, but I cannot...

"Who is in the library?" I asked Nadia, our librarian at Anthology Film Archives. That was circa 1975.

"It's Gregory, Gregory Markopoulos. He wants to take a look at his folder." I hadn't seen Gregory for some time, so I said I will go to say hello to him.

I go upstairs, where our library was located at that time, and there is Gregory, with the folder bearing his name. I was about to say hello but even before the hello, to my horror the first thing I saw was Gregory taking a photograph from the folder and tearing it to pieces. There was a little pile of torn photos on the table. "Gregory," I said, "what are you doing! You cannot do that!" "I hate this photograph! I look so ugly in it!" said Gregory, in a voice that was a mix of total innocence and disgust. I pulled the folder out of his hands, almost violently. "Gregory, you cannot do that! This is history. This is the property of the library now." "I know that," said Gregory, in the same mix of politeness and disgust. "But I look so ugly in these photographs."

Since that day I have, of course, forbidden the librarian to make files available to any film-maker who asks to see their files...

OPPOSITE: Gregory Markopoulos, 1964.

282

For Jonas
and Anthology Film Archives
Good Luck
Charles J Levine

Plt by Yasunori Yamamoto

# CHARLES LEVINE CONSIDERS SUICIDE

May 5, 1984

Charles Levine called. Said he has to see me urgently. He's about to commit suicide. "Come to Café Roma," I said. "We'll talk."

He comes and I order an espresso, for myself, and a cappuccino for Charlie.

"Is it OK for you, with your heart condition?" I had in mind the cappuccino.

"I figure the way I feel and I'll die maybe tomorrow anyway—it's OK to drink coffee," he says.

So he tells me he had decided to commit suicide during Frampton's show at Millennium.

"Why do you want to do that?"

"Nobody gives me any grants. Nobody recognizes my talents. And I have no means to live. I am down to my last penny. Here I am, with all the talents, and nobody wants to use them." And he begins to cry.

Then again he says he will commit suicide.

I ask him: "Do you have a good means to commit suicide? Many have just crippled themselves. I hope you have some failsafe way."

"Yes," he says, "I have razor blades and poison and guns and everything else, don't worry about that."

And he starts crying again. Everybody's looking at us, all the Italians. I am wondering what they are thinking.

"I deserve a job like anybody else in this country! But nobody will give me one. I can do as good a job as anybody on Channel 13, ABC, CBS or any other place. But they fail to see what I can contribute to the world, and the world is going down and down."

He cries.

"Charlie," I said. "I really have to go. I told you that I have only fifteen minutes. I have to go. Just relax, drink your cappuccino, and we'll talk again."

So I go. Charlie sits alone. I look back, he's staring at his cup. Italians stare at him.

Oh, Charlie...

283

The author with Al Pacino at Anthology Film Archives, 1997. Photo: Peter Sempel.

# AL PACINO AND ME

In 1992 at Joe Papp's Public Theater, Al Pacino held a small private screening of his film *The Local Stigmatic*. After the screening a reception was held at a bar across the street.

At some point during the reception a guy comes up to me and begins to talk, paying me compliments for something I have done—one of those people that you don't know but they know you and admire you and they corner you and you can't escape them. So I say to the guy, "I don't want to hear about myself. This is an evening when we should talk about Pacino. He was really great in the film. Actually I think he should get an Academy Award for this performance," etc. The guy listens, blinks, then we talk a little bit more, and then I walk away. I go to Fabiano Canossa, who seemed to run the evening—he was the film programmer at the Public at that time—and I say, "Fabiano, I would like to meet Pacino, is he here?" Fabiano looked at me a little bit strangely and then said: "But Jonas, you were just talking to him."

I couldn't believe him. But yes, he said, that guy you were just talking to was Pacino.

Hell, I was talking to Pacino about Pacino.

You see, I have one of the worst memories for faces and names. I have to see a person at least four or five times before I can begin to recognize the face. Or name. Sometimes I think I began my film diaries just in order to remember faces, places—when I re-see it on film, I never forget it again.

I cannot resist telling you another anecdote related to my unfortunate short memory of faces.

In 2008, on April Fools' Day, the president of Austria, Heinz Fischer, held a ceremony during which Marina Abramović and myself were honored with medals in Arts and Sciences, Österreichisches Ehrenzeichen für Wissenschaft und Kunst. The ceremony was held at the Austrian Presidential Palace with attendance of prominent guests fit for the occasion.

I was taken to the palace by Peter Kubelka, who had received similar honors a few years earlier. We arrived at the palace, we crossed several lavish but democratic halls and arrived at the room where the ceremony was to take place. A humble, neatly dressed doorman let us in. I was pleasantly surprised how humbly it all proceeded.

Usually, in similar situations, there is always a committee of three or four important people by the entrance greeting the guests. In this case, there was none of that—it was just a simple doorman, that's all. I thought that was wonderful! Very democratic.

The ceremony proceeded. There were speeches, and pictures taken, and toasts. I even had a toast with the doorman... I hoped that the president himself would appear at some point, but there was no president. "How come the president is not here?" I asked Peter. "What?" Peter seemed to be surprised. "He was here. He just left," he said. "You met him; he let you in." "No," I said, "I thought the guy was just a doorman." Peter had a big laugh. "Yes, the president himself opened the door for you! He is very democratic, our president. I thought you knew that." "No, I didn't," I said.

Peter found the whole incident very funny. But I didn't feel that good about it, not at all.

I have to add a footnote to the above anecdotes. Not long ago I had to go through a cataract-removal surgery. Both of my eyes, for years, have been suffering from worsening cataracts. My left eye eventually went totally blank and could not be saved. I joined the ranks of other one-eyed film-makers— John Ford, Nick Ray, Raoul Walsh, Fritz Lang, and André de Toth, the maker of the first big 3-D movie, *The House of Wax* (1953). But my right eye was saved, just in time. After the surgery, I opened my eye and I could not believe the colors and details I saw! It's like in that famous paragraph by Stan Brakhage, in which he asks himself how many colors a newborn baby can see. When I told the doctor my problem with the faces, I was told that it had definitely a lot to do with my cataract, which reduces subtleties of faces to tabula rasa— they begin to look the same. So this may have been the reason. At least, one of the reasons.

OPPOSITE: Marina Abramović and the author in Vienna, 2008. Photo: Sebastian Mekas.

288

## JEROME HILL, THE FLORIDA KEYS,
## AND THE HOME OF ANTHOLOGY FILM ARCHIVES

Early in January 1968, I received a call from Jerome Hill. Would I consider doing something with cinema in one of the unused spaces of the Public Theater building on 425 Lafayette Street? His army-days buddy Joseph Martinson is the Chair of the Board there and he had just made an offer to Jerome of one of the spaces.

Me being what I am, with no second thoughts, "Of course!" I said, "Yes, sure!" And that's how Anthology Film Archives was born. All thanks to Jerome Hill and Joseph Martinson, of Martinson Coffee, Jerome's army-days buddy... I won't here go into the story of Anthology Film Archives at 425 Lafayette Street. That is a different story. This anecdote is somewhere else. It's about how Jerome Hill, who died of cancer in 1972, in his last will left to Anthology a small piece of land on one of the Florida Keys. I was too busy at that time relocating Anthology from 425 Lafayette to 80 Wooster Street to give much thought to the Florida Keys. But Allan Masur, our lawyer, did keep it on his mind, and one day he said, "Why don't we take a look at it?" So he goes, comes back, and I ask him how our little Florida Key is doing. He says, "Let's sell it immediately! The ocean is eating our property, soon there will be little left of it!" "OK," I said. "Let's sell it." It's said, it's done. We got $50,000 for it. I put it all in the bank and said, OK, this is very special money that Jerome gave us. Let us sit on it until a really important need arises. Time passes, three years. Anthology is doing fine on 80 Wooster Street, in the very heart of Soho. But we are cramped. Our paper materials and film library was expanding so rapidly. We desperately needed more space. I made a decision to sell the 80 Wooster space and look for a larger home.

As I was scouting for available buildings, I discovered that the Second Avenue and Second Street corner small courthouse building was still there. It was briefly used by St. Mark's Church in the late sixties. The Bread and Puppet Theater did some performances there, and so did Ken Jacobs. In its basement Jack Smith developed his film *No President*, hanging strips of developed film over the basement pipes to dry... Andy Warhol shot *Henry Geldzahler* there and, I think, his *Beer* film. Now it was empty and totally vandalized, stripped of everything inside and outside, but it was still there!

OPPOSITE: John McGettrick, who helped the author acquire the Second Street courthouse building and transform it into a film museum. Later, he helped transform the dilapidated Brooklyn Red Hook area into a living neighborhood. Photo: Hollis Melton.

So I go to the Building Department and I ask if it's for sale. The guy tells me that they are going to put that building on an open sale and I am welcome to bid for it like everybody else. "No," I say. "I cannot compete with the real estate sharks." "Too bad," he says.

I go home a little bit depressed. I meet my old Irish friend John McGettrick (later he became known for developing Red Hook) and I tell him my problem. "Don't worry," he says. "We are going to do some work..." First thing we did, we persuaded Henry Geldzahler of the Office for Cultural Affairs to persuade Mayor Koch to restrict the sale of the courthouse building to not-for-profit cultural organizations. But the word went out... Before we knew it, the legendary Ellen Stewart of La MaMa Theatre decided that the building should go to La MaMa. The local community board had to approve our importance to the community in order to legitimize us as worthy bidders for the building. Community board votes nineteen for La MaMa, zero for Anthology. I report this to McGettrick. "Do not worry," he says. "We have to do some work..." We do our work. We meet every political person that has anything to say in the city. Next voting, at the Board of Estimate, Anthology gets, if I remember it right, seven votes, La MaMa gets two. We are both in.

On August 21, 1979, we both, Anthology and La MaMa, go to the city auction. Just before the auction starts, the La MaMa guy comes to me and asks how high I am willing to go. I don't know why he asked me that, but I immediately felt that La MaMa is not able to go very high... "As high as it takes," I said. I knew I had only my Florida Keys money, my $50,000, but why not play a millionaire? There was always a rumor going around in the New York underground that I was a millionaire in disguise, and I never discouraged that rumor.

The auction begins. Some other buildings are sold. Then comes the courthouse... "Fifty thousand!" cries the City auctioneer. I lift my hand and shout, "Yes!" Silence... Silence... *Clunk* went the wooden hammer. Thank you, Jerome! You just gave us a new home!

Next day I go look at our new home. I come and I see a guy standing in front of it, looking at it. I recognized Jasper Johns. "I think I am going to buy it for my studio," he says, "I always liked this building. Now I am sure about it."

"Sorry," I said, "very sorry, Jasper, the building is gone! I just bought it!"

The author with Ed Koch, former mayor of New York City, at Anthology Film Archives'
film preservation dinner, 2007. Photo: Robert Haller.

Yuri Zhukov, editor of *Pravda*, in his Moscow office, 1971.

## YURI ZHUKOV AND *PRAVDA*
## AND A TRIP TO LITHUANIA

In 1944, due to the unfortunate circumstances of the Second World War, myself and my brother Adolfas, we ended up in the Nazi Germany forced-labor/war prisoner's camp near Hamburg.* To make things worse, the Big Four—England, France, USSR and the United States—decided at the Yalta Conference to donate my country, Lithuania, to the Soviet Union, which was very nice, very nice of them. This nice act of thievery made it impossible for me and my brother, after the war's end, to return home to our little village of Semeniškiai. It took fifteen years until we could even begin to correspond with our parents. And it was only in 1971 that, due to what I should call funny circumstances, me and my brother finally could visit our mother and brothers again. And it happened, as I said, in a funny way.

This is how it all happened...

Although it was impossible for me to go to Lithuania, in 1971, as editor of *Film Culture* magazine, I was invited to attend the Moscow Film Festival. I managed to get an invitation for my brother too. While in Moscow, looking at a copy of *Pravda* in front of me, I remembered that in 1967 in New York, I had met its cultural editor Yuri Zhukov. He had come to interview Allen Ginsberg and Abbie Hoffman, but had difficulties reaching them. Then someone gave him my number as one who could give him an introduction to both of them. So he calls me. And, of course, I introduced him to Allen and Abbie. We had several good conversations together and some good vodka too. It was all described later in a book Zhukov did about his visit to New York. He was a jovial guy, very curious about many things, including LSD and ESP and Warhol and the Velvet Underground.

---

\*    This chapter of my life I describe in a volume of my diaries, *I Had Nowhere to Go* (Black Thistle Press, 1991).

So now I remembered him in Moscow. I decided to give him a call. I asked my Moscow hosts, who happened to be the festival's Lithuanian film delegation, to connect me with *Pravda*.

I would never have guessed the reaction my casual, innocent request provoked! There was a panic! They almost trembled... Imagine, I was asking to talk to the editor of *Pravda*, the source of the Ultimate Truth of the Communist Party! Like asking to talk to God. Or the Devil. One has to remember that in 1971 the Soviet Union was still under the hammer and sickle.

But they managed to get a grip on themselves and connected me with Zhukov, who jovially invited me to join him at his office for a cup of tea.

So there I was, drinking tea with Yuri Zhukov, editor of *Pravda*, most feared paper in the Soviet Union, while my hosts were waiting for me in the lobby, trembling...

Later, back at the festival, I asked the Lithuanian film delegation to arrange for me and Adolfas a side trip to Lithuania so I could see my mother. They shook their heads and said no no no, that was absolutely impossible, I had first to apply in writing, it all had to be approved, and etc. and etc. So I say, "Could you please connect me with *Pravda*, with Yuri Zhukov...?" There was a brief panic again, and the guy in charge made some anxious telephone calls, and then said, "No, everything is fine, no problem, we'll take you to Lithuania."

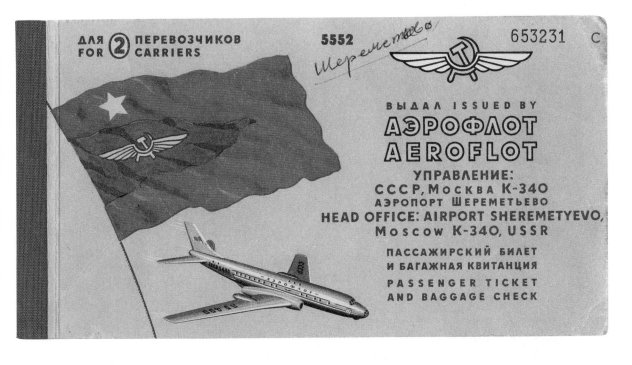

ДЛЯ ② ПЕРЕВОЗЧИКОВ    5552   *Шереметьево*    653231   C
FOR ② CARRIERS

ВЫДАЛ ISSUED BY

# АЭРОФЛОТ
# AEROFLOT

УПРАВЛЕНИЕ:
СССР, Москва К-340
аэропорт Шереметьево
HEAD OFFICE: AIRPORT SHEREMETYEVO,
Moscow K-340, USSR

ПАССАЖИРСКИЙ БИЛЕТ
И БАГАЖНАЯ КВИТАНЦИЯ
PASSENGER TICKET
AND BAGGAGE CHECK

The author in Lithuania, 1971. Photo: Antanas Sutkus.

So there we were, myself and Adolfas, and his wife, Pola. We were in Vilnius, in Lithuania! So I say to our Lithuanian hosts, "Can you please arrange a car to Semeniškiai, our village?" So the guy in charge says, "No no no, that is absolutely impossible, it's against the rules, all visitors to Lithuania, and especially ones from the United States, they must stay in Vilnius, they are not permitted to go into the provinces. We'll bring your mother to Vilnius." So again I say, very casually: "Please, could you connect me with *Pravda*?" Another small panic ensued, and the telephone calls, then the guy comes back to me and says, "No no, no problem, we'll take you to Semeniškiai."

So that's how, after twenty-five years, thanks to Yuri Zhukov, I was finally able to see my mother and my brothers again.

It was after the Moscow tea with Zhukov, watching the reactions of my hosts, that I realized that suddenly I had a card in my hands that, in the Soviet Union, could open for me any door. I realized that I had managed to confuse my hosts about who I was. It was clear to me that they took me for a double agent. In any case, they could not ignore that possibility. I decided to use this card without blinking.

One more funny detail.

Before leaving for Semeniškiai, I informed my hosts that I was not only going to my village but I was also going to film it all. This sent them into another mini-panic and a spree of telephone calls. When all that was done, they informed me that it was fine, it was OK to film, they will put at my disposal an entire professional film crew, and they would be happy to do it all for me. "Thank you very much," I said, "I do not need a professional film crew, I have my Bolex, and that's all that I need." I thanked them kindly for their offer and I thought that was that. But no, that was not the end of it: During my entire stay in Semeniškiai there was always a truck with a lot of equipment half a kilometer away. "We have here a fine film crew at your disposal, in case you'll need it," my hosts said. I was not sure what other equipment was there in that truck, so very often while talking with my brothers and mother we had to talk in whispers. And there was a helicopter always circling over our heads, not very far away... That was still a very, very real Red reality in the Soviet Union in the year 1971... The footage I took on that trip made up my film *Reminiscences of a Journey to Lithuania*, now part of the National Film Registry.

OPPOSITE: Elžbieta Mekas, the author's mother, 1971. Photo: Antanas Sutkus.

299

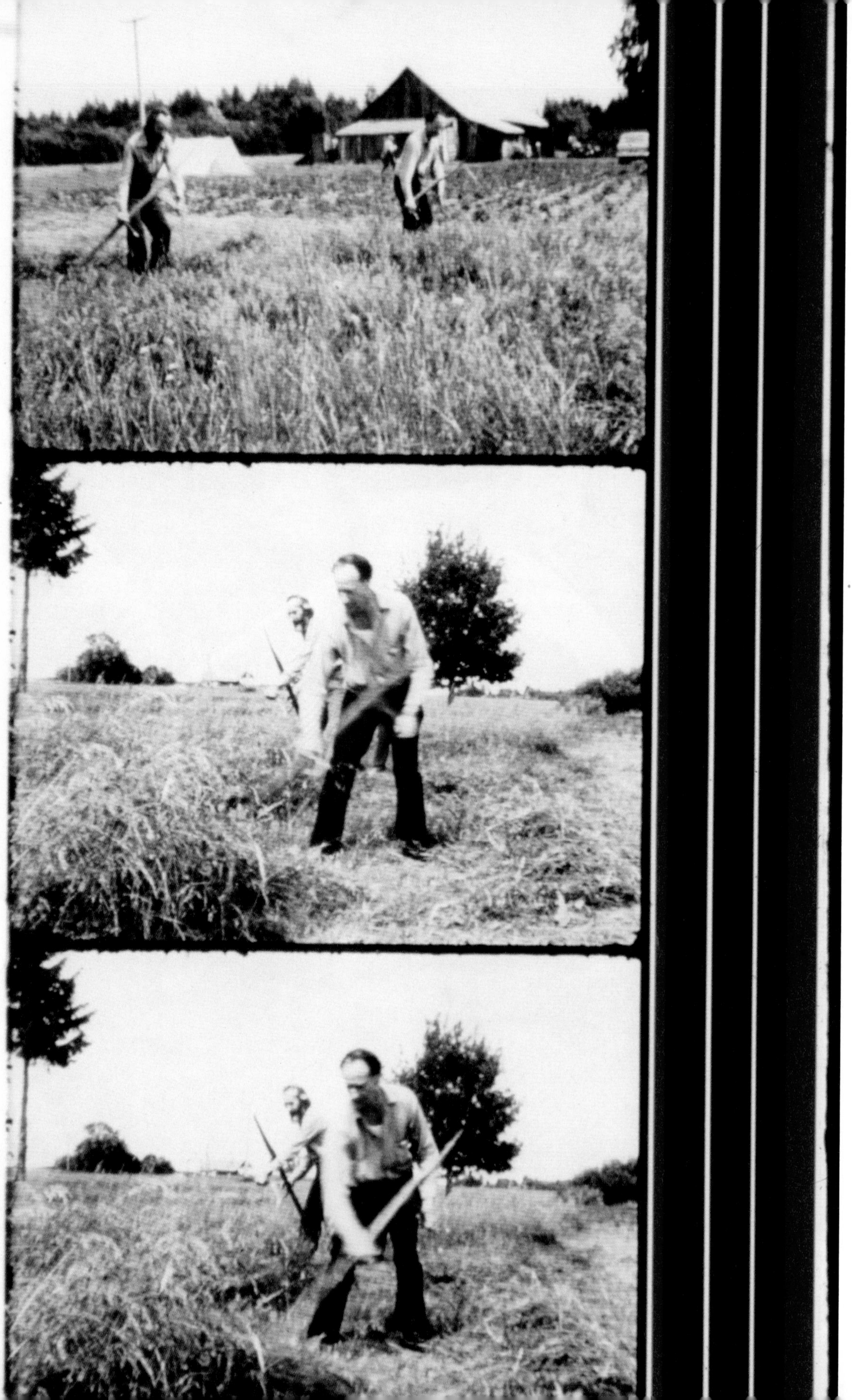

To The Poetry Project:

Re. the enclosure:

In November of 1985 Allen Ginsberg visited Lithuania, which in those days was called the Lithuanian Soviet Republic. Allen called me after his return to New York. He said he was always being followed by the secret police. They even forbid him to see his translator. I do not remember the name of his translator, I have to do some research on it, but Allen told me that one night he managed to escape the eyes of the secret police and to secretly visit and even have a drink with the translator.

A young photographer by the name Algimantas Žižiūnas managed to take several pictures of Allen during that visit. On one of them, which I am sending to you—a clipping from a current Lithuanian newspaper on the occasion of a photo exhibition in Vilnius this July—Allen wrote a poem/text which—it's very possible—has not yet been seen here. So here it is.

Jonas

"Sentient beings numberless, I vow
to liberate all;

Obstacles are countless, I vow
to cut them thru;

Dharma Gates infinite, I vow
to enter all;

Buddha-Path endless, I vow to
follow through."

—Bodhisattva's Vows

Vilnius 11/22/85
Allen Ginsberg

OPPOSITE: During the 1971 home visit, the author takes time out to mow hay.

Allen Ginsberg in Vilnius, 1985. Photo: Algimantas Žižiūnas.

"Sentient beings numberless, I vow
    to liberate all;
Obstacles are Countless, I vow
    to cut them thru;
Dharma Gates infinite, I vow
    to enter all.
Buddha-path endless, I vow to
    follow through!!
        — Bodhisattva's Vows
Vilnus        11/22/85        Allen Ginsberg

## AVANT-GARDE FILM IN RUSSIA

September 22, 2000

Dear Masha, and Andrei,

Congratulations with the extraordinary Exhibition you have put together. Of course, it's only a beginning, but I think it's a good beginning.

But if we'd bring some humor into this event, then I'd call it the Third Exhibition of American Avant-garde Film to travel to Moscow.

The first show took place in 1972. During my stay in Moscow, in 1971 (I was a guest at Moscow Film Festival) I had lengthy discussions about the American avant-garde cinema with Mr. Karaganov. Since he was full of misconceptions about what kind of animal that avant-garde was, I suggested to him that I'd be willing to bring a few selected programs to Moscow and he and his friends could find out firsthand what it was all about. He said, of course, it was a terrific idea and when I go home, I should select the films and contact him. There will be no problems, he said, to present such a selection in Moscow.

I returned to New York, and prepared four or five programs. I sent the list to Mr. Karaganov suggesting that I was ready to come any time. I also indicated that all films were 16mm.

Two months passed. A letter arrived from Mr. Karaganov.

It said, "Sorry but we do not have 16mm projectors in Moscow. We only have 35mm." I immediately wrote back and said, "OK, I'll bring both: the films and the projector." Again, a long two months' silence followed. Another letter came, and it said, "Sorry, but we searched for an auditorium and we could not find a free auditorium available for the show in Moscow."

I got the message and stopped the project.

In 1988 another occasion came up. The Riga Film Festival called me and said they would be very very interested in a mini-survey of the American avant-garde film for their festival. OK, I said, I will prepare a few programs for you.

I selected some key works by Michael Snow, Brakhage, Gehr, Menken, Maya Deren, etc., and shipped it all, via Moscow. Of course, it had to be through Moscow. A couple of days before the opening of the festival, the Riga woman calls me, all in panic. She says, "Where are the films?" "But I sent them to you a month ago," I said.

No, the films never arrived in Riga. They "disappeared" in Moscow or Leningrad. My inquiries about their whereabouts never got very far. Second Exhibition of the American Avant-garde Film was seen only by the officers of the Secret Establishment.

So I am very happy that the Third One is finally taking place for real. Good wind!

Jonas

P.S.

In 2000, Masha Godovannaya, a young film-maker from St. Petersburg, and Moira Thierney, a young film-maker from Dublin, took six programs of American avant-garde film to Russia.

# SAYING GOODBYE TO HOLLIS FRAMPTON

April 2, 1984

We buried Hollis [Frampton]. A small crowd of about thirty or so, family circle, relatives, cousins, mothers (Hollis' mother, and Marion's mother), a few
film-maker friends, university friends—they placed the coffin on a little hill, in
the Fresh Meadows cemeteries—I think that's the name—with a little brook
scurrying past, right there, a few feet away, actually about the nicest spot in
the cemeteries, which I found quite beautiful, not depressing at all, as some
sometimes can be.

We met at 10 a.m., at the Funeral Home, 2540 Main Street, not very far from
where Hollis lived (on 75 Greenfield St.) and there was the coffin covered with
many flowers—a lot of bird of paradise, chrysanthemums—and then we all got
into the sad car caravan and we took Hollis along the route worked out by
Marion, which took Hollis past his home, and past the zoo, with the heads of
giraffes sticking out above the fence, and past the Frank Lloyd Wright building
and some other places that Hollis liked and passed by everyday, and out to the
Fresh Meadows.

Two humble, five-sentence goodbyes by two friends, and then we went to
Marion's and played with the little mechanical wind-up toys, a couple dozen
of them that Hollis had collected. We played with them on the floor... Hollis'
mother sat there, her head swaying gently, and I had an impression that she was
completely somewhere else. I was not sure she was aware of what the occasion was all about, but she must have had some kind of peaceful awareness of
it. But she wasn't upset or too sad, only very, very quiet. This may have been
her way of being sad, and Marion was very brave and down to reality, handling
everything and trying not to collapse. Yes, Hollis knew all about it, for a year or
so, about the lung cancer, but he didn't want to spend the rest of his life talking
about cancer to sad-looking faces... He died at home, and without pain, and
very relaxed about it all, and there was Bruce Jenkins, somebody that usually
has to appear in situations like this and do and handle it all in a calm way and
selflessly and be very strong and just do it—because it all has to be done—
and keep it all under control and keep it moving; the day was sunny, beautiful.

We all spent some time, later, at Bruce's, permitting Marion to rest, and at 3:00 p.m. we all went to Albright-Knox Gallery where there was a modest tribute arranged for Hollis with little statements from Bruce, Annette, Huot, and Hollis' cousin, David (Hamilton). Some other friends made statements, some even told Hollis' favorite jokes, and it was all very simple and not big.

And then we all went our own ways, wherever—carrying each with us a flower: a rose, a chrysanthemum, a bird of paradise that we had picked up from Hollis' coffin, as he lay there, on the little sunny hill, next to the brook ready to carry him across.

P.S.

I remember asking Hollis, some time ago: "Would you like to be buried or cremated, when you die?" He said cremation wouldn't be fair to the worms. He would like to give them some fun too, after he had his.

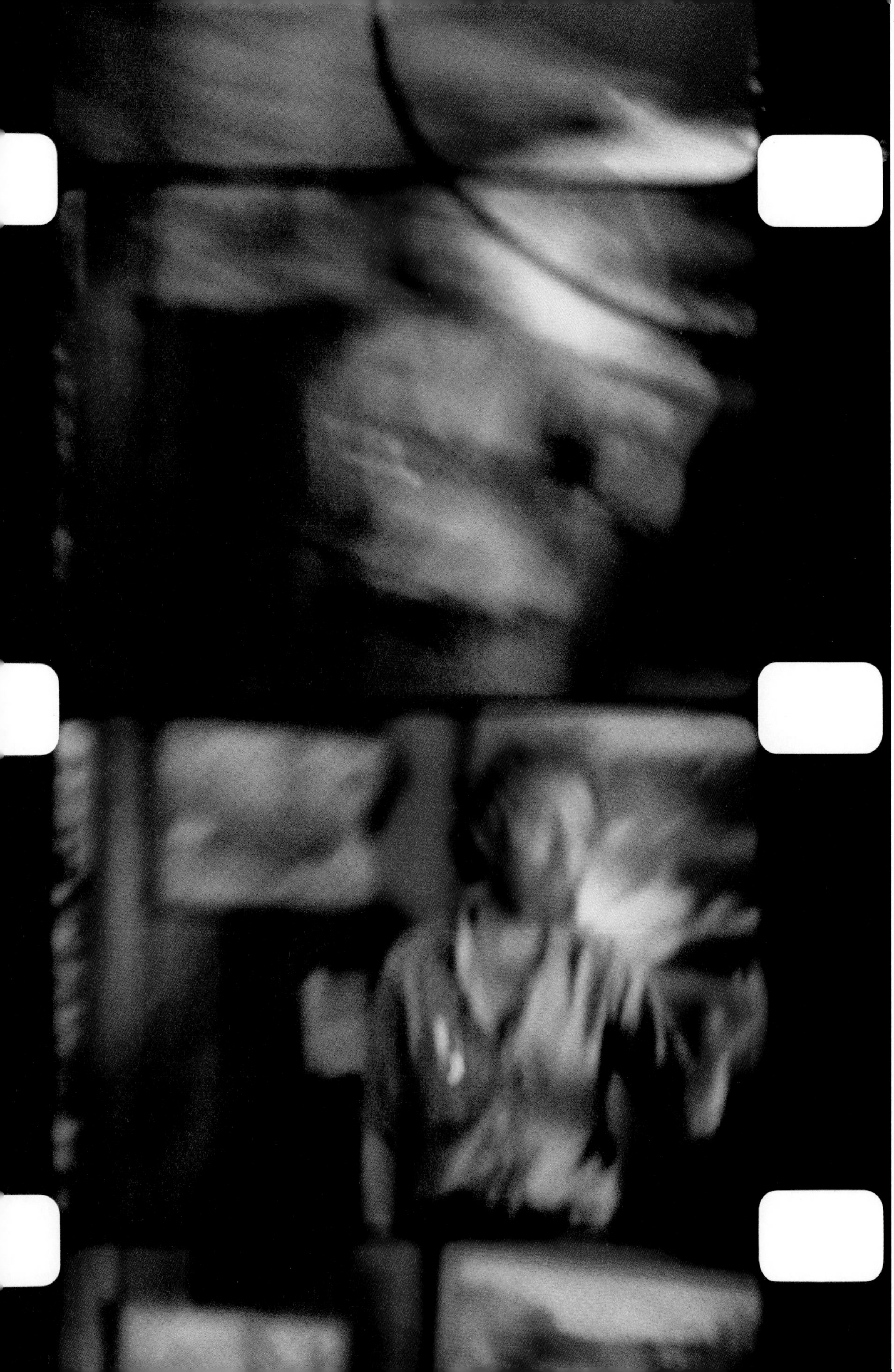

# AN ANAGRAM OF IDEAS
# ON ART, FORM AND FILM
## by MAYA DEREN

## TWO MEMORIES:
## MAYA DEREN AND SASHA HAMMID

### Memory One

The year was 1953. I had just moved into my 95 Orchard Street place. The rent was $14.95 a month. During the days I worked at Leonard Perskie's Graphic Studios on West 22nd Street, doing camera work. We did work for the international edition of *Life* magazine. I remember making for Archipenko copies of his old photographs. But my real work was to catch up with the best of New York's culture. In particular, beginning that day that I landed in New York—October 29, 1949—I submerged myself in the world of cinema. One of my universities was MoMA and its 5:30 p.m. daily screenings. Another was a film society called Cinema 16 and its monthly screenings of experimental films at the Needle Trades School on West 24th Street. I had to see—and did see—everything that was screened in New York and I had to read everything that happened to be published on cinema in English. One publication that was always mentioned with great respect, in special publications on film as an art, was a mysterious book entitled *An Anagram of Ideas on Art, Form and Film*, by a certain Maya Deren. I combed all the bookshops and libraries, but could not locate it. I got so frustrated in my search for it that I decided to locate the author of the book. I had heard that she actually lived here in New York on Morton Street. I was so obsessed with the book that I decided to call and ask her to lend me a copy of the book. And so I did.

A husky voice came on the line. She was Maya Deren, she said. I presented her with my problem. "Come, of course I'll lend you the book," she said. We made an appointment.

At the appointed time I arrive, ring the doorbell and begin to climb up to I think the fourth floor. I arrive at the top of the stairs and there is this woman, Maya Deren, staring at me very weirdly. I expected to meet her very simply and normally. Instead, I found this woman who seemed sort of panicky. I looked at her strange stare and I didn't know how to react. She was really panicky.

"Anything wrong?" I managed to stammer.

The silent panic continued another moment, then Maya said:

"I really thought you were Sasha. You looked so much like Sasha and I had not expected him."

I was a bit confused. But as she received me and we talked it became clear that Sasha was her recently divorced husband, Sasha Hammid. Still in my old European Displaced Persons camp clothes, I was very European looking, and when she showed me some pictures of Sasha I understood how close our resemblance was.

That's how I met Maya Deren. Not as myself, but as a Doppelgänger of Alexander (Sasha) Hammid. But we became very good friends immediately. And, of course, I walked out that afternoon clutching in my hands the thin volume of *Anagram*.

Memory Two

I met Sasha Hammid in real life in 1961. I was in the process of making my first "real" film, *Guns of the Trees*. Adolfas, my brother, thought we should get a car to help us move around. I don't drive, but Adolfas does. We were told that Hammid had a car he was trying to sell. So we went to see him.

The first thing that we really appreciated was that the Hammids, Sasha and his wife, Hella, treated us with a good meal. We were always hungry in those days; we put every penny either into our filming or *Film Culture* magazine. So a meal was always very welcome. Hella even gave us a big bag of food to take home with us. We especially liked her bread, which she baked herself. And, of course, we bought their old used car. They sold it to us for practically nothing. Their children called it Papacar. The Papacar served us faithfully during the filming of *Guns*. Whenever we visited the Hammids, the children always were asking about Papacar. They were very attached to it.

Sasha helped us in another emergency. We had a need of a tripod. When we told this to Sasha, he went to the closet and brought out a beautiful giro-tripod. "Here it is, use it." So we took it and used it for a lot of shooting. But one night we were stupid enough to leave it in the Papacar in the street. Next morning it was gone. Luckily, Adolfas was smart enough to insure it. For months we hid from Sasha the fact that his tripod was stolen. Then three months later, we got the insurance money, $300 of it. So we stopped to see Sasha at 1 West 89th Street, where he always lived, and we handed him the money, apologizing profusely.

Sasha looked at us in disbelief, then he began laughing. "Yes," he said, "thank you very much, but that tripod was worth only thirty dollars."

We couldn't believe it. We were quite ignorant about the prices of movie equipment. But we had to believe Sasha. So we had some good food and some good wine and we celebrated the stealing of the tripod. I think we split the money.

As years went by, we had many good days and evenings with the Hammids. He was one of the nicest people I have ever met in my life.

Alexander Hammid.

Dear Jonas Mekas:

Ever since your wonderful review appeared I have been wondering how to Thank you.

It's also been delayed by being very busy and also out of town to lecture (in Vermont).

But I thought perhaps you would enjoy having a good print of The Primavera moment from "Meshes".

Once more, Thank you so much —

Maya.

313

Roberto Rossellini, Tavern on the Green, Central Park, 1968.

# TWO DIARY ENTRIES ON ROSSELLINI

July 2, 1968

Drinking beer in a Christopher Street bar: Rossellini, Annette [Michelson], someone from *E.V.O.* paper. Rossellini arguing that there is no really new cinema in Italy. But he is completing a twelve-hour movie on... nutrition. Really, he said, on survival. Three steps of the Revolution: the young Christians; the troubadours; and the student revolution. All three revolutions, he believes, were conducted, primarily, by young people.

He is producing *Nutrition* himself and he doesn't care how it will be shown: in installments, or in longer or shorter parts—like he doesn't care how he reads a book, in thirty-, fifty-, or ten-page sittings.

He still remembers the last Christmas screening we had for him at the Cinematheque. I tried to tell him that there is a budding film underground in Italy too, but he said there is nothing in Europe like Brakhage's *Window Water Baby Moving* or Bruce Conner films or Nelson's *Oh Dem Watermelons*. Films like these, this type of film aesthetic and style and content are completely revolutionary in cinema, he said. He said, there is too much of the old, empty style in the European avant-garde film-making. But in Brakhage the form and content merge totally and produce a totally new cinema, he said. "If I wouldn't be making the films I make now, I think I'd be making films like Brakhage and you."

July 26, 1971

The most important thing I have heard anybody say last week, or recently, was Rossellini, during our last conversation, when he said, I don't remember in what connection, that education is an effort, that in order to learn something you have to make an effort to learn it: Nothing worthwhile comes without an effort. You have to seek things out. Get closer to them. Open yourself to them. He was speaking to that effect, even if not in exactly those words. And I thought that it's about time that people realize that we expect too much for nothing when in truth we can get only nothing for nothing—nothing is the most you can get for nothing.

Oct | Nov 30 | Jan | Feb | Feb 15 | March

Special Events: at 9:30 pm on dates above
Central Needle Trades Auditorium, 225 W. 24th St., bet. 7th & 8th Aves.

1954/55
**Cinema 16** 175 Lexington Avenue, NYC MU 9-7288
**Membership card** Complimentary
**Tuesday series** *Jonas Mekas*
name of member

Regular Performances: at 9:30 pm on dates below
Central Needle Trades Auditorium, 225 W. 24th St., bet. 7th & 8th Aves.

Oct | Nov | Dec 14 | Jan 11 | March 15 | April 12 | May 10

nov. 16 | jan | feb. | feb. | march 7 | 21 | may 10

special events (9:30 pm on above dates at the
Central Needle Trades Auditorium)

**cinema 16 membership card 1953/54**
issued by cinema 16, 175 lexington avenue, nyc, mu 9-7288
**wednesday series — 9:30 pm**

*Jonas Mekas*
name of member

regular performances (9:30 pm on dates below at Central Needle Trades
Auditorium, 225 west 24th street, between 7th and 8th aves., nyc)

oct. | nov. | d | jan. | march | a | y

this certifies that *Mr. Jonas Mekas*

is a member of the

**cinema 16
film society**
OCT    1951

signature of member
*Amos Vogel*
president of cinema 16

cinema 16, 59 park avenue, new york 16, n. y.

# JEAN RENOIR AT CINEMA 16

December 15, 1952

Jean Renoir spoke at Cinema 16. Screening of *La Règle du Jeu* followed. Even after eleven years in America he looks 100 percent French, in his short gray suit, his continuously gesticulating arms, and his whole body moving and swinging when he speaks. He speaks freely and in an improvisational manner, a stream of consciousness of sorts. He likes to talk, just talk, simply and without fuss.

He didn't say this was his best film, only that he likes it very much. He said his friends in Europe think this is his best. He spoke about the rottenness of life in France when he was making the film.

Some expressions I wrote down:

"In all my pictures I improvise much. Lines, movements, etc."

"This picture (*La Règle*) can be considered a depiction of stupidity of a dying society."

"This is a normal picture about abnormal people."

"This film is about the ruling class of France just before the catastrophe. They don't feel any responsibility to others, like all classes of the catastrophe. In that sense, this film is an accusation. They (Vichy) understood the film best... and they banned it."

318

## JOHN F. KENNEDY'S CAMERA

Jackie Kennedy was one of the most special women I was privileged to know in my life. I do not mean her position in society: I mean her intelligence, a very special intelligence with a deep sensitivity, and her elegance, her style, her generosity, her simple, straight, magic human quality. I could go on and on.

There were several occasions that I met her and spent time in her presence. But I want to relate here to you one memory that is relevant to the theme of this book.

This event took place the very first time I visited Jackie in her Fifth Avenue home. Somehow the talk turned to John F. Kennedy and movies. "You know," Jackie said, "just a few months before he died somebody gave him as a present a little 8mm movie camera. He always carried it in the pocket of his raincoat. You know, as I am thinking now, it must still be there."

319

She went to the closet and found a beige raincoat and there it was! In the raincoat pocket there was a small 8mm movie camera! She brought it to me. I regret I do not remember now the brand of the camera.

"He did some filming. But he never finished the roll, it's still in the camera," she said.

She put the camera back into the pocket of the raincoat.

Caroline was present, on that occasion, during that little event.

Later I forgot all about this little camera. Years later, I think it was around 1995, I told this story to Professor Gerald O'Grady of Harvard University. He got very interested in it and spent some time trying to find out what happened to that camera. He said nobody could tell him anything about it. Nobody knew anything about it.

OPPOSITE: Jackie Kennedy and Caroline Kennedy at their Fifth Avenue home, 1970.

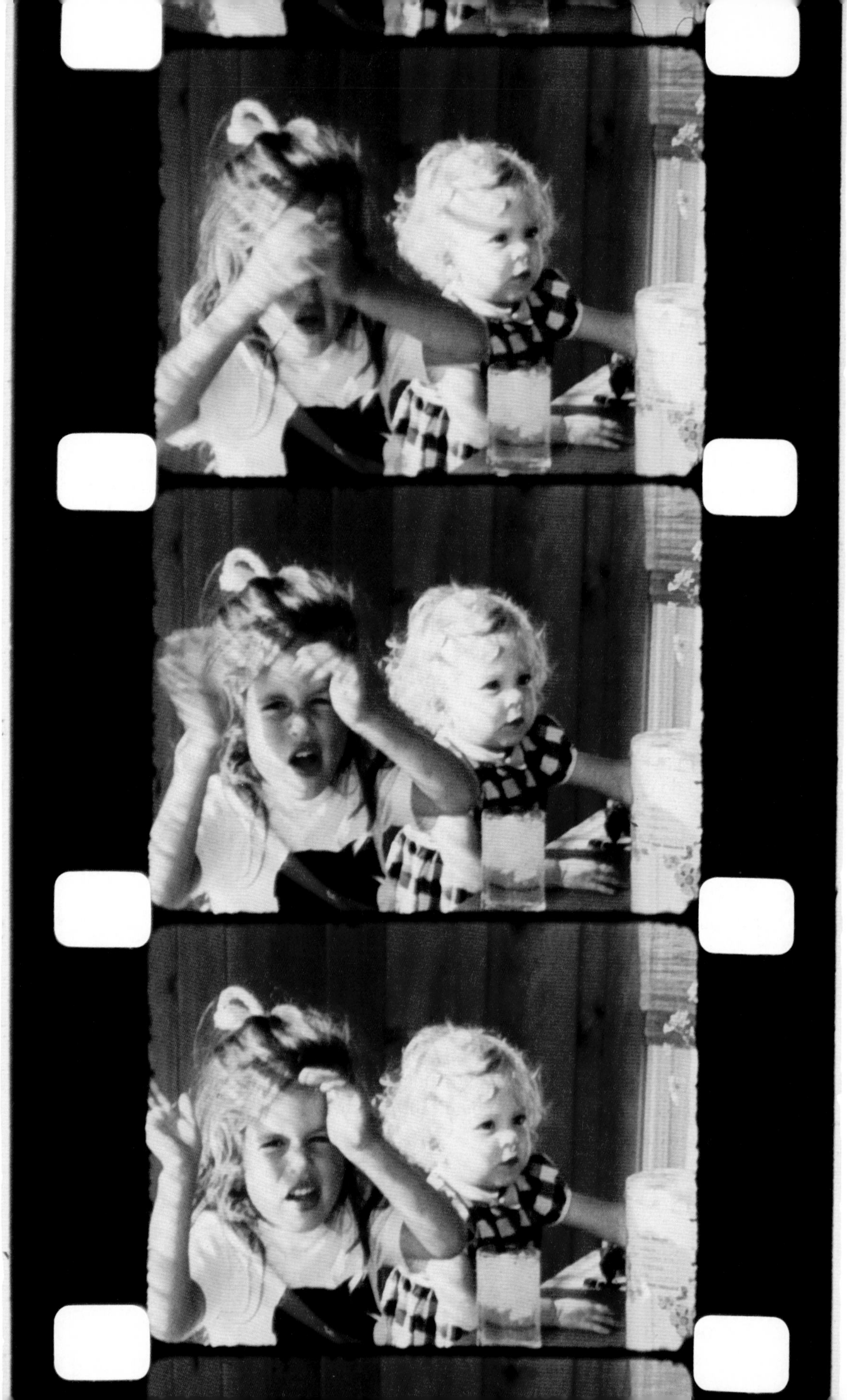

## JACKIE ONASSIS AND OONA

November 11, 1978

An opening of Peter Beard's photography exhibition took place at the International Center of Photography, in New York. Since my wife, Hollis, was out of town, I came to the opening with my three-year-old daughter, Oona.

Jackie Onassis was on the board of the ICP at that time, so she had to come to the opening. She was also a close friend of Peter's.

Jackie happened to come alone. So she asked if I could be her guide to the show. What she actually meant was that I would stay with her to protect her from unwanted admirers and pesterers. Thus, for a part of the evening, until Peter replaced me, I became Jackie's companion and protector.

But what I really wanted to tell about this evening was completely something else. And that is, my little Oona, who was going through her third year, was also going through a period when she used to pick up a certain word she had heard and repeat it, and that special evening, I don't know where she picked it up, the word was "shit." So, as we were walking with Jackie through the thickening crowd, Oona kept saying, "Shit shit shit."

I looked at Jackie, feeling a little bit uncomfortable about the situation. But before I could say anything, Jackie smiled in her inimitable way, and said:

"They all do that. My children did the same..."

And we continued through the crowd.

OPPOSITE: Jade Jagger and Oona Mekas, 1977.

322

# A VISIT TO MAYA DEREN'S MOTHER

May 7, 1977

Mother's Day. Three of us—Hollis, our little daughter Oona, and myself—decided to pay a visit to Marie Deren, Maya Deren's mother. The day was sunny but a little bit windy. We passed the West 90th Street flower market and came to one of those modern tenement buildings, where Marie lives.

Marie is eighty-eight and her hearing has been getting worse during the last few years. She is very brave and good-humored about it. She is such a great little woman. By "little" I mean she is just like Maya was, on the short side, and stocky. And the face: the same structure of face, sort of roundish.

On the little table, in the kitchen, this morning's edition of *The New York Times*, with the arts section open. Maya's photograph on the wall. She brings a postcard Maya sent her on Mother's Day in 1959.

"I used to be very sad about it, when Maya died. Here I am, and it's Mother's Day, and Maya is dead. But now I am not sad anymore. Now I know Maya is alive. There are so many people who care about her, about her work, her films. She is very alive."

Marie still goes to work. She works as a volunteer in an accounting department of the old people's home, nearby. Today is Sunday and it's Mother's Day, so she is trotting around the kitchen in her little careful steps.

"I am very lonely on Sundays," she says. "These are the longest days. Everybody has family, friends. But I am all alone here. I feel very, very lonely on Sundays."

She is very agile and very composed. Her mind is sharp, her humor always present, often biting. Oona strikes an immediate friendship with her and attacks her peppermint candies. Television is going loud and strong in the bedroom. It sounds like Panatta and Gerulaitis are losing to Stockton and Amritral. Marie's cane is hanging on the door knob.

"The bad hearing affects my balance. I need the cane because of my bad hearing," she says.

OPPOSITE: Marie Deren, Maya's mother, May 1977.

"How do you go to work?" I ask.

"By bus. I take the bus. I cannot walk much. But one has to work. When you are eighty-eight you have to work." She laughs.

We sit silently for a moment.

"Sorry I am not very talkative today. I had a bad night. I didn't sleep well. I am not in my best health today," she says.

Marie watches Oona sitting on Hollis' lap.

"You two are like Today and Tomorrow," she says to Hollis.

We have more cake. She makes me coffee and sees that it's strong.

"When Maya was alive, I used to go and help her, sometimes, with things like mailing. But then I couldn't see her for long periods. Her life was so busy. She used to say, 'Mama, I'll make you a tape one day. I'll tape my entire day and I'll send you the tape so you can listen and see how busy my days are.'"

"Is the house in which you live in Kiev still there?" I ask her.

Marie cannot hear. I repeat the question louder. It's still difficult for her to hear it. She gives me a batch of little pieces of paper and a pencil. I write down the question, she reads.

"I don't know. I never went back. People are asking me sometimes why I never went back to visit my home. But I think that if I'd go now I'd feel like in the cemeteries. Everybody's dead, everything has changed, nothing is there the way it was then. I had no brothers, no sisters. I grew up alone."

"Did Maya ever feel alone because she had no brothers and no sisters?" asks Hollis.

"No, no. She was always surrounded by others, in the school, later by her other friends. No, not Maya."

She brings us some ginger ale and some cake. We sit and we look at the window, the sun pouring through the laced curtains.

"No, I don't feel sad now," she repeats, "I know Maya is alive, very alive."

Maya Deren.

She sits there, by the table, in silence. In deep silence. Not a single sound from the street below penetrates that silence. It's very, very quiet there, deep, very deep. Only her mind is ticking all the time. I can almost hear it. Almost like Maya's mind. Ticking, ticking. I remember, suddenly, Elfriede Fischinger's remarks, the other day. She said, "Oh, I remember Maya very well when she was in Hollywood. She used to come and sit in front of Fischinger, on the floor. Sometimes she sat in Buddha position. But she never said a word. She just sat and listened and said no word."

"She really didn't say a word?" I asked, in amazement, because we all knew Maya only during her "talking" period.

"No," said Elfriede, "she *never* said a word, that's how I remember her."

I looked at Marie again. Yes, the same face, the same impishness, the same mind. In a different way, at a different time. Here was Maya's mother, and she preceded it all. I am watching the beginnings of Maya.

We planned to stay until 3:00, but it's 3:30 already, and it's Oona's siesta time so we have to go. Oona is having a great time bringing from the living room into the kitchen all of Marie's pillows, and eating more of her peppermint candies and putting cake into Marie's pocket. But it's time to go, and Marie suddenly is very serious and sort of sad as she stands in the door, alone, as we wave from the elevator, as she stands there, her little brave figure in the door, on West 90th Street, in New York, on May 7, on Sunday and on Mother's Day.

"Don't forget to visit me again soon," she says.

It's still windy and sunny and the children are playing loudly below, in the tenement's playground.

## SOME NOTES ON *EMPIRE*
## AND ANDY WARHOL

It was the spring of 1964. I had just brought out a new issue of *Film Culture* magazine. There were stacks of it at 414 Park Avenue South, in Manhattan. Park Avenue sounds very rich. But this was Park Avenue South, 28th Street. Not rich at all. It was a taxi-driver luncheonette area. The Belmore Cafeteria was just across the street.

414 P.A.S. was my apartment/loft; Film-Makers' Cooperative office; *Film Culture* magazine office; and a hangout of underground film-makers, poets, people in transit. Bob Kaufman, Barbara Rubin, Christo, Salvador Dalí, Ginsberg, LeRoi Jones, Corso, George Maciunas, Warhol, Jack Smith—you could find them there. The only private place that was still left for myself was in the very back, where my editing table stood. I slept under the editing table while the parties were going.

In any case, a new issue of *Film Culture* was out and I had asked John Palmer, a young film-maker, age eighteen, who had just arrived from Boston and had settled down in New York, or, rather, in my loft, to help to carry bags full of magazines to the post office. The nearest post office was in the Empire State Building.

As we were carrying our heavy loads, the Empire State Building was our Star of Bethlehem: It was always there, in front of us, leading us...

Suddenly we both stopped. We had to stop to admire the Empire State Building. I don't remember who said it, John or myself, or both of us at the same time:

"Isn't it great? This is a perfect Andy Warhol movie!"

"Why don't you tell that to Andy?" I said.

I had just introduced him to Andy and he was helping now at the Factory with some daily work.

"I will," he said.

Next day he calls me.

"Andy is very excited about filming *Empire*. Can you help us? We need a camera that could run for many hours."

"OK," I said.

I rented an Arri and got a lot of film. Saturday, July 25th, we gathered in the Rockefeller Foundation's office. It was run by Henry Romney, a friend of Andy's. And there we were, on the 41st floor of the Time-Life Building. I set up the camera and framed the Empire State Building. It was 8:00 p.m., early evening. Andy was there to check framing. He peeked through the viewer, and said: "It looks great, go ahead."

I pushed the button and the camera started.

We had a lot of beer and some crackers. So we all—some six of us—Andy, John Palmer, Romney, Gerard Malanga, my girlfriend Marie, and myself—we relaxed and settled down for a long evening and into the night. It was not so relaxing for me, though, since I had to keep track of the rolls and had to change the film every thirty minutes and had to reload the magazines. But we all had a good time.

The premiere of *Empire* had to wait for almost a year. The filming was done, and we felt that that was it. We knew what it was, what it would look like—why see it? In addition, it was a very, very busy period of the sixties; we kept doing new things, and we had no time to look at what we did yesterday. Ahead, ahead we moved!

So it was only March 6th, 1965 that *Empire* was first screened. The premiere took place at the City Hall Cinema, an old movie house at the bottom of Manhattan that was about to be torn down. I had rented it for the Film-Makers' Cinematheque screenings.

Some two hundred people came, but they trickled out, one by one. Still even many hours later there were at least fifty people, with beer and sandwiches, and everybody had a great time. Andy was there too.

This past July, on its thirtieth anniversary, I saw it again at Anthology. We had some fifty people. Five or seven stayed to the end.

The film looked greater than ever. Even today, thirty years later, it remains one of the most radical aesthetic statements in cinema.

The film begins very quietly. Yes, almost nothing happens in it—meaning, nothing in the usual, conventional movie-watching sense. Some lights, film scratches. The film keeps running, time goes, the anticipation begins to mount: What will come next, maybe nothing will ever come. I had completely forgotten what happens in the film. I was sitting there full of anticipation of the unknown. Suppose nothing will happen...

An hour later, suddenly: An ecstatic moment! The whole Empire lights up! What a moment! What a visual ecstasy! The audience bursts into applause...

Later, six or so hours later, when all the lights suddenly go out: Amazingly, *Empire* is still there! It's all burned deep into our retinal memory, by now, we still see all those lights, even in the darkness of the night...

"EMPIRE" by Andy Warhol and John Palmer / World Premiere Sat. March 6th, 8:30 P.M., Adm. $2.00
CITY HALL CINEMA, 170 Nassau Street

Advertisement in the March 4, 1965 issue of *The Village Voice*.

Later I was thinking, why did we, that day, with John Palmer, why did we look at Empire State Building and say: *Ah, this is an Andy Warhol movie!*

Already in 1964, Andy had established himself as celebrator of publicly recognizable, iconic images, images that everybody saw every day and which had become imprinted in our minds, in our eyes. Andy was attracted by such images. Be they people—Elizabeth Taylor, Jackie Onassis, Mao, Elvis Presley—or objects such as electric chair, Empire—he was attracted by these images of mythic proportions. Not to make money with them, no: He didn't need any money. He was obsessed by images. Like the 54th Street discotheque. He had to be there. It was also a mythic place. Not to dance: I never saw him dancing. He, actually, seldom even went inside: Most of the time he remained in the lobby, with his Polaroid camera, snapping, snapping. He had to record these Beautiful People. He was the perfect Watcher or Gazer. Not a voyeur, really, but a seeing and recording eye.

I think it was during the winter of 1962–63 that one day I met Andy on Second Avenue in lower Manhattan. He asked me where I was going. I said I was going to a La Monte Young concert. He said he will join me. So we went. La Monte played one of those very, very long pieces, four- or six-hours-long variations on a single note. Andy sat through the entire piece.

330

Andy was already doing serial pictures, repetitions of the same image. Stretching time. Jackson MacLow had already written his script/note about filming a tree for twenty-four hours. It was all in the air, *Empire*. Andy was no amateur artist. He was very up-to-date with what was happening in the arts. One could say that *Empire* was his conversation with other avant-garde artists of his day. It was a conversation with minimalists, conceptualists, real-time artists and, at the same time, an aesthetic celebration of reality. As such, it will never date, it will always remain alive and unique.

Sat, Jan 23, 2010, at 2:54 p.m. February 4, 2010

From: Neil Hennessy

To: L. Burchill

I contacted Caillie and she gave me some great info:

"Jonas Mekas is reflected in the window at the beginning of Reel 5, approximately 3 hrs. and 14 minutes into the film. At 4 hrs. and 51 minutes, the reflection of Andy Warhol appears at the beginning of Reel 7. And at 7 hrs., 17 minutes, you can see the reflection of John Palmer at the beginning of Reel 10."

So, now I'll be ready when the action starts.

## EMPIRE IN VIENNA

It's October 22, 1994. I was in Vienna to introduce a Warhol exhibition at the Museum Moderner Kunst.

As a part of the exhibition, the Warhol film *Empire* was scheduled to be shown. I introduced the film by telling about its premiere at the City Hall Cinema in New York in 1964.

"Good to see so many of you [the place was full]. At the premiere in New York, I had some two hundred people. At the end of the film I had some thirty or so. I am curious how many of you will be here at the end of the film."

They all looked a pretty determined bunch. So I went to the Apostelkeller for some wine. Two hours before the end of the film I went back to review the situation. I found that everybody was still bravely there. That amazed me greatly but there was still a lot of time to go. So I went back to the Apostelkeller and had some more wine.

I came back to the theater some fifteen minutes before the end of the film. I could not believe my eyes: Everybody was still there!

The film ended and nobody had left. I walked in front of the audience, almost in shock, and I said:

"You Viennese, you are amazing. You are really amazing. You are amazing..."

And as I was talking like that, standing there, there comes this woman on my right and she begins to talk to the audience, ignoring me completely as if I wasn't there at all, and she says:

"I represent Austrian Airlines. OK now, since you are all still here I have no choice but to have a lottery for the ticket."

I shut up and listened in amazement to what she was saying and, of course, the following became clear to my stupid head:

The screening of *Empire* in Vienna was taken by the press as a big joke, as a challenge to the audience's patience. Austrian Airlines joined in the joke by announcing that the person who will be able to stay to the end of this most boring film ever made will get a free round-trip ticket to New York...

I was pretty crushed by this turn of events. I had to go back to the Apostelkeller for more wine.

Later I was told that the lottery took place and a young Viennese film-maker, Kurt Palm, was the lucky one.

332

# A NOTE ON ROBERT FRANK

October 21, 2003

At Cremcaffe with an art curator from Luxembourg. The talk turned to Robert Frank and how he's doing these days. Then my Luxembourg friend said: "I remember this very funny story about Robert Frank that my friend, a photographer, told me." It was some years ago. He came to New York especially to take a portrait of Robert Frank. He called Frank before coming and made a date at a restaurant on Bleecker Street. So he arrives, and it happened to be a horribly rainy day. It was pouring like hell. So he walks along Bleecker Street searching for the restaurant, and it's raining, and the street is empty, and it's night, and he's all paranoid about New York—you know, the Europeans. And as he walks, he notices that two guys in black are following him. To escape them he speeds up his walk, turns into the street of the restaurant and realizes that the two guys do the same. And the street is totally empty. He really panicked. He comes to the restaurant and, horror! The door is locked; the restaurant is closed. Meanwhile the two guys are closing in on him. So he starts running into the next street and there is a bar of some kind. So he runs into the bar. The bartender asks him if anything is wrong. "No," he says, "it's OK; I was about to meet this guy Robert Frank but I ended up about to be mugged."

So the bartender turns to the clientele and at the top of his voice shouts: "Is there anybody here by the name Robert Frank?" and a voice comes from the door, "I am Robert Frank," and the photographer looks at the man who says he is Robert Frank and he sees that it's one of the black-dressed muggers that he had just escaped!

OPPOSITE: Robert Frank, Prince Street, Soho, October 27, 1975.

334

The author with Robert Frank on the set of *Pull My Daisy*, 1959. Photo: John Cohen.

# SURREALISM ALIVE: DOROTHEA TANNING

August 8, 2003

Dorothea Tanning, Max Ernst's wife, now ninety-three years old, called about Hans Richter's film *Dreams That Money Can Buy*. She just viewed it on video and found out, so she said, that the video was a horrible, mutilated version of the film (she is in it).

But that is not why I am writing this down now. Why I am writing this down is because while I was talking to her—and she was very energetic and, she said, in perfect health, only her sight is a little bit failing—later she sent me a fax in LARGE type...

Yes, as I was talking to her, and later all day long, I had this feeling I was in contact with history, with art history, not a real person. I had accepted the fact that all the important people of the surrealist period had been dead for many years, all those great surrealists—and here, suddenly, here is a real living voice from the great past, from that great history, a voice on my telephone: very, very real, full of life. Suddenly it all became very real, that whole period, through this woman who was still here, and who was so much a part of it all, that great period of art history—no, she was real and alive and here!

Suddenly all that period became very, very real, as if it were still here and I had access, a connection to it, very, very real and direct—not from the pages of books but through this real person, who was part of the art of the period, and part of Max Ernst, she was an inseparable part of it all. What till now was only history to me, suddenly it all became a reality.

The voice on the telephone was real, very real. It was right here and now.

**Dorothea Tanning**
FAX 212-254-0299

to Jonas Mekas, Anthologie Film Archives.
2124772714

Dear Jonas Mekas:

After a couple of phone tries, I will resort to
writing a letter, in spite of my poor vision (I am
93).

My hope is to find two films we made, my
husband, Max Ernst, and I, with Hans Richter,
back in 1943: *Dreams That Money Can Buy*, (A so-
called copy of this film was brought to me to see
two days ago. It was a blatant forgery, very long,
vary bad, and had no relation to Hans Richter's
movie. Do you know about this, who made it, how
did it pass the estate rights, etc.?)

The other one was called, *8x8*, made a few years
later, which I would so like to see again after all
these years.

So if I call you again, Jonas, I hope you will help
me with information, if nothing else.

very truly yours,

*Dorothea Tanning*

Aug 3. 2003

337

338

## PIER PAOLO PASOLINI

Before I knew Pasolini as a film-maker, I knew him as one of the most important modern poets of the Italian language. Important as his work in cinema is,
he will remain, primarily, a master of Italian poetry. Nevertheless, cinema has
been graced and inspired by several men and women who came to cinema from
literature—Cocteau, Prévert, Broughton, Pagnol, McLaine. And we shouldn't
forget that Maya Deren and Stan Brakhage began as poets. Stan may not want
to admit it, but Hans Richter showed me one of the long poems that Stan had
sent to him, dated circa 1957. We read it together and we were quite impressed.

Anyway, I first met Pasolini in July 1967, in Rome. I came to Rome with some
twenty programs of the American avant-garde cinema. He came to practically every program. He usually came early, even before the door of the Centro
Sperimentale opened, and sat on the street curb usually with the curly haired
star of *Uccellacci e Uccellini*. My Italian was primitive and his English matched
my Italian. But we understood each other perfectly. His intuition and intelligence
had a lightning-speed quality. Three words in a sentence of twelve was enough.

I visited him in his Roman Mussolini workers' apartment. We had a lengthy
conversation on different subjects. He was especially interested in what was
going on in the radical political movements in America. He sincerely believed
that there would be a real revolution, a real revolution in America soon. If not,
America would gradually become a fascist country... I tried to persuade him
that cinema was the real revolution, but he thought that cinema lacked "ideology" and that there can be no revolution without ideology. I said, "Yes, but
there are six million movie cameras in America..." "But there are also six million typewriters in America," he said—"but are they producing a revolution?"

We met again, this time in New York, three or four years later. I do not remember which of his films was shown at the New York Film Festival. The film ended,
I walked out; he stood there, on the side, by himself. Since he didn't speak
English and since, it seemed, nobody around him spoke Italian or French, he
was left alone. So we went to the bar and had a drink. After one drink I told him
that my favorite film of his was still *Accattone*. To which he said, "Yes, it's also
my favorite but only in the same way as to a mother her firstborn is the dearest,
even if it's a brat." Then he added that he was still a brat of the Italian cinema—
that's why he was alone here this evening. On that note, we had another drink.

339

OPPOSITE: Pier Paolo Pasolini at his Rome apartment, summer 1966.

*Film Art Fund*

Requests the pleasure of your company at the inaugural party for

## Anthology Film Archives

### Monday evening, November 30th, 1970

from five until eleven p. m.

### at The Public Theater, 425 Lafayette Street, South of Astor Place

A film program of thirty minutes will be shown throughout
the evening in the newly constructed
Invisible Cinema

This invitation admits two

R.S.V.P. Jonas Mekas, P. Adams Sitney
677-3197   11:00 a.m. to 3:00 p.m. weekdays

341

Anthology Film Archives, 425 Lafayette Street. Invisible Cinema designed by Peter Kubelka.

At the opening of Anthology Film Archives, November 30, 1970. FROM LEFT: Boris Kaufman (Dziga Vertov's brother), Otto Preminger, unidentified, the author. Photo: Michael Chikiris.

Anthology Film Archives' Film Selection Committee, 1970. FROM LEFT: Ken Kelman, James Broughton, P. Adams Sitney, the author, Peter Kubelka. Photo: Stephen Shore.

# AT THE OPENING OF THE INVISIBLE CINEMA

November 30, 1970

Anthology opened at Papp's Public Theater on 425 Lafayette Street. Peter Kubelka had designed for Anthology a very special movie-projection space that became known as the Invisible Cinema. It contained very specially designed seats that gave you a view of the screen but you could see neither your neighbor nor the people in front of you: It was only the screen and you (see the picture).

Now this situation, this fact that you couldn't see anyone in the theater, required that nobody was permitted to enter the theater after the film began. Reason: You wouldn't know where the empty seats are.

December 1, 1970

Anthology held its opening party. Everybody was there. Even the Big Otto (Preminger) was there.

At the announced time a screening of films selected specially for the opening—a Joseph Cornell, a Méliès, a Brakhage, a Jerome Hill, and a Kubelka—took place. The audience took seats, the door was closed, the screening began. It was at that time that a bulky man came to the theater door and was about to enter. A woman who took care of the entrance informed him politely that the policy of the Invisible Cinema did not permit anyone to enter after the film started. The man ignored her and proceeded towards the door. At that point Peter Kubelka, who happened to be there, asked him not to go in. The man turned to Peter and said: "Who is going to stop me?" To which Peter answered very politely but emphatically, "Me." The guy, who happened to be taller and weightier than Peter, ignored Peter and proceeded to the theater door. At which point Peter approached him, and before we knew what was happening, the guy was lying on the floor wrapped up in his own overcoat. The guy stood up and proceeded again to the entrance into the theater. In a second he was again on the floor. In disbelief the guy stood up and this time went for Peter. Again Peter had him down on the floor in a second. This time Peter held his finger on the man's chest and the guy couldn't get up. Realizing that he was dealing with someone who knew what he was doing, the guy got up and proceeded towards the exit. As he was walking out, in a fury he smashed all the trays from the waitresses' hands.

What he didn't know was that three years earlier, while serving as head of the United Nations Film Division, Peter had won the judo championship of New York State.

OPPOSITE: Andy Warhol at the opening of Anthology Film Archives, November 30, 1970.

The Charles Theatre, Avenue B and 12th Street, 1962. Photo: The author.

# ABOUT SUN RA: TWO MEETINGS

It was in 1961. I was in Chicago. Why, I don't know, because Chicago, in my opinion, is one of the five most boring cities in the world. Others being Rotterdam, Brussels, Toronto and San Francisco.

After the screening, a guy comes up to me and invites me to his house to meet some of his friends. This guy was the composer Ed Bland, who later made the film *The Cry of Jazz* that caused quite a storm wherever it was shown.

Anyway, it's through him that I met Sun Ra that evening.

A year or so later, two eccentric young men, Walter Langsford and Edwin Stein, rented the Charles Theatre, a movie house on the corner of New York's 12th Street and Avenue B. They ran commercial movies there but they were about to fail. Since I lived around the corner, 515 East 13th Street, we became friends and soon began working together. They did the regular commercial stuff, and I added the "auteurist" cinema and the underground. Suddenly the Charles became one of the most exciting movie places in downtown New York. I don't think I will exaggerate by saying that what became known as the New York independent/underground film scene began there at the Charles, thanks to these two innocent, adventurous, permissive idealists, Langsford and Stein. These two guys gave me free hands to do what I wanted.

At that point Ed Bland already had moved to New York. Details begin to blur— I think it was Ed Bland who brought Sun Ra to New York, and when I suggested to the Charles Theatre guys to give him a show, of course they said yes. We had already inaugurated special late-night weekend shows with theater and music people. Bob Downey did shows there. In any case, that's how Sun Ra got his first New York show. The rest is history.

Thirty years later:

I am at JFK Airport waiting for the arrival of my brother Petras from Lithuania via Moscow. As I am standing there, waiting, I see this huge airport cart loaded with as much as it could take, with drums and other percussion instruments and suitcases, and this guy is pushing it by himself. It was Sun Ra. So I helped him push the load and we exchanged a few sentences until I saw my brother Petras, whom I hadn't seen for many years, coming out too, so I said goodbye to Sun Ra.

I didn't know at that time, when we met at JFK Airport, that fate had brought us together at the very beginning of his amazing career and then again at the very, very end. He was coming back from his concert in Moscow, his last concert.

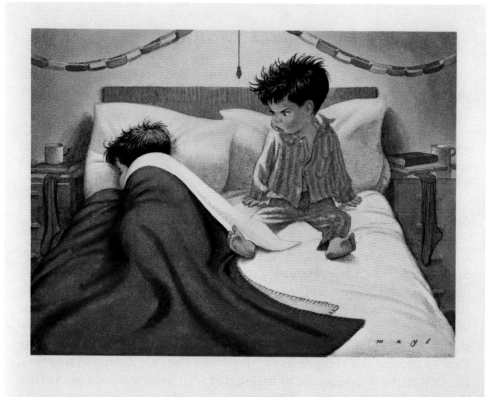

*With*

CHRISTMAS GREETINGS

*and all Good Wishes*

*for the*

NEW YEAR

*Chrystine Doyle (Jack Smith's mother)*

## MOTHER OF JACK SMITH

The first time she called me, it was in 1962. David Brooks, who was helping me at that time at the Film-Makers' Cooperative, picked up the phone, and said there was this woman on the phone, she insists on talking with me. So I picked up the call. She said she was Jack Smith's mother, and how is he, how is Jack. I said he is fine, he is just fine, he's doing great. "He never calls me," she said. "Would you mind if I call you once in a while just to check how he's doing?" "No," I said. "I don't mind it at all." She said she was working as a nurse in a Chicago hospital and was doing OK herself, but she misses her son, Jack. He never calls her and she has no telephone number for him.

So she used to call me once a month or so just to hear something nice about Jack. Her name was, she told me, Chrystine Doyle, and she lived on 200 East Chestnut Street in Chicago. She was always so happy to hear that Jack was healthy and doing well. She asked me not to tell Jack about her calls to me. I never did. It remained our little secret.

March 2o 1991

1040 Fifth Avenue

Dear Jonas

I am very gratful that you sent me an inscribed copy of your book.

It is so moving, so sad. I remember when you showed us some of your film of Lithuania at Lee's apartment - and how it affected me.

I am sure I Had Nowhere to go will deeply affect everyone who reads it. Everyone should read it today. My admiration to you for writing it. It must have been hard - but you should be very proud - always your friend
Jackie

Note from Jackie Kennedy, 1991.

## NOTES ON AN UNFINISHED BIOGRAPHY
## OF JACKIE AND LEE

It was in 1971. Or was it in 1972? It was Peter Beard who came up with the idea of a film biography of Jackie Kennedy and Lee Radziwill, two sisters. And I was the one to make it.

Jackie had seen *Walden* and *Reminiscences of a Journey to Lithuania*. Not only had she seen the two films: She told me she was very taken by them. So much, actually, that in 1972, on Mother's Day, she gathered her whole family clan to watch *Reminiscences*. Many years later Jackie still remembered it, and in 1991 she wrote me a note.

What surprised me the most was that Jackie not only liked *Walden*, but she liked my single-frame way of filming. She kept talking about it.

So when Peter came up with the idea of the biography, Jackie insisted that it should be me and no one else. I thought it was challenging, so I said yes. It was very challenging.

So I began slowly moving into it. Family photographs, letters were made available to me. We were all very excited about it.

What happened next has been later reported in gossipy bits by Jackie's biographers, such as Heyman, who tells that the autobiography was eventually abandoned because its production ran out of money... Now, only a fool who doesn't know that my way of filming doesn't cost any money could say that.

No, it wasn't the money: It was the TV moguls.

What happened was that the rumors had reached the TV networks that Jackie had entrusted this unknown guy to make her film biography.

I have to tell you at this point that I had so little interest in television in those days that I didn't know any of the big names that were running those channels and programs. But soon it became clear that some of them were very close to the Kennedy family, and when they heard about the biography project entrusted to somebody else, they felt snubbed.

So the first thing they did, they called Jackie and tried to find out what's this all about. Next, they got interested in meeting me. We met at some big hotel, the name of which I forgot. The conversation went something like this:

"Ah, so you want to make a film on Jackie?"

I said yes.

"But you are not a professional. It's OK, you can be the film-maker, but we are going to make it for you. We have all the technology, you know."

"Thank you," I said, "I don't need any help. I know what I am doing, I don't need any help."

The meeting lasted a couple of hours, during which they tried to persuade me and Peter Beard to let them do it: We could just sit there and do nothing—they will do it for us.

Later I met Jackie. I told her what happened. She confided to me that they are also talking to her, trying to persuade her the same way. She said those are very powerful people.

This went on for a month or two. I began to fear that this idea of this film biography might affect Jackie's relationship with some of these people, and I thought that the project should be temporarily put on ice. I did not want to complicate Jackie's life because of her relationship with me. I relayed this to Jackie and Peter. We discussed it and we decided to postpone the project. As for the TV people, I think it was Lee who suggested, like a bone that one throws to hungry dogs, maybe they could instead make a film about their aunts—which eventually was done under the title *Grey Gardens*.

Jackie never agreed to give the biography project to anyone else. That was something only between her, me, and Peter Beard. She was an amazing human being.

The author with Peter Beard, Montauk, c. 1995. Photo: Peter Sempel.

354

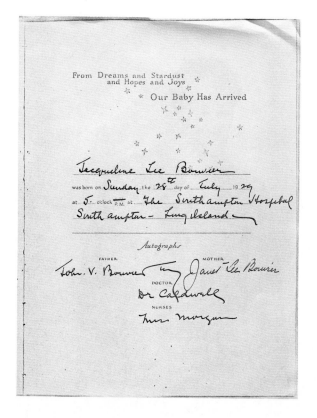

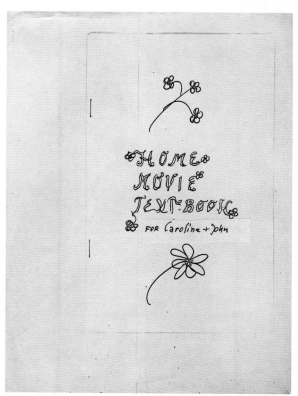

From Jackie Kennedy's baby book.

Baby's Birth-Stone

*Ruby*

Baby's Birth-Stone

*Ruby*

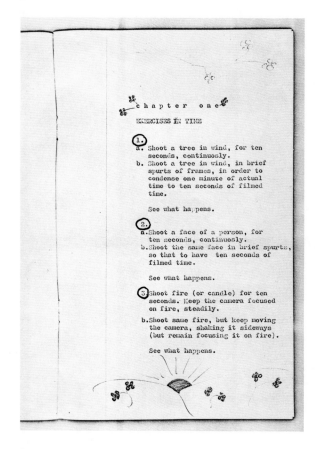

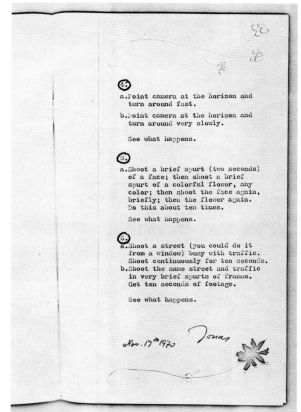

**chapter one**

EXERCISES IN TIME

**1.**
a. Shoot a tree in wind, for ten
seconds, continuosly.
b. Shoot a tree in wind, in brief
spurts of frames, in order to
condense one minute of actual
time to ten seconds of filmed
time.

See what happens.

**2.**
a. Shoot a face of a person, for
ten seconds, continuosly.
b. Shoot the same face in brief spurts,
so that to have ten seconds of
filmed time.

See what happens.

**3.** Shoot fire (or candle) for ten
seconds. Keep the camera focused
on fire, steadily.
b. Shoot same fire, but keep moving
the camera, shaking it sideways
(but remain focusing it on fire).

See what happens.

**4.**
a. Point camera at the horizon and
turn around fast.
b. Point camera at the horizon and
turn around very slowly.

See what happens.

**5.**
a. Shoot a brief spurt (two seconds)
of a face; then shoot a brief
spurt of a colorful flower, any
color; then shoot the face again,
briefly; then the flower again.
Do this about ten times.

See what happens.

**6.**
a. Shoot a street (you could do it
from a window) busy with traffic.
Shoot continuously for ten seconds.
b. Shoot the same street and traffic
in very brief spurts of frames.
Get ten seconds of footage.

See what happens.

Nov. 17th 1970    Jonas

OPPOSITE: The author having a good time with Anthony Radziwill, John Kennedy Jr.,
and Lee Radziwell in Montauk, at the Andy Warhol Estate, 1971.

Dear Mr. Mekas —

You can't know the happiness you have brought to my children — and to me — a whole new world opening —

It would have been more than enough just to see your films — but your giving us (I include myself because I am equally or more thrilled by it than they — if that is possible) that magical camera —

I never knew cameras could do

2)

things like that — zoom in and out — fast and slow — all so easy to hold in one's hand — We used 2 reels following your directions — on the fire — the night Peter and Minnie brought it too — !

Your primer of directions to motion picture acolytes is something so poetic and touching —

I just hope you know how happy you have made us all — and how wonderful it was to see your films and to meet you — With our deepest thanks — I feel

3)

sure that you have touched a chord — and I think my children are very lucky to have had that happen —

Most Gratefully

Jacqueline Kennedy Onassis

## A LETTER TO CALVIN TOMKINS

April 21, 1972

Dear Calvin:

Just to bring you up to date.

Yesterday I paid a visit to Jackie [Kennedy] to see how they are doing, film-wise. I found out that my little Super-8 camera is in constant use. More than that: Now they all have cameras, Jackie, John and Caroline, and they keep shooting wherever they go. The film-maker in the family, of course, is John. He made a 3-minute movie called *The First Shave* which is a smash success. John plays the leading part, with plenty of soap all over his face, and the cook plays a supporting part, he is the barber, and he shaves John with an ax, and chops his beard off, and does a good job in general. There is some argument going whose film it really is because Caroline says she did the filming while John had to act. But it was John's direction and script. In any case, it looks like a real "auteur" work... I gave them a copy of my *Movie Journal* book, which they are studying now. I did this, of course, in order to prevent them from gravitating to Andrew's [Sarris] camp...

Best to you –
Jonas

P.S. Next time when there is a show of *The First Shave* I'll try to get you a seat.

360

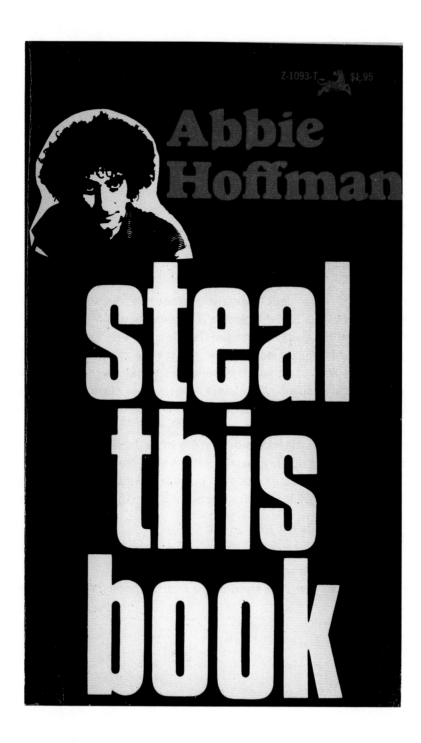

## ABBIE HOFFMAN AND A NOTE FROM BENN NORTHOVER

The year was 1962. I had just completed my first film, *Guns of the Trees*. But what do I do with it now? Where and how to show it? Sheldon Rochlin, my cameraman, had an idea. He said his good friend Abbie Hoffman had just become a manager of a movie house in Worcester, somewhere in Massachusetts or Connecticut. He thought he may want to show the film.

So we pack up and drive to see Abbie. My brother Adolfas, myself, Sheldon, and Edouard, our Polish friend.

We arrive and Abbie's wife gets panicky to see the whole gang of us, with nothing to eat or drink in the house. So we say we'll go and buy some grub.

Abbie takes us to the local chain food store. We walk around the store, we buy some bread, some beer, and some canned ham. None of us had any money, so that's a lot—bread, ham and beer.

We return to Abbie's place and lo and behold, Adolfas opens his coat and he has all kinds of goodies stacked in there. I had a couple of pieces too and so had Sheldon. We displayed it all proudly on the table in front of the shocked owners of the house.

"How could you do that, how could you?" kept repeating Abbie. "How could you steal it?"

Both of them, Abbie and his wife, were really shocked by our behavior.

I have to tell you that during the making of our first film, living on East 13th Street, and with no money, on many a hungry day we learned to go next door, to a chain food store called Safeway, and steal some basic food. We became very good at it. We had even worked out a theory for ourselves that it's not a crime to steal food when one is really hungry and has no food but it had to be a chain food store, not some small private store. We used to laugh that we steal only Safeway.

It was years later that I walked into a bookstore and saw a book displayed titled *Steal This Book*. I looked at the author's name. It said: Abbie Hoffman. Later, in one of his memoir books he described our visit. But there was no mention of the food-stealing event.

From a letter by Benn Northover, January 15, 2006:

"You mentioned Abbie Hoffman, when we spoke a few days ago, it made me think of when I first arrived in New York. For three months I stayed on the sofa of my friend Donna Ranieri, at 30 St. Mark's Place, right across from the Dom, and fifteen minutes walk down 2nd Avenue to Anthology Film Archives.

The apartment 4D was up on the 4th floor, facing out to the street. During the sixties the building saw a mix of people moving in and out. One of these was Abbie Hoffman. By all accounts Abbie moved through different apartments of the building, his last abode being 4D. This was his last New York home, before he went underground, leaving all his possessions as they stood, leading many of the tenants to believe that the occupant had died! When I stayed there, there was a scar in the ceiling of the living room. Donna told me that a few years earlier there had been some kind of leak from the ceiling, so the super was called. Opening up the ceiling, they found it riddled with wires, old FBI bugging equipment evidently placed there sometime during the sixties, keeping track of Abbie. Obviously, Abbie wasn't aware of it."

The author with his brother Adolfas, 1960, during the filming of *Guns of the Trees*.

364

## KENNETH ANGER AND ANNETTE MICHELSON

There are stories and anecdotes that, as years go, attain almost the status of a classic. One such anecdote, so the legend says, originated in Paris circa 1970.

Kenneth Anger had invited Annette Michelson to join him at a rare screening of part three of Eisenstein's *Ivan the Terrible,* which had just opened in Paris. So they go, the film ends, and they are walking out of the theater. At that point, Annette, so the legend goes, turns to Kenneth and says something to the effect of, "Kenneth, what do you think of it?"

Kenneth says nothing. They walk out. They go to eat at some place. Kenneth is silent, not very talkative. They finish eating, they part.

Years pass. Several years, so the legend goes.

Kenneth is silent.

Occasion arrived when there was another event taking place, again in Paris, during which Kenneth and Annette Michelson meet again. Annette, who is very perplexed about Kenneth's long silence, decides to break the ice.

"Kenneth," she says, "what happened that evening when we saw *Ivan the Terrible*? Something must have happened, you seem to have kept a distance from me."

Kenneth, so the legend goes, turns to Annette and says (my words):

"But Annette, how could you dare to talk about a film as great as *Ivan the Terrible*? How could you talk in the words you did, when we were just walking out of it? We should have both walked out in silence."

OPPOSITE: Kenneth Anger, c. 1975.

366

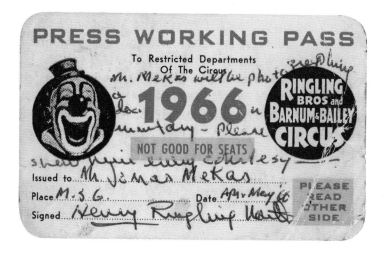

## FILMING THE RINGLING BROS.
## AND BARNUM & BAILEY

In April of 1966 Kenneth Anger sent me a few rolls of Ektachrome film. He was not planning to film anything soon, so maybe I could use it, he said. It was like sent from Heaven! The Ringling Bros. and Barnum & Bailey Circus had just arrived in town and I don't know why, but I always wanted to film circus. But I was in one of my dry periods; I just had no money to buy film. So this was my lucky chance.

So I go, I buy the ticket, and just to be sure, I inquire whether it's OK for me to bring my Bolex and film…The answer comes firm and clear: No cameras of any kind are permitted. Strictly verboten!

That came as a totally unexpected blow to my dream. As I stood there by the ticket window, trying to absorb the shock, I see Elenor Lester, a writer from *The New York Times* whom I happened to know, passing by. I told her the bad story. "Let me see what we can do about it," she said. "Come with me." As it happened, she was there to do the main story on Ringling and Barnum for the weekend edition of *The New York Times*.

We go, and we are taken to the circus office. And who is there, behind a heavy office desk, if not Mr. Ringling himself!

So Elenor says to him, "Meet my friend Jonas. I want you to give him a press pass for filming the circus. He works for me." Of course, Mr. Ringling needs that piece in *The New York Times*. With no questions, he picks up a card from the desk, scribbles on it and hands it to me. I thanked them both and left. It all happened so fast—it was, again, like sent from Heaven!

Since the Ringling and Barnum circus is a three-ring circus, I went to it three times and I filmed it three times on the same film rolls, and I was permitted to move around on the circus floor freely wherever I wanted. Thank you, Elenor Lester!

I have to tell you a sequel to this anecdote.

A year or so later, I sent a copy of the film to the Boston Cinematheque. I said, "It's silent but if you want, you can play some music with it." After the screening, they sent it back to me and included an audio tape that Jim Kweskin had made to go with it. I screened the film with his track and I liked it. So I decided to put it on film. And that's what now makes the sound track of the film *Notes on the Circus*.

A few months later I sent a copy of the film to Stan Brakhage. Months later, he wrote me that it had become his children's favorite movie. They want to see it again and again.

As it happened, Peter Kubelka came to visit Stan. He sat together with the children through the movie. After the screening, an argument ensued between Peter and Stan. Peter insisted that the film should be screened silent and that it was criminal to run it with music. Stan, who had seen it by then many, many times and had gotten used to seeing it with music, defended it as strongly. The arguing reached such a crescendo that, according to the legend, Peter left the room and walked into the woods and didn't come back for six hours...

To end the story of *Notes on the Circus*, here is the last of it, as told to me by Stan:

Later the same year, the real circus came to Denver. And, of course, Stan had to take the children to the real, live circus. Which he did. The children went with great excitement. After ten minutes or so they began crying and asked to be taken home. "This is not Jonas' circus!" they cried. "We want to see Jonas' circus!" Stan took them home and they watched once more Jonas' circus...

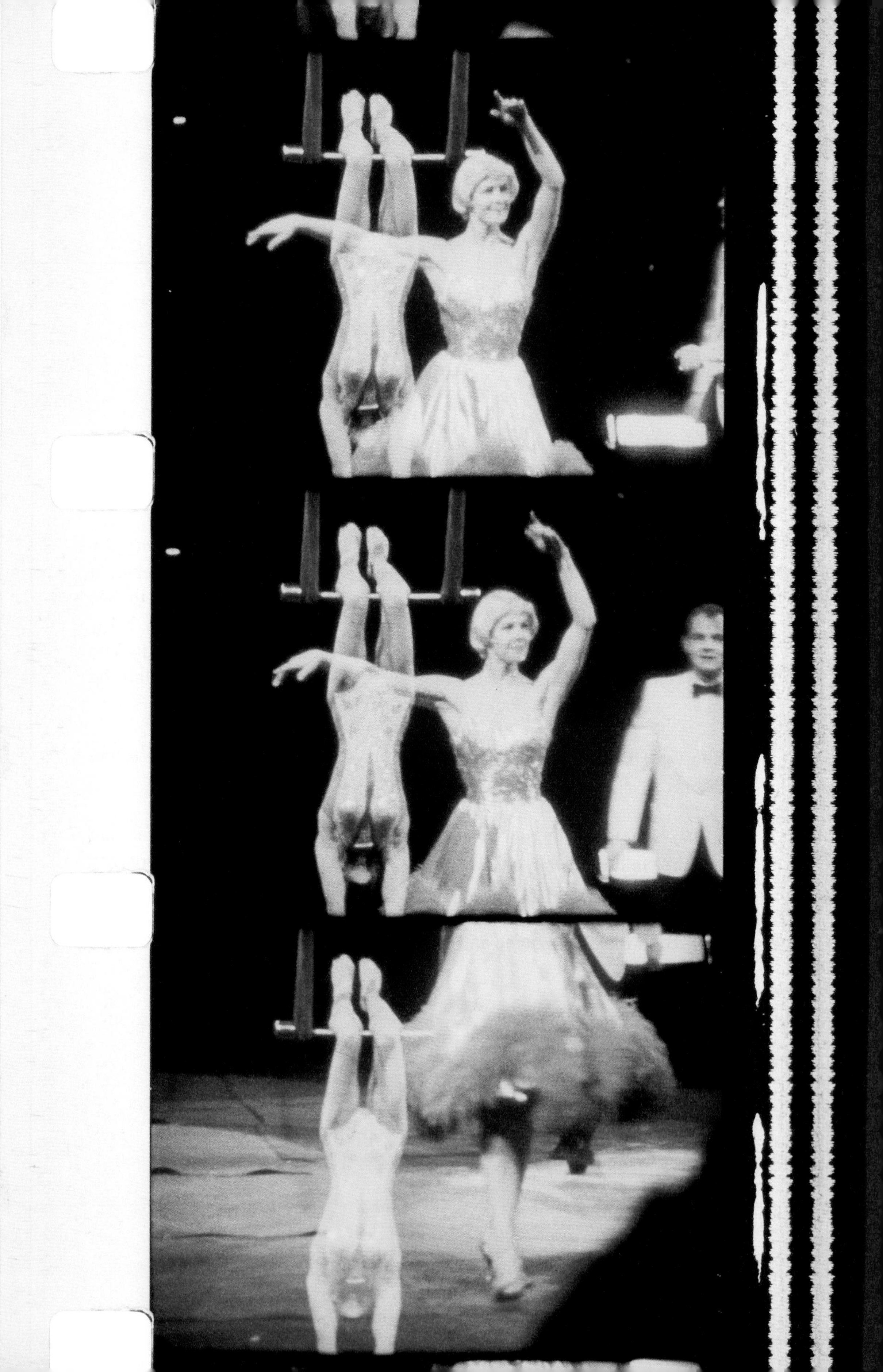

OPPOSITE: From *Notes on the Circus* (1966).

CLOCKWISE FROM TOP-LEFT: Myrrena and Neowyn, Bearthm, Crystal, Rarc and Neowyn.

The New York Times Magazine

JANUARY 28, 1979 / SECTION 6

# JOHN McENROE

**The Teen-Age Tennis Whiz Vows: 'I'll Follow Jimmy Conners To the Ends Of the Earth'**

## JOHN McENROE

I am obsessed with basketball, long distance running and tennis. Especially tennis. And especially the tennis of McEnroe. To me he was the greatest. I liked his totally unpredictable, irrational playing. He was my Rimbaud of tennis.

So when I had a chance to meet him at a dinner thrown by *The New Yorker* magazine for Calvin Tomkins, I could not resist telling him that he was my Rimbaud of tennis.

"I always considered you to be the Rimbaud of tennis," I said.

He looked a little surprised. Actually a lot surprised.

"How come? In what way?"

He seemed to be very perplexed by it. I tried to explain it to him. Then suddenly I noticed that he was pronouncing the name of Rimbaud very weirdly.

It's at that moment that Sebastian, my son, who was with me, whispered to me: "I think he thinks you are talking about Stallone."

Suddenly I got it! He thought I was comparing him to Stallone in *Rambo*!

"No," I said. "I don't mean Stallone... I mean the French poet..."

He said he'd like to read him, and I promised to send him a volume of Rimbaud. I haven't done it yet, but I plan to do it some day. He may have bought it meanwhile anyway, who knows.

## POLAROID CINEMA

It must have been around the year 1971. The Polaroid company had decided to introduce a Polaroid movie camera. As a promotion piece, they sent one promo camera to Andy Warhol hoping to get back the roll with some society people— a good promotion gimmick. But Andy didn't feel like doing it. He asked me to do it instead. He said, "You do it."

A special party was arranged by Polaroid people at Sam Beard's place (Peter's brother). A top society crowd was invited, including of course Andy and Jackie Onassis.

But I did it, of course, in my own style, that is, a lot of single frame and color activity. After I shot it, this being a Polaroid film, we could, of course, review it immediately. Jackie liked it, Andy liked it, but I saw from the faces of the Polaroid agents that it was not what they had hoped for. It was all too fast! They had expected something regular, routine, like one long pan showing all the celebrities, clearly and recognizably.

I don't know what happened to that first roll ever filmed on the Polaroid movie camera.

## THIS IS NOT HERE SHOW

### Part One

October 9, 1971

I was in a taxi on my way from the railroad station to the Everson Museum of Art in Syracuse. I was coming to the opening of a show that David Ross had curated for Yoko Ono and John Lennon.

Here I was, in a taxi, on a highway, on my way to the museum. And I see a man running along the highway in the opposite direction. I recognize him: It's George Maciunas. My taxi window was open and I managed to shout, "GEORGE!" I was not sure he heard me. But later he told me he heard me.

On my arrival at the museum this is what I found out.

It was George who had designed the Yoko Ono/John Lennon exhibition. It was George who had made every piece in it following freely Yoko/John instructions and scenarios. But it was also George who, once he did something, he did it so perfectly and so precisely that there was nothing, not a smallest minute detail that could be changed without destroying the whole thing. That was 100 percent George.

375

PAGE 376: Yoko Ono at the Everson Museum show, October 9, 1971.

PAGE 377: October 9, 1971, Syracuse.

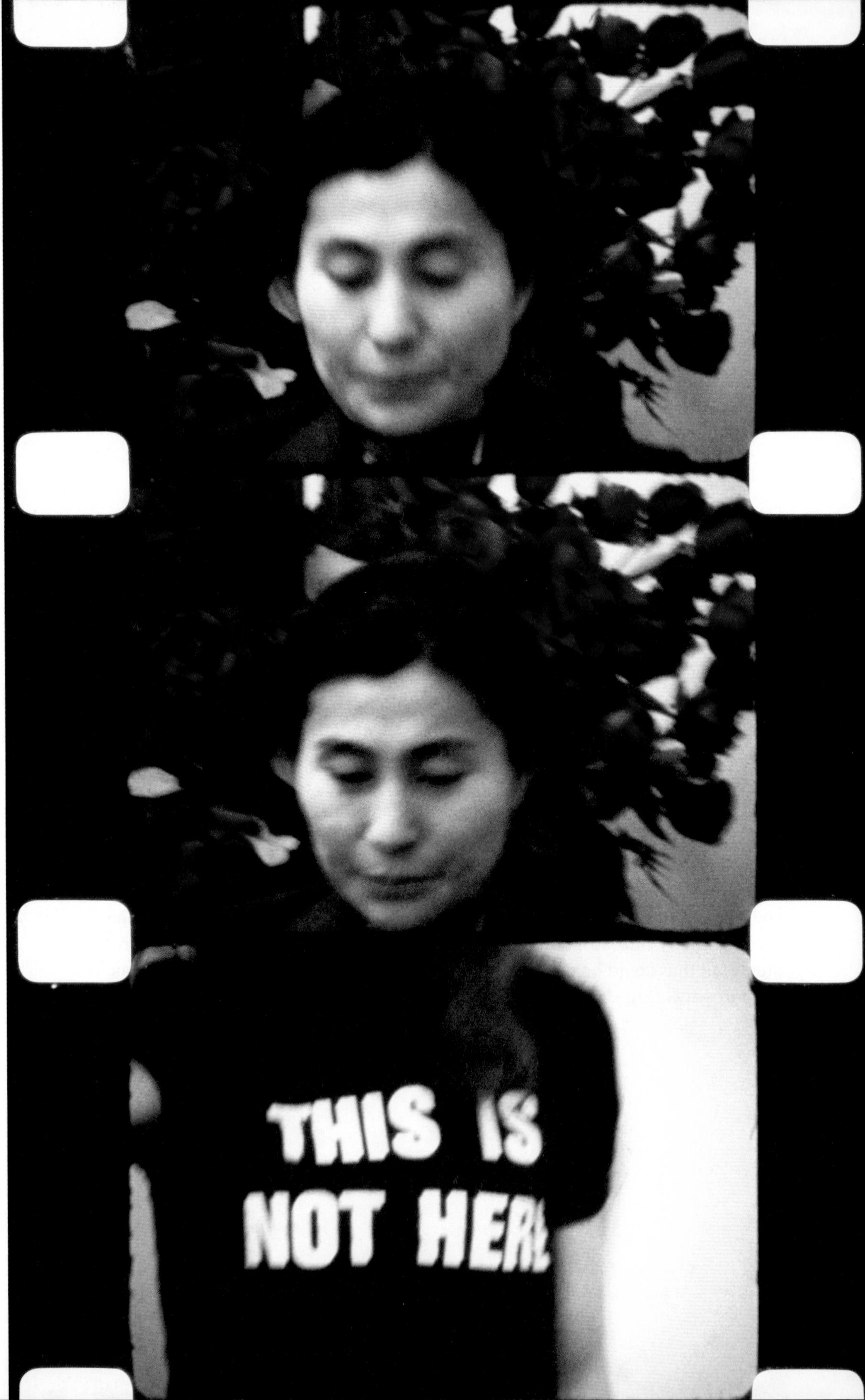
THIS IS
NOT HERE

John Lennon's birthday, October 9, 1971.

Miles Davis with John Lennon, June 12, 1972.

Part Two

October 5, 2004

I called David Ross. He was the director of the Everson Museum of Art in 1971. "What really happened that day when I met George running along the highway?" I asked. This is what David told me:

One of the pieces in the exhibition was *Portrait of John Lennon as a Young Cloud*. George conceived it as a piece consisting of many, many little wooden boxes stacked together. Now, what happened is that Yoko saw it the night before the opening, and decided that the little boxes should be painted white. So she asked David to get some white paint and paint them white, which he did. "I did a horrible job on it," he remembers. Now, in the morning George comes in and sees his beautiful wooden boxes all painted white. George went into a rage: "How did she dare do it? How could she!"

In a fit of rage, he grabbed a fire extinguisher and threatened to fill the gallery with chemical fumes. When he was persuaded not to do it, he asked David to take him to the airport. On the way to the airport, on Route 81 at some 60 mph speed, George opened the door, jumped out and began running along the highway. That's where I met George.

379

This happened on October 9, 1971, on John's thirty-first b-day.

Part Three

Some weeks later, Klein, Lennon's New York agent, threw a party at his estate for John and Yoko Ono on the occasion of the Everson show. The cream of New York avant-garde arts were all there. And of course, the center of it was John and Yoko.

But the Syracuse show was all George; everybody knew that, including John and Yoko. George had to come to the party, he had to!

So a Polaroid was made right there with John and Yoko on their knees begging George to forgive and come to celebrate the occasion. The Polaroid was delivered to George in a limo to 80 Wooster Street, where George lived.

George never came.

George never forgave anyone who tampered with his art.

380

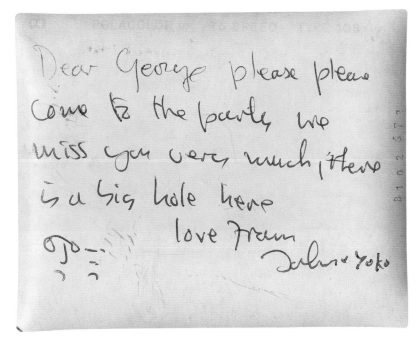

Dear George please pleas come to the party we miss you very much, there is a big hole here
love from
John & Yoko

OPPOSITE: John takes time out at Allen Klein's party, June 12, 1972.

ABOVE: A Polaroid delivered by Yoko Ono and John Lennon to George Maciunas, asking him to come to their party.
George didn't come. He was still angry at Yoko for changing, without his permission, one item in the Everson Museum show.

Larry Edmunds Bookshop, 2015. Photo: Scott Cambridge.

# MEETING ALDOUS HUXLEY

Los Angeles. The year: 1958. Summer.

I was visiting a friend. One evening we were joined by Richard Fleischer, the film director. It was a time when he was agonizingly obsessed with Freud. Somehow the evening turned to psychedelics and chemically induced perceptions. Fleischer mentioned a book by Huxley, *The Doors of Perception*. I had never heard of the book.

Next day, not having much to do, I decided to go to Edmunds Bookshop and see if they had the book.

And there it was, *The Doors of Perception*, right there on the shelf, in front of me. I picked it up and began skipping through some pages. I was sort of distracted by a tall man who was just right on the opposite side of the shelf. There he stood, tall, gray-haired, this very, very impressive person, who seemed to also be holding a book. My friend nudged me and whispered, "That's Aldous Huxley..."

Amazing as this coincidence was, I stared at him in disbelief. Of course, he didn't look at me, he just looked at some book he was holding. That was it. But I was thinking: What was the probability of such a chance meeting? One in a billion? Probably.

# A FEW NOTES ON ANDY WARHOL

In a way, Andy and the Factory were a huge psychiatrist's couch. Andy himself was, basically, a listener. Anyone could tell him, reveal to him, anything and everything, knowing that he will never disapprove of anything. He was an ideal father... So they came to the Factory, all those sad and confused souls, knowing that they will be accepted for what they are. And they revealed, opened themselves, either in real life or on the movie sets. Because there was this thing about Andy, this thing that made you feel absolutely free. All the lost, confused souls floated to the Factory, from all over the country, and found there a new home and a patient, listening father... And many of them were saved, I mean literally saved. I have read some nasty newspaper people saying how Andy's Factory destroyed people. I have seen just the opposite. There were exceptions, of course—there were a few cases of someone too far gone, and nobody could help them. But in most cases, these fragile souls found a new family, friends, recognition, even fifteen minutes of fame.

And then all those talks about Andy and the Beautiful People, the Society People. But I've seen Andy many times, at Studio 54, the disco place, but he was never really in the middle of it. And I've never seen him dance, either. But he was always there, on the edge of it, on the outside, in the lobby most of the time, near the entrance, with his Polaroid camera, watching, seeing everything. A perfect 100 percent voyeur, or, more correctly, gazer. He was an unblinking gazer seeing everything that was happening around him, neither approving of it nor disapproving. He was like a garbage can into which anything could be thrown: He accepted absolutely everything. At the same time he was like a sieve with very precise holes which permitted everything to pass through except some images, some items that he cared about, and they did not pass through, they remained stuck in that sieve of his mind, his eyes, and became his art.

I have a feeling that the same blank, open gazing stare and the absolute acceptance of everything was what attracted to him all those Beautiful People. What I am saying, really, is this: It's not Andy who chased the Beautiful People, it was just the opposite: The Beautiful People chased Andy. I know this from my own personal experience, from my own life of the mid-sixties, when some people used to say that I was chasing the press and the publicity. The truth is that the

OPPOSITE: The author and Andy Warhol during the filming of the
*Award Presentation to Andy Warhol*, December 1964.

energy, the intensity and passion of the period, was magnetic: It attracted the press, it attracted the young people, and it attracted the Beautiful People. The mid-sixties in New York was such a magnetic period. Andy couldn't have cared less about any of the fuss surrounding him; he had no time for it. On the other hand, he couldn't do anything to prevent it either.

I'd like to end this entry on Andy by saying that I have known very few people as sweet as Andy. And I always appreciated his sense of solidarity. He stuck with his friends. When I really needed help, it was enough to just say that I needed help. He asked for no explanation. He was a true friend.

The funny thing is I don't really know when I met Andy.

The story of Andy and me began, I think, in early 1962, when a film-maker, Naomi Levine, called to invite me to her birthday party. Actually, she was not only a film-maker—I liked her film *Yes* very much—but she was also a good, a very good painter. And she always said that Andy had stolen from her the flower image motif. In any case, she called to invite me to her birthday. "Come," she said, "there will be some other of your friends, Warhol and others." "Warhol?" I said, "I don't know him." "What do you mean you don't know him?" said Naomi. "He has been sitting there in your loft on the floor for months, watching all those movies, and you say you don't know him?" "No," I said, "I don't know him, there are all kinds of people coming to my loft."

Now, I have to tell you something about my 414 Park Avenue South loft, between 28th and 29th Streets, opposite from the Belmore Cafeteria, where all the taxi drivers used to stop for late-night meals. (It was a very large cafeteria with good, cheap food, where you could sit all night even if you ordered nothing.) I moved into the third floor of 414 Park Ave. South in 1961. In January 1962, "underground" film-makers, that's what they used to call us then, decided to create their own distribution center, the Film-Makers' Cooperative, and since the decisive meeting took place in my loft, they decided that my loft should become the newly created Co-op's headquarters. As a result of that decision, my loft soon became one of the busiest places in New York. The film-makers would bring their finished and unfinished films practically every evening to show to each other and to anyone who cared. The audience, on any given evening, could include Allen Ginsberg, Robert Frank, Salvador Dalí, Jack and

The author in 1962 at the Film-Makers' Cooperative (his loft), 414 Park Avenue South.

The author introducing the Velvet Underground, psychiatrists convention, New York, January 14, 1966.

388

Harry Smiths, Gregory Corso, Peter Duchin, LeRoi Jones, the Warhol gang, etc., etc.—in short, the Who's Who in New York's Old and New art scene. It became so crowded that I had to sleep under my editing table; there was no other place left for me. And then they all went to the Belmore Cafeteria: Warhol, and Rauschenberg, and all of them. Belmore was an all-night place.

So I went to Naomi's and, of course, Andy was there and I recognized him, this guy whom I saw sitting on the floor, in my loft, for months, watching movies by Jerry Joffen, and Jack Smith, and Ken Jacobs, and George Landow, and Harry Smith, and Ron Rice, and etc. and etc... That's how we met, Andy and me, and our friendship was lasting.

In 1964, at *Film Culture* magazine, we decided that our sixth yearly Independent Film Award should go to Andy Warhol for his films *Sleep* and *Empire*. Our idea was to have a special screening of one of Andy's silent movies at Dan Talbot's New Yorker theater and have Andy there to receive the award.

"No, no," said Andy when I presented him with this idea. "Too many people... too many people..." "OK," I said, "then why don't we do it at the Factory? I will present the award there and we'll film it, and then we'll show the film at the New Yorker! You don't even have to be there..." "That's great," says Andy. "Let's do it! How exciting!"

So we make a date. I arrive on 47th Street and I am about to walk in when it comes to my mind that yes, I have my Bolex, but I have nothing, no "award" to give to Andy. I have an idea... I go to the corner grocery store and fill a basket full with vegetables and fruit, carrots, cucumbers, mushrooms, bananas, all kind of stuff, and I arrive at the Factory.

The Factory gang is all there. I set up the camera, Gregory Markopoulos offers to help me as the second cameraman. So I present the basket of fruit and vegetables to Andy, and he thinks it's a great award and he passes the veggies to the Factory gang, to the Superstars, and the camera is rolling, and the Supremes music is loud, as any other day at the Factory, and we are all munching on the veggies, and my Bolex is purring happily (I had motorized it for the occasion). And that's how the *Award Presentation to Andy Warhol* film was made. We completely forgot about the New Yorker. This was the event, this was it. We all had a great time that day at the Factory.

390

## NOTES ON SHIRLEY CLARKE,
## NEW YORK WORLD'S FAIR AND BIG OTTO (PREMINGER)

October 16, 1967

Shirley plodding across the morning grass, all wet, with her red shoes, lagging behind me. Her shoes were pressing—"Those net stockings," she was complaining, with our hearts half-broken about all the unused buildings and stupidity of man. We visited the old NY World's Fair grounds, in Flushing. The city's office for Cultural Affairs called and said maybe we could do something with the U.S. Pavilion. So very early this morning, Shirley and I, we proceeded to Flushing, by subway. A desolate place, with only three or four structures left. We had to walk for a good mile to the U.S. Pavilion, and when we arrived, we couldn't get in. After finally locating the guard, we had no light—the electricity was disconnected, or didn't work. We checked the projectors and the auditorium by lighting matches. Later a flashlight arrived. Six huge, modern 35mm projectors sitting without any use, and the round auditorium. We couldn't figure out what we could do with it. Best for music jam sessions, or Stan's DOM theater. Only that it's all 35mm, what a pity.

They build those structures without thinking how they will use them after the fair is over. Incredible. How goddamn stupid, we thought, all that money. Just for upkeeping alone. The guards said they have to raise 120 flags on festivity days, and there are flags that need six men to raise them. We could run the whole Cinematheque just on flag money. Anyway, we looked at it, then we had a hot dog, and back we went.

OPPOSITE: Andy Warhol at his studio, Union Square, c. 1985.

PAGE 392: Shirley Clarke, June 1972.

392

393

The author with Otto Preminger, 1970. Photo: Michael Chikiris.

6:00 p.m. Shirley and I, we went to see Big Otto. He apologized for having canceled the last Thursday's meeting. He said he took LSD and forgot our appointment, lost all sense of time. It was his first trip, and Tim was there. He thought it was only 9:00 a.m. but it was really 3:00 p.m., he said. That was the only thing he lost control of during the trip: the sense of time.

Anyway, he sat there behind his long, huge table, a tremendous and good table, a good feeling—there was a very good feeling about him. Otto kept talking, telling stories; he was in a very good mood. Chuck Wein came in with a friend. There was no long talk about money: He understood everything perfectly, and said he will send $5,000 this week. He said, any Hollywood director who gets older wants to be with younger people. It would be good, he said, if he could teach cinema two months out of twelve every year.

As he rambled, he said he doesn't like to edit films. It comes from his stage background. When he shoots, he avoids too many different angles. He gives to his editors only one choice, so that anybody can edit his films. Because of this self-protection from editors, he said, sometimes he himself gets stuck: It would be good to have a closer shot, but he didn't shoot any closer shots... Shirley said she could sit all day and all night in the editing room. She shot Jason in twenty or so shots, but then spent months in the editing room.

We left the Big Otto and the day was good and shining. It was good, we thought, that he remembered us under LSD...

# WARHOL, A DAY AFTER

(My column here is reprinted from the August 7 issue of Andy's *Daily Star.*)

Last evening I was among the lucky many who attended Andy's 75th birthday party. I am not sure I should call it a party. I should call it a pandemonium. What with all those people converging on the Brillo Box building designed by Andy himself—the magnificent structure that covers all of 9/11 downtown. New York has seldom seen such an event. Prominent were the tables of all the Warhol conglomerates from Africa to Bangkok to Vancouver. President Ventura was very visible. Bill Gates, Andy's closest rival in the computer industry, was, of course, not excluded from the party, as befits Andy's by now famous all-inclusive style of life.

Henry Geldzahler, looking like a Buddha with a cigar, still going strong, was speaking to some television people, telling how Andy's art is still going strong, especially his work in the computer and laser arts to which he has devoted much of his time these past ten years.

And there was Andy himself, looking very much like I remember him from the first meeting in 1962—now standing under the palm trees in the building he had designed himself—yes, a replica of the famous Brillo Box—surrounded by installation artists, politicians, industrialists and, yes all those gorgeous young women and boys. He was holding in his clasped hands—yes, the cliché image that has appeared on so many billboards—clutching the latest AW Zap camera he introduced five years ago, the amazing post-Polaroid miracle toy that amazed not only Letterman, on whose program he first presented it, but also Wall Street when the stocks next morning shot through the ceiling.

For me a very special moment was around 10:00 p.m. when who arrives but... all dressed up, frock and cane and yes, the monocle—George Maciunas himself. He was carrying a plate of dumplings which he presented to Andy. Of course, this was, for all of the present the same as Rosebud in Orson Welles' film. I knew the meaning of it. Andy knew it. And George knew it. To all others it was and it will remain *our* secret. George now runs a dozen Fluxus stores in New York's bustling shopping Paradise. Maciunas is having a great time running his joke stores selling Fluxus chairs in which you can not sit, Fluxus clothing, Fluxus ice cream that sometimes baffles, confuses, and sometimes infuriates the tourists. His most recent addition to Soho came just this past January when he opened three Fluxus restaurants—one that serves only white food, another one with blue food, and the third one with red color food. Anyway, it was good to see these two provocateurs of the 60's, now both celebrities and multi-billionaires, getting together again, still good friends. Yoko Ono, George's wife, was having her own good time with President Ventura who seemed to enjoy the occasion very much.

In the midst of all of this commotion and bustle Andy's art was ignored. Slightly overshadowed by his latest computer art blockbusters, you could see two of his best films, *Sleep* and *The Chelsea Girls*; both were running at the Scorsese Theater across the Brillo Square. A huge sign by the entrance announced that beginning today a special radio channel is being inaugurated that will run 24 hours a day non-stop airing all of Andy's incredible audio tapes. It will take exactly 365 days to run them all. What a feast for the social, etc. scientists and anthropologists and anyone who likes fun. It's incredible what this guy has done.

So I lift my glass of Andy's wine (Vintage, 1995, the great year for Andy's Montauk vineyards) to you, Andy, and I wish you many more!

Jonas Mekas

Tribute to
Andy Warhol
on his 75th Birthday

A DIAMOND JUBILEE
FOR ANDY!

# FILM CULTURE

JANUARY, 1955   Volume I   No. 1

ERICH VON STROHEIM / Queen Kelly; Walking Down Broadway
ORSON WELLES / For a Universal Cinema
HANS RICHTER / Film as an Original Art Form
EDOUARD L. DE LAUROT / Towards a Theory of Dynamic Realism
HERMAN G. WEINBERG / The New Films
GEORGE N. FENIN / Motion Pictures and the Public
WILLIAM K. EVERSON / A Family Tree of Monsters
     also articles by GORDON HENDRICKS, FRANCIS BOLEN, ROGER TILTON,
     JOSE CLEMENTE, RICHARD KRAFT. and others

## ALL ABOUT MONEY: STARTING *FILM CULTURE* MAGAZINE

December 10, 1954

Still looking for money. Last week our books showed that we had only $120. The sum needed to pay for the next issue of *Film Culture* is $700. During the last few days, I've approached at least thirty people in the "film business" for sponsorship. I got names but no money.

While preparing the first issue, I was mostly concentrating on the content. Money seemed such a secondary thing. But now I am facing the song.

I reported on the sad financial situation to the editorial board. I simply proposed that each of us come up with $100—and the problem is solved! The idea didn't work. George is going to South America and doesn't have a single dollar extra. Louis said he is willing to give any help to the magazine except financial. Gordon said he has money but he wouldn't give because of his principles. "Why," he said, "why did you start the magazine at all without money! You can't start a magazine unless you have money for at least three or four issues." If he'd known we didn't have money, he wouldn't have helped from the start. So I said, if we'd all think that way, *Film Culture* would wait another two centuries. There are thousands of people with money and business brains, but it had to be us, without money and without business brains to do the job. Gods are cruel... I didn't dare tell him that this morning we received a summons to appear in court. Pacific Printing is suing us for the printing of the first issue. We have seven days to find $723.91...

December 11, 1954

I am continuing the money Odyssey. Perry Miller said she spent all her money on a trip to Europe; she owes money to her mother. We called dozens of people without any results. I tried to see Marlene Dietrich, but was thrown out by the doorman.

So now I have to work full-time, and often overtime too, at the Graphic Studios, on West 22nd Street. We walk around hungry, live on coffee, saving money to pay the printer.

Editorial board of *Film Culture* magazine, 1955. STANDING, FROM LEFT: Andrew Sarris, Eugene Archer, George Fenin, Adolfas Mekas. SEATED, FROM LEFT: The author, Arlene Croce (*insert*), Edouard de Laurot.

## Affidavit of Service on Individual(s)

State of New York, County of                    ss.:

being duly sworn, deposes and says, that he resides at

and that on the
day of              , 19    , at No.

in the Borough of              , City of New York,
he served the within Summons and Complaint on

the Defendant therein named, by delivering to and
leaving a true copy of each thereof with said defendant personally; deponent knew the said person so
served as aforesaid to be the same person mentioned
and described in said summons and complaint as the
defendant therein; deponent is over the age of 18
years and not a party to the action.

Sworn to before me this
day of              19

Commissioner of Deeds, City of New York
Notary Public, County of

## Affidavit of Service on a Corporation

State of New York, County of                    ss.:

being duly sworn, deposes and says, that he resides at

and that on the
day of              , 19    , at No.

in the Borough of              , City of New York,
he served the within Summons and Complaint on

a              corporation, the defendant therein
named, by delivering to and leaving a true copy of
each thereof personally with

an officer of said corporation to wit, its
deponent knew said corporation so served as aforesaid to be the same corporation mentioned and described in said summons and complaint as the defendant therein, and knew said

to be such officer thereof; deponent is over the age
of 18 years and not a party to the action.

Sworn to before me this
day of              19

Commissioner of Deeds, City of New York
Notary Public. County of

---

Index No.                    19

## Municipal Court of The City of New York

Borough of  Manhattan: 2nd    District

PACIFIC PRINTING CO., INC.

Plaintiff

**against**

JONAS MEKAS, individually and
d/b/a FILM CULTURE

16 W169

Defendant

# Summons

## COMPLAINT

*A statement of the nature and substance of the
plaintiff's cause of action is as follows:*

Action to recover for work,
labor and services rendered and
materials furnished by plaintiff
to defendant consisting of printing matter, magazines, etc., at
the agreed price of $923.91, on
which defendant paid $200.00,
leaving balance due of $723.91,
no part of which has been paid,
although duly demanded. Said
work and materials furnished at
defendant's special instance and
request.

SIGMUND MOSES
*Attorney    for Plaintiff*

*Office and Post Office Address*

Borough of 33 West 42nd Street New York City
Manhattan

White to Play and Win

**Look through from other side against light**

# 8x8

Rudolf Arnheim, Luis Bunuel, Rene Clair, H. G. Clouzot, Jean Cocteau, Carl Th. Dreyer, Marcel Duchamp, N. Gabo, Fritz Lang, Norman McLaren, Jean Painleve, Herbert Read, Mies van der Rohe, Jose L. Sert, James Johnson Sweeney, Josef von Sternberg, Herman G. Weinberg, Cesare Zavattini

invite you to **THE FIRST PRIVATE PREVIEW OF HANS RICH-TER'S NEW SURREALIST FILM POEM** **8x8**

in the auditorium of the Museum of Modern Art, on March 7th, 1957, at 8:30 p.m.

**8x8** will be introduced by
**SHELLEY WINTERS**
**BOSLEY CROWTHER**
**SALVADOR DALI**
**HANS RICHTER**

for the benefit of **FILM CULTURE**, America's independent motion picture magazine, devoted to the aesthetic and social aspects of the cinema.

**8x8** is a fairy tale for grown-ups, mixing Freud and Lewis Carroll with Venice, Venus and Old Vienna.

An impromptu art film by Gjon Mili on Salvador Dali will precede the screening of **8x8**

---

Please send ............ tickets to the address below. My contribution ($5 minimum for each reserved seat, payable to FILM CULTURE) is enclosed.

NAME ..................................................

STREET ..................................................

CITY ..................................................

*Film Culture* benefit at the Museum of Modern Art, 1957.
FROM LEFT: Frederick Kiesler, Hans Richter, Lillian Kiesler, Alexander Calder.

*Film Culture* benefit at the Museum of Modern Art, 1957.
FROM LEFT: Marcel Duchamp, Hans Richter, Frances H. Flaherty, Elsa Maxwell.

$2.95 • SEPTEMBER 19, 1994

# *New York*

404

**Sous Chef
$55,000**

## WHO MAKES HOW MUCH

**Supermodel
$7 million**

**Private
Investigator
$150,000**

**Coach
$1.25 million**

**Street Musician
$15,000**

**Advertising V.P.
$978,001**

**Photographer
$2 million**

**Newspaperman
$586,589**

**Prison Inmate
$8/week**

**Tenant Lawyer
$25,000**

*A peek at the paychecks of
hundreds of New Yorkers.
Where do you rank?*

**Poet
$96,228**

**Subway Track
Walker
$43,000**

**Socialite/Planning
Commissioner
$40,000**

**Peter Lightbody** $45,000
*business manager,*
*Profile Records*

**David Lincoln** $105,000
*senior rabbi, Park Avenue Synagogue*

**Charles LoBello** $34,325
*English teacher, I.S. 119*

**Donald Schul**
$53,000
*chief projectionist, Walter*
*Reade Theater*

**Richard Lopuzzo** $55,000
*executive sous-chef, Aureole*

**John R. Loring** $290,919
*senior V.P. and design director, Tiffany & Co.*

**Michael Lowenstern** $12,000
*free-lance bass clarinetist and founder, Portable*
*Electronic Coffee House,*

**Mary Lowery** $49,500
*NYPD helicopter pilot, aviation officer*

**Mike Lupica** $600,000
*Daily News sports columnist*

**Peter Lynch** $102,682
*director, N.Y. State Lottery*

**Bruce Lynn** $50,000
*publicist*

**Rosemary Maciel** $31,593
Green Book *editor*

**Mike Maddux** $1,250,000
*Mets pitcher*

**Sergeant First Class Reginald Manning** $44,184
*army recruiter, Lincoln Center*
*Recruiting Station*

**Donald B. Marron** $11,059,200
*CEO, PaineWebber*

**Spiros Mastoras** $17,000
*hot-dog-and-pretzel vendor*

**Don Mattingly** $3,620,000
*Yankees first-baseman*

**Frank Mazzetti** $51,042
*English teacher, Mabel Dean Bacon High School*

---

**"Anne McAdams"** $25,000
*street musician*

**Mike McAlary** $330,000
Daily News *columnist*

**Claude McAulay** $47,000
*nurse administrator, Creedmoor*

**Eugene R. McGrath** $931,900
*chairman, president,*
*and CEO, Con Edison*

**Colleen McGuire** $25,000
*tenant lawyer*

**Michael McKeever** $100,000
*private investigator*

**Steven Meisel** $2 million
*fashion photographer, Condé*
*Nast*

**Jonas Mekas** $0
*president and program director,*
*Anthology Film Archives*

**Myra Melford** $50,000
*pianist and composer*
*(free-lance musician)*

**Mark Messier** $2,633,000
*Rangers center*

**Ruth Messinger** $95,000
*Manhattan borough president*

**Michael Metry** $31,000
*Olympia Trails bus driver*

**E. H. Meyer** $2,909,578
*chairman/president/CEO, Grey Advertising*

**Fred Meyer** $1,446,156
*chief financial officer, Omnicom Group*

**John Miller** $94,000
*deputy commissioner for public information,*
*New York City Police*

**E. Leo Milonas** $111,125
*chief administrative judge*
*of the courts*

**Guy Molinari** $95,000
*Staten Island borough president*

**Dr. Yolanda T. Moses** $116,550
*president, City College*

**Daniel Moyer** $19,200
*chairman of guitar department*
*and guitar teacher, Third Street Music*
*School Settlement*

**Jennifer Jo Moyer** $31,000
*pre-kindergarten teacher,*
*Grace Church School*

**Daniel Patrick Moynihan** $133,600
*U.S. senator*

**Gregg Mulpagano** $11,000
*sales supervisor, FAO Schwarz*

**José Navarro** $400,000
*jewelry thief*

---

**Steven Meisel**
$2 million
*fashion photographer,*
*Condé Nast*

---

**Jeffrey L. Neal** $42,200
*physical therapist, Sports Training*
*Institute*

**Andrew Neil** $600,000
*co-anchor, Full Disclosure*

**Charles Nelson** $20,000
*self-defense instructor*

**Lauraann Nicoletto** $48,000
*head nurse, adolescent psychiatry,*
*Bellevue Hospital Center*

**Matt Nokes** $2,250,000
*Yankees catcher*

**Robert C. North Jr.** $175,000
*chief actuary*

**Stephen Novick** $978,001
*executive V.P.,*
*Grey Advertising*

**Eric Ober** $714,053
*president, CBS News Division*

**John Cardinal O'Connor** $0
*archbishop of New York*

**Vendela**
$250,000
*contract model,*
*Elizabeth Arden*

405

## WORKING WITH ANDREW SARRIS

The year was early 1955. The first issue of *Film Culture* magazine was just out. We hadn't paid for it yet and we had no idea how we were going to pay for it. But we were all very excited and were proceeding with plans for issue No. 2.

There was a young brilliant film-maker by the name of Roger Tilton. I don't remember how we met. He had just made a film together with Ricky Leacock, *Jazz Dance*. He saw the first issue of the magazine and said, "You know, I am teaching film at Columbia University, and I have these two crazy students in my class, they seem to be just right for you." "Why do you think they are the kind of people I need?" I asked. "Why? One of them has just demolished *Potemkin*, and the other one, in his paper, totally demolished *Cabinet of Dr. Caligari*." "Yes!" I exclaimed enthusiastically, "I want to meet them!"

I do not remember, by now, which one of them had demolished *Potemkin*. If I am not wrong, it was Andrew. In any case, I met them both very soon, Andrew Sarris and Eugene Archer, and I invited them both to review new films for *Film Culture*. They were both totally obsessed with movies, and as with myself and Adolfas, their favorite street in New York was 42nd Street, where during any given night you could see at least thirty movies, and I mean night, not evening, because they were running movies there twenty-four hours a day. We sat there, in those dingy movie houses: Andrew, Adolfas, Eugene, a crazy Pole by the name of Edouard, and Peter Bogdanovich, until our eyes couldn't take any more. We sat there with all kinds of sad lost souls, pimps and bums and hookers—and we had incredible, great, ecstatic movie nights.

OPPOSITE: Andrew Sarris and the author, 1966. Photo: Elliott Landy.

But life went on and we continued. And Andy, of course, he always completed his reviews on time, even if we had to lock him up in our room to force him to finish his piece. And when I began reviewing films for *The Village Voice*—it was me who introduced regular movie reviewing into *The Village Voice*, in 1958—and when the independent film movement exploded in New York around the turn of the sixties and I couldn't honestly cover both the independents and the commercial cinema, I decided that the only person I could really trust doing the job was Andy, so I invited him to join me at *The Village Voice* to review the "commercial," "public" cinema. Ironically, some years later, after Felker took over *The Village Voice* and when it began moving towards a more commercial public, and when at every editorial meeting I came under the attack—*Why the hell do we need this guy and his "Movie Journal?"*—it was Andy who defended me. And that's why my "Movie Journal" continued for a few more years at *The Village Voice*.

But let us forget cinema for a moment. Cinema or no cinema, I always liked Andrew's kind of clear humor, very intellectual humor, and his very carefully constructed critical language. And myself being an immigrant, I envied him, as I always envied Arlene Croce and Parker Tyler their linguistic skills.

Amazingly, just the other weekend I was listening to Andrew on the WBAI radio talking about some film, and he sounded just like in 1955, same humor and ironical twists and subtle, detailed analyses: no abstract talking, like so many others do. Andrew is always so very concrete, down to earth about what he's talking about, be it actors, or camera angles, or direction, or ideas expressed in the film, the plot, etc., etc. I admire that kind of quality very much. No baloney, it's all very factual, same as when Berenson discusses some Renaissance painting.

A great guy, Andy. I learned a lot from him. I have the *American Cinema* book on my table, the only book on cinema that I have on my table. We have had arguments about the avant-garde—but that's not his ground, and he knows it. But as far as the narrative cinema goes, I still go by Andrew Sarris. Thank you, Roger Tilton!

# MOVIE JOURNAL

*by Jonas Mekas*

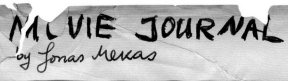

## THE MORAL CLARITY
## OF ANDREW SARRIS
### (demonstrated in three chapters)
### Chapter One

"THE POINT BEING MADE IS UNCLEAR. IT'S ALL FRENCH PROPAGANDA"

Relaxed, far from Vietnam, Andrew Sarris has a political revelation

[see last week's review of "Far From Vietnam"]

### Chapter Two

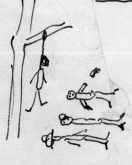

"By contrast, the Vietnamese peasants are neat, alert, and dedicated"

A. SARRIS ibid.

### Chapter Three

"How curious this cult of the peasant abroad"

A. Sarris

409

7 N Goodman St
Rochester NY
14607

17 Feb 1965

Jonas —

Surprise! and thanks
for the Danish Pabst
program — your Poker
F.C. was a darling —
I've switched from variety
obits to laughs with
you — Herman has chick
voice Brooke —

410

Louise Brooks with Gustav von Seyffertitz in Malcolm St. Clair's film *The Canary Murder Case* (1929).

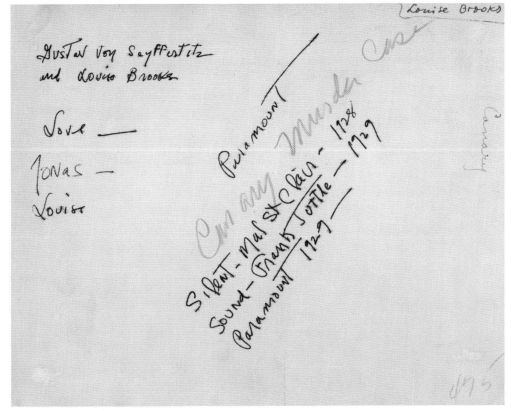

7 N Goodman St
Rochester NY 14607
20 November 1965

Dear Jonas

The Steichen photograph on the Berlin
program you sent me is my favorite. In the
50 stills Pabst has just sent me there are
50 Louise Brooks, but Steichen got to the bottom of me. First because, when I went to be
photographed, I wandered all over the Ambassabdor
Hotel in Los Angeles before I found that he was
waiting for me in one of the bungalows.

To make me crosser, Steichen suggested that
I take off the grease paint that covered my
hated freckles. A great photographer is a
great director. I was steamed up.

Yesterday, for dinner I had Gerald Pratley,
Joan Fox, and Andrew Sarris.

My darling landlady had rehearsed me on
a wonderful Italian dish. I made out. And it
was wonderful too to get out of my hole and see
PUSSY CAT which reminded me of an old time
Shubert Revue.

Love

Louise

---

Dear Jonas — As an editor you
fascinate me even more than
your divinely crazy magazine —
How do you keep your head clear
of the muck that makes most
film magazines the work of silly
show offs who write nonsense
totally unconnected with anything
they see on the screen — If they
ever _do_ see anything on the
screen — you must come to see
me so that I can stuff you with
roast chicken and pick at your brain —
Love Louise

Thanks for returning my photo —

13 July 79

Dear Jonas — What a charming Surprise —
14 beautiful Red Roses —

Film Culture is mentioned twice in Tynan's Brooks Profile (June 11) — Once among the magazines publishing my articles; Once as the source of a quote from Charlie Chaplin Remembered. The Profile also ran from July 8 – 12 in the L.A. Herald Examiner, all of which should help to sell back numbers of F. C.

Did you become an instant Celebrity when your extraordinary Profile appeared?

413

2.

over
come ~~finally~~ The New Yorker's magic power has even Eastman House's blindness to my existence here.

All this is nothing compared to the greatest of editors, William Shawn phoning me weekly, answering my questions, telling me, "you can, you CAN!" to my Memoirs.

Of only my new electric typewriter could write the damned book.

Love Louise

# Merry Christmas

20 December 1971

Dear Jonas
Thanks for the $50 check.
        Please send me 4 copies of <u>Film Culture</u>.
And don't forget to send back my stills.

==============

Unlike Hemingway, I never had to go out with
sex and gun and booze to find a subject to write
about.  But articles are subject to libel--"What
is against the public interest" which novels
are not.

        I have in mind a Garbo article...
<u>The Comedy of the Garbo Mystery</u>.
        But your magazine is not, I think, interested in
Garbo.  It seems a very masculine magazine.
Still you are one of my favorite editors.  You have creative outlets which release you from messing with other
people's scripts and moving commas around.


        Love


        Louise

414

Jonas Mekas
80 Wooster Street
New York NY 10012

415

15 June 1980

Dear Jonas — Good luck — but I cant help — I am dying with emphysema — only drugs keep me breathing. ~~You cant~~ ~~~~

Love
Louise

22 questions by Sophie Calle-Grégoire Bouillier:


-When have you died already ?
Once Yoko Ono did my horoscope, Japanese style. She said I am a very
-What makes you get up in the morning ?    young soul. Lived many times
Waking up.                                 but hasn't yet died.
-What's become of the dreams you had as a child?
They all came through except one.
-What makes you special ?(What makes you stand out/different from others ?)
My hat.
-Is there anything missing in your life ?
A beautiful woman.
-Do you think anyone can be an artist ?
No. Because it's not easy to be crazy.
-Where do you come from ?
The Big Bang.
-Do you consider your lot as a tempting one ?
Not especially.
-What have you given up ?
Hope to learn Japanese.
-How do you spend your money ?
Poetry, wine and women.
-What daily/house chore is the most putting you off?
I don't have any.
-What are your favorite pleasures ?
to drink, eat, sing & dance with friends
-What would you like to get for you birthday ?
A beautiful woman.
-Name three living artists that you hate
I gave up hate when I was seven
-What cause or whatsoever do you defend ?
The right to tell politically (in every way) incorect jokes
-What are you able to/can you turn down/refuse ?
Food at  airplanes
-What part of your body is the most fragile ?
Probably my nose, it bleeds a lot
-What have you ever been able to do for love's sake ?
My loneliness To give up my loneliness.
-What are you usually blamed for ?
For finding things.
-What use do you make of art ?
I met my first New York girlfriend in front of a Tchelitchew; my
-Write your epitaph              second -- in front of Brancusi.
Some of me is Here
- What would you like to be if reincarnate ?
Adam. If that is not possible then Eve.

Dear Jonas,

you asked me for a letter saying why I thought
the work of Filmakers should be helped.

Actually I am astonished that you need a letter
of this kind. What can I possibly add about the work of
your extraordinary group, which is famous all over the
world.

It is incredible that you should have to fight
against these economic difficulties.

I believe that the success of many commercial
films to-day is because they have been influenced by
underground movies.

Anyway, I feel that you should absolutely have
all the help you need, in order to continue your experi-
ments and researches, without which cinema could not continue to *evolve* in the way it has so far.

Yours
Michelangelo Antonioni
5th July 1969

418

## TASTING GREAT WINES

Sometime around 1983 I was having a dinner with Tim Forbes. We planned to go out, but at the last minute Tim made an offer to dine in his wine cellar.

So there we were, having a nice dinner, surrounded by walls stacked with hundreds of bottles of the most expensive, most famous wines in the world. Malcolm, Tim's father, was an obsessive wine connoisseur/collector. I looked at some of the labels and they went all the way back to Napoleon times.

Tim, noticing my interest, pointed to the bottles and sort of nonchalantly said:

"Choose any bottle you like..."

My heart jumped. I could not believe it. Here was my chance to drink with Napoleon.

At that point, Tim smiled and completed the sentence:

"...but you should know that they are all vinegar, you wouldn't want to drink them."

That, of course, ended my chance to drink with Napoleon.

My second wine-tasting adventure took place at Konstantin Frank's wine cellar in the Finger Lakes region. My wife, Hollis, and me, we happened to drive past Frank's place, so we thought this was the occasion to taste the famous wine right where it came from.

So we stop, we say hello and we tell Frank how much we'd like to taste his wine right there, in his cellar.

He seemed to be flattered by our wish. And to please us and himself, he leads us to a shelf stacked with books of clippings and encyclopedias in many languages and began pointing out all the places where his name was mentioned. Same time, of course, he was telling us his entire biography. At the age of seventeen, he said, he was already in charge of Tsar Nikolai's wine cellar in Petrograd. And, of course, we heard all what followed: how he ended up in the Finger Lakes and revolutionized the wine industry, and how Jackie Kennedy serves only his wine to her guests, and etc. and etc... Now, this lasted some forty minutes or so. All this time we were getting more and more eager to taste the wine.

Just about the time when he was about to complete his biography, a nice happy family walked in. So he greeted them and, noticing that they also had great interest in him, decided to start the biography tour from the beginning so that they too would learn firsthand something about his incredible life. Clippings, encyclopedias, Petrograd, etc., the whole thing. Actually, he got so excited and inspired by it all that he went into even greater detail and subtleties than before.

After an hour and a half, or maybe even more, we decided that maybe we should be leaving. Our decision was made final when we noticed that another couple was coming in. We were absolutely sure that our host would have no choice but to start the whole thing from the beginning. So we politely bid our host goodbye and left. As we were leaving we heard Frank's voice still going strong. He was about to arrive in America.

On our way out from the lakes we stopped at a wine store and bought a bottle of Konstantin's wine to take home with us.

422

## STEAL THIS FILM: HENRI LANGLOIS

The other day we were talking about film preservation. And about to what lengths some producers and film-makers go to make sure that nobody makes bootleg prints of their films. Jack Smith, for instance, was dead sure that I was making copies of every film I projected at the Film-Makers' Cinematheque, and that I had a secret lab in the projection room...

This reminded me of a story involving Henri Langlois of the Cinémathèque Francaise.

In 1971, we ran a complete retrospective of the film-maker Jean Epstein. Langlois himself brought the films and introduced the retrospective. New Yorkers had a rare chance to see the work of one of cinema's greats. Incidentally, Epstein's film *Fall of the House of Usher* was the first film I saw when I arrived in New York in 1949. It was at the New York Film Society run by Rudolf Arnheim. It made my first day in New York great.

So we saw the films and we sent them all back to Langlois. And that was it. But three years later I decided to re-screen two of the films. I sent a message to that effect to Langlois, asking for the films. A telephone call came in. It was Henri himself. He was almost furious as he spoke:

"You stupids, you had all those films I sent you and you didn't make copies of them!"

I was crushed. Here I was with P. Adams Sitney, two innocents trying to be really correct and honest, and here is Henri, the great lover of cinema, scolding us and giving us fatherly advice: Steal the films you love! No matter where they come from...

Ah, yes, you'd be amazed how many great films have been saved for posterity by lovers of movies who managed to steal the films they loved. Ask the American Film Institute or any film archive. You'll be amazed.

OPPOSITE: P. Adams Sitney and Henri Langlois, New York, 1971.

Henry Flynt, Anthology Film Archives, 1992.

## UNABOMBER AND ME:
## HENRY FLYNT, TONY CONRAD

Remember the Unabomber? We all do, of course. Remember the three or four full-page political rant he sent to *The New York Times* and it was published? I read a good part of it. I read it and I stopped in the middle of the first page. That was it. I knew who the Unabomber was. Of course, it was Henry Flynt, the Fluxus artist, mathematician and musician. Every word I read in the statement sounded exactly like it was Henry Flynt talking.

A few days later I meet Henry Flynt on the street.

"Admit it," I say. "Admit it, you are the Unabomber."

So he laughs, and I laugh, we joke, and we part.

Then it came that the bomber got caught.

Long court procedures followed. I don't remember all the details. I didn't exactly follow it. But a year or two later, Tony Conrad, film-maker and musician, visits me. I don't know how the talk turned to the Unabomber. "You know," says Tony, "we went to Harvard together. In the court he mentioned several times his friend Tony, but nobody paid attention to that. That Tony was me. And you know who else was in that class? Henry Flynt was also in the class. We were all friends."

I could barely believe what I was hearing! I was right! I should have reported my suspicion to the police! I was that close to it in my detective intuition, incredibly close! By one chess move, that close.

425

## BRUCE BAILLIE COMES TO NEW YORK

April 17, 1983

Bruce Baillie came to town, and is staying with Charles Levine. He came on Wednesday. I called him yesterday. He said he has the flu and hasn't left bed since he came to town.

He called to say that he tried to go out but didn't make it.

I decided to pay a visit to Bruce.

Charles opened the door. He has a dog now, a big sweet dog that he found lost a week ago, so he took the dog in. He calls him Dog, has no other name.

Bruce was in bed in some kind of semi-yoga position. The room was dark, window shades closed. There was a moldy, stuffy smell in the room. Bruce was an image of sickness. So I say, "Bruce, but why don't you at least have a peek through the window? Look, it's a nice day outside; the sun is rolling on the ground." And I pulled all the shades up. Bruce's first reaction was, "No, no, no! Don't do it!" But then he said maybe he should have a peek. So he comes to the window and sort of looks out. He looks out, he mumbles, then he says, "Hmm... maybe we should go out for a walk."

And so we went for a walk. And there was absolutely nothing wrong with Bruce, I wished I was that healthy...

OPPOSITE: Happy family of Bruce Baillie, 1989.

428

# FROM THE LIFE OF PAUL SHARITS

July 19, 1982

Paul Sharits, July 8, 1982: Ridden with bullets in the doorway of some dingy Buffalo bar. Mistaken identity, they mistook him for somebody else. Spleen removed.

Paul Sharits, 1981: Lost his keys, tried to get into his house through the roof window. Fell down. Broke his pelvis.

Paul Sharits, 1980: Stabbed in Buffalo bar, during an argument with a stranger. I was with Paul in a New York bar once when he turned to a young woman who was there with a man and he said, "Why are you with that guy? Have a drink with me." The woman ignored him. That time he was lucky.

Paul Sharits, 1979: Decided to learn roller-skating. On his first try he fell, broke a leg, for weeks walked in a cast, on crutches.

Paul Sharits, 1978: Crashed into a cemetery near Buffalo, ended up in the hospital for several days. Said he saw the cemetery and the sight of the cemetery took him into a deep meditation on death and he lost driving concentration.

Paul Sharits, 1990: At a party at the University of Buffalo, where he was teaching, Paul, completely drunk, came up to the president of the university and told him how much he hates him and that he is resigning right there.

Next day Paul came to his usual class and was met by some university official who asked him what he was doing there. Paul informed him that it was his class. The official informed him that he, that is, Paul, resigned last night, so what was he doing there?

Friends, other professors tried to reinstate Paul to his position, but the president didn't give in. Paul was out.

Paul Sharits, 1990: Smoke was noticed in Anthology's lobby. Manager called the Fire Department. The smoke was coming from the toilet room. There was Paul Sharits with a fire thrower in his hands and young woman in a strange garb. Paul was burning holes in her dress. He had decided to become a fashion designer. He was producing his first dress.

OPPOSITE: Paul Sharits in an early photograph.

I could go and go and go about Paul's adventures. Oh, yes, I have to tell you one more.

Paul Sharits, 1971: Paul needed a place to sleep overnight, so I decided to permit him to sleep in Anthology's office. In the morning I came in and I could not believe what I saw: There was Paul, all naked, Xeroxing himself, every part of his body, on our huge Xerox machine...

As I am typing this down, I receive a phone call from Gerald O'Grady, University of Buffalo. He says no, there should be no permanent damage to Paul after the shooting, so the doctors say. The bullet didn't touch the heart, or lungs, or any other "vital" organs to really make an invalid of him. So he'll be OK and ready for another catastrophe.

And ah, said O'Grady, Paul's father is with him, he came. "What?" said I, surprised. I thought Paul's father went the way of all the other Sharitses long ago, they are all so accident-prone. "No," said O'Grady, "but ten days ago he fell out of a tree and broke a few ribs. That's why he couldn't come to see Paul the first few days. He was in a hospital himself. But now, he's here, with Paul, even if he can't move much and is all wrapped up in bandages."

P.S.

A clipping from a San Francisco newspaper informs that Greg Sharits, Paul's brother, was shot by the police. According to the paper, Greg bought a rifle, and started shooting, standing in his doorway, just shooting. Police asked him to stop, he refused, so they shot him.

Greg was a manager of Film-Makers' Cinematheque for a few months in 1966. He fell in love with Carla, the ticket taker. She didn't answer his love. So he boarded a train to Buffalo. Near Buffalo, as the train was passing one of the high elevations, he jumped out. Survived. Spent one year in hospital.

430

# ABOUT MY EDUCATION

I feel this volume wouldn't be complete without some notes on my education...

The reason why I want to bring this subject in is that it contains some practical, useful tips.

It's all about sneaking into the classes and lectures that have nothing to do with what you are actually, officially studying.

At the University of Mainz, where I had enlisted myself in 1945, after I was liberated from the forced-labor camp, the subject of my studies was philosophy, don't ask me why. Soon I discovered that philosophy lectures were so dull that I needed some escapes. So I used to spend most of my time in the classes of other disciplines, such as art history, anthropology, even medicine. I discovered that seldom anyone checks whether you belong in that class or not.

One of the most ecstatic moments of my Mainz studies happened when one afternoon, being totally bored with a lecture on Maritain, I snuck into some class—I had no idea what it was about. I thought I'd just take a blind chance.

I discovered it was a class where some Swiss guy was talking about what he called a genius, a genius writer whose name was James Joyce. Since I had spent all my teenage life under the Russian and German regimes, I had never heard the name of James Joyce. But this guy was talking about him with such excitement that I had to listen to him. What made his lecture even more Joycean for me was that my German was still pretty bad so I was filling the empty spaces with my own imagination of Joyce. I don't have to tell you that this lecture, into which I had snuck by chance, had changed my life drastically.

When I came to New York, in late 1949, I soon discovered that Hans Richter was teaching at the City College. I dropped him a letter. "I am here in Brooklyn, I am a displaced person, I have no money, but I want to attend your classes," I said. A few days later I received a note from Richter, a note of two words: "Just come."

So I came. But I discovered that Hans Richter did not teach at all, he was only running the school. That was very, very disappointing. But I stuck around for a month or two. One of the students was Shirley Clarke.

And we became good friends, Hans Richter and myself, and our friendship lasted till his death. I couldn't have received more from any lecture.

Around the same time I happened to hear that a certain George Amberg was teaching film at New York University. I did some detective work and found the room in which the film classes were held. I did the Mainz trick. I just walked into the class and sat there—usually in the back—just like any other student. And, of course, nobody bothered me.

One of the great things about George Amberg classes was that to each of his classes he used to bring a guest film-maker who screened and discussed the films screened. That's how I met Gregory Markopoulos, Curtis Harrington, Ian Hugo and a few other film-makers who became my friends. Amberg was a great teacher. He began as a writer on dance; he actually did a book on ballet. We eventually became good friends.

Around the same time someone told me that another guy by the name Arthur Knight was giving a course on "experimental film" at the New School. So, of course, I used the Mainz trick. I attended all of his lectures too. For free.

It was more difficult to sneak into Cinema 16 screenings, so we usually paid. But we, I mean my brother Adolfas and myself, we looked (and were) so hungry and shabby, we were still in a transitional stage between being displaced persons and Williamsburg, Brooklyn immigrants, that Marcia Vogel, who usually took care of the door, often let us in for free, bless her heart.

That is how my education in the arts and cinema began.

The author with Hans Richter and Pola Chapelle (*front, left*), 1970. Photo: Adolfas Mekas.

Waterbury Hospital          15 Nov 73

Dear Jonas you wrote me such a lovely article + so full of friendship, that I wanted to answer immediately. But you guess what happened. 2 days after you visited us I got terrible gallbladder attacks. They took me to the hospital here + cut the gallbladder out (with much, much pain).

At the moment I am lying here in Bed and a wonderful motherly nurse takes care of me and she is from Lithuania (like her husband). She is a real gift from heaven. Fresh like a fullblown rose + with lots of intelligent humour. Anyhow thank you + your family for the lovely party + the affectionate article.

Love Heinrich R +

Kaip ainus Jonas? Kaip grazus Zodelos parashai api mano milimu patient Ir musu

Conn. Mr. Richter ira Kaip
Jus zinote labai milimus
zmogus ir ira privelege
Ji zinote. Ush dauk
zodzu ush mirshau. Mes.
gimami i chita pusu
ale tavele ish Litauos.
Dauk Labu Dainu
Martha Hermonat

I could go on and on: A list of my transgressions is long. It included even the Arts Students League on 57th Street, me sitting there and trying to draw from live models, etc., etc., etc.

But I want to describe here only one more transgression.

When I came, or rather was brought to New York by the UN's International Refugee Organization (IRO), for a few years I didn't miss a single theater, ballet or music performance, I was like a dry sponge absorbing everything that I had missed in my youth. But opera was usually more expensive, so I had to figure something out. I discovered the New York Opera House, which at that time was located on the corner of 40th Street and Eighth Avenue. At the end of Act One the side door was usually opened onto 40th Street for all the smokers to catch up on air and some puffs. As the bell for the beginning of Act Two sounded, they all streamed back in, and, of course, I streamed in with them... There was always a standing place in the back, in those days. There were many operas of which I missed the first acts, but missing the first acts made the operas for me more mysterious.

Ah, the life of a young artist and in New York! How exciting it was! I could do it again!

I had so many good memories from that period of the New York Opera House that when it was demolished, a decade or so later, as I happened to pass by, by pure chance, I picked up a big chunk of it, a piece from the ceiling cornice. I still have it, a piece of the New York Opera House, impregnated with some of the greatest voices of the first half of the twentieth century. Maybe they could be retrieved from it, some day!

## RE: MY EARLY DIARIES

This is for the students of archaeology, for you who like to dig. Please read this carefully.

I began keeping a diary when I was approximately six. I didn't know yet how to read or write, I was a latecomer... My diaries of that period were in pictures.

When I learned to write, I began keeping a daily written diary/record of what my father or older brothers did that day. It was a very factual diary. It included references to the weather and cows and sheep. I grew up as a good farmer boy.

Then, in 1940, the Russians/Soviets came. And a little later, the Germans/ Nazis came. And I was entering my teenage period. My diaries began taking a different shape. Being politically naïve and still trusting the world—until I learned it better—I wrote down in my diaries thoughts and details that, if seen by Russian/Soviet or German/Nazi eyes, would have caused me and my friends and family a lot of trouble. But I was already smart enough to hide well my diaries, usually in the barn.

It's a long story about why in June of 1944 I had to run away from my town and Lithuania. I describe it in some detail in my book *I Had Nowhere to Go*. I will only tell you here that I was given no choice. My underground friends had told me that I may be facing an imminent arrest by the German military police and I should disappear as soon as I can. And so I did, taking my younger brother Adolfas with me, who I felt may have been endangered too.

Now, what I am going to say next is for you, the students of archaeology...

Since my diaries contained a lot of incriminating information—our underground activities were directed equally against Germans/Nazis as against Russians/Soviets—in order to protect my underground friends, I decided to bury my diaries. There was another good reason to do that. Only a few days earlier, my underground friends had entrusted me with a package of sensitive documents. So I dug out a hole in the tool shack of my uncle, in whose house in Biržai I was staying at that time. I wrapped it all in newspapers, and I buried it some two feet deep. Twelve years of my diaries. My uncle helped me do it. We both hoped that the war would end soon, Lithuania would be free again (America would see to that...) and we would dig it all out again. Happy ending.

But things went badly for Lithuania and my diaries.

When in 1971 I was allowed to visit my mother and uncle, I discovered that where in 1944 there was a small tool shack, now there was a much bigger barn erected. Since I was never left alone during that brief visit to my uncle—there was always an official Party person close by—I could not ask my uncle about what happened to the stuff buried in the old shack, what happened to it when the new barn was built on top of it.

Soon after my visit, my uncle died. Since nobody else knew about the burial of my stuff, the fate of it will remain a mystery. There are three possibilities: a) my uncle dug it out and destroyed it so that it wouldn't fall into the hands of the Soviet police; b) it rotted; c) it's still there, in whatever shape.

439

Close-up from a class photo, 1940.

440

One of the earliest pictures taken by the author: his father, Povilas Mekas, and his mother, Elžbieta Mekas, in 1940.

# HOW IT ALL BEGAN: MY FIRST STILL CAMERA

Now I will tell you how it all began.

I was sixteen.

My older brother Povilas had just given me a present: my first still camera!

It was a very, very exciting moment of my life. I kept it under my pillow, treasuring it, waiting for the moment to use it. I had only one roll of film so I didn't want to waste it on just anything. I wanted my first pictures to mean something to me.

I didn't have to wait long. Only a few weeks.

It was the summer of 1940.

Our village woke up to the rumble of tanks and heavy trucks full of Russian soldiers as they moved, enveloped in a cloud of country road dust, past our village into the heart of Lithuania, the event that became known as the first occupation of Lithuania by the Soviet Union.

I took my camera from under the pillow and ran to the road. The moment had come! It was an event I couldn't miss! I was still blessed by innocence, as I sat on a stone wall at the edge of the road and began recording this historic event, as my parents and older brothers watched it all, hidden behind the closed windows. No, I couldn't miss this event, the dust, the soldiers, the tanks. *Click click click* I went.

This ecstasy lasted only a minute or two.

I saw a Russian soldier running towards me. He violently tore the camera out of my hands, he violently pulled the film out of it, he threw the film roll on the ground, in the sand of the roadside, then he rubbed it into the ground with the heel of his boot. Then he pointed his hand towards my house and shouted what I understood, not knowing Russian, as *Run, run, you stupid, run, or else...* Which, of course, I did. Later I was told, by older people who knew better, that the Russian soldier was very, very nice to me, he could have been much worse, much, much worse...

This was how my life in photographic arts began.

This was also the beginnings of my political education...

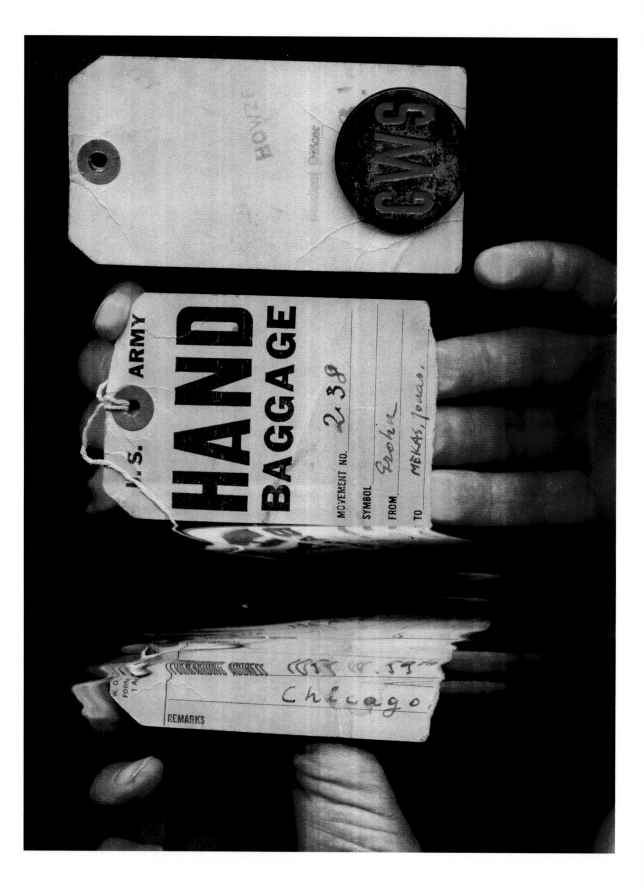

442

# ABOUT LANGUAGE AND MYSELF

Now I'll tell you something about myself.

A mini-biography. It's all about language.

I grew up in a small farming village, in Lithuania, in an area that spoke its own dialect. We used to laugh at the official Lithuanian language, make jokes about it.

Then I went to primary school. There I had to learn and speak the official, literary Lithuanian language.

Then I went to high school. There I began learning Latin and French. Two years of each.

In 1940 the Soviets came. They declared that French and Latin were no good. Russian was good.

So I began learning Russian. Two years of Russian.

In 1942 the Germans came. The Germans declared that Russian was no good, German was good. So I began learning German. Two years of German.

Then it happened so that I ended up in Hamburg, in Germany, in a war prisoner's camp together with Italian and French prisoners.

Ah, I thought, now I am in Germany so I can progress with my German. It didn't take much time to discover that I was in an area of Germany that spoke a very special dialect of German called Plattdeutsch which even Germans had difficulty understanding. So I said, since I live with Italians, I will learn Italian. Then I discovered that the Italian I was learning was really Italian of the Sicilian Gypsies that my other Italian friends didn't understand at all.

At that point the war ends and the Americans come. So we all begin learning English. But by that time I had reached a point where I knew many languages and I knew them all badly. So, my brother and myself, we come to a genius conclusion: Now we are going to learn the language of cinema, a language that everybody understands.

So we come to New York, get a Bolex and begin to film. We begin to meet other young people who also film. And we begin to show our films to our older and wiser friends. And they look at our movies and then they look at us, and they shake their heads and they say: We don't understand what you are showing us. What is this? This is not cinema. We know what cinema is; we go to movies.

We were crushed: We had learned the wrong language of cinema! The language of the avant-garde, of poetry...

At that point we decided to quit all languages, including that of cinema, and just do what we like, even if nobody understands us except our friends. Like in my old village.

ON HAPPINESS

August 17, 1974

Dear Jane:

You asked what makes me happy.

I have been thinking about it. Of course, it changes. Usually, it makes me always happy, very happy to be in nature. Among the trees, to lie down under a tree, or in the fields. To lie down on my back and follow the clouds. No product of man, no artifact of culture has ever made me as happy.

Then, I am very happy to be with three, four, maybe five friends, and have something to eat and something to drink and then just talk and do nothing, fool around; no serious talk, only friends' nonsense, talk of four, five friends who have said everything to each other, discussed everything, and now they can put it all on the shelf and just be themselves. I remember such happy evenings with Peter Kubelka, and P. Adams Sitney, and Raimund Abraham and Nitsch, and Leo Adams.

I am happy when I am walking the streets of New York, alone and by myself. I am walking slowly, and with no particular plan, and with no purpose. I am just walking. Sometimes I stop and maybe I film something. The first thing I do when I come back from distant journeys, I drop everything and no matter what hour of the day, I go out and I walk through the city streets. It makes me feel so good.

Author with Lou Reed and Phil Glass, at Anthology Film Archives, 1995.

At the opening of Anthology Film Archives, November 30, 1970, with Hollis Frampton, Florence Jacobs,
Ken Jacobs and Peter Kubelka behind the author. Photo: Michael Chikiris.

And, of course, one of my instant ecstasies is when my brother bakes some kugelis, a Lithuanian potato dish (on which he works a full day and the art of which he has mastered completely). You give me kugelis, a lot of it, brown, burned, crusty—and you can have all your cinema, I'll stick to my pot of kugelis, stuffing myself full, burning my tongue, and sweating like a pig—nobody will be able to pull me away from it. And then, of course, you are so full of it that you can't do anything but sit full of happiness, nodding yes to everything, content with everything—a feeling which I could best describe with the words of this fantastic woman who came to Anthology's opening on Lafayette Street in 1970, of whom nobody seemed to know who she was, she was just one of the many people who came to the opening, and she ate and she drank and everybody was very happy and the evening was very good, good movies and good people and good food (cooked by Peter) and good wine (made by Raimund), and it was already very late, maybe three in the morning, there was only this small group left, and this woman, she said, very, very casually, "I saw movies. I ate. I drank. I am very, very happy. Now I can go home and fuck." And as we looked at her with stunned admiration, she walked out.

What makes me happy? Oh, dear Jane, there are so many things that make me happy. Really, sometimes anything can make me happy. It's almost easier to enumerate what makes me unhappy. When two people argue, it makes me terribly unhappy. I don't understand it, it confuses me, I am totally lost. To see the unhappiness of someone, that makes me unhappy. Yes, maybe it is unhappiness itself that makes me really unhappy.

A day later:

I was eating some grapes today. Late this evening we sat with Hollis, my wife, and we ate grapes. We had a big plate full of them, and they tasted fantastic. And they looked great too. And I knew I could eat as many of them as I wanted. I couldn't finish them all, there was a big bunch of them. Two days ago I also had grapes, a lot of them.

Suddenly, I was thinking about our early days in New York, myself and Adolfas, dropped here from postwar displaced-persons camps, our hungry days when we were dreaming of apples, and strawberries, and cherries. We were never able to afford them.

And now I was eating grapes and I really enjoyed them and I knew I could eat as many of them as I wanted. I looked at them, green and sweet and inviting, and I said, "Yes, I think I deserve them. After so many years of hard work that I put into this world, I really think I deserve some grapes."

449

When we grew up, our father's farm was new and there were no apple trees that bore fruit, nor any other fruit trees—in any case, not like on the old farms. As children, we always had this desire for apples and pears; it was always a luxury to have some. I remember when my brother and I moved to town, and he got his first job, in the hardware store, and I myself the same day, I think, started working in a drugstore, packing toothpaste—I remember, with my first salary, or maybe it was his—we went during the lunch hour and we bought a lot of currants. They were red, transparently red in the sun—and we ate and we ate until we felt sick.

450

Yes, the berries... The things you finally get in your life. The things you dream of all your life and never get...

I remember now all this, while eating my grapes and feeling happy. No, I don't regret that I worked so hard all these years, no. It was all worth it. This plate of grapes, this final compensation. I am perfectly happy with it. This plate is my Paradise. I don't want anything else—no country house, no car, no dacha, no life insurance, no riches. It's this plate of grapes that I want. It's this plate of grapes that makes me really happy. To eat my grapes and enjoy them and want nothing else—that is happiness, that's what makes me happy.

Author, circa age five, on the knees of his father.